WARPLANE

WARPLANE

How the Military Reformers Birthed the A-10 Warthog

HAL SUNDT

LYONS
PRESS

Essex, Connecticut

An imprint of Globe Pequot, the trade division of The Rowman & Littlefield Publishing Group, Inc.
4501 Forbes Blvd., Ste. 200
Lanham, MD 20706
www.rowman.com

Distributed by NATIONAL BOOK NETWORK

British Library Cataloguing in Publication Information available

Library of Congress Cataloging-in-Publication Data
Names: Sundt, Hal, author.
Title: Warplane: how the military reformers birthed the A-10 / Hal Sundt.
Other titles: How the military reformers birthed the A-10
Description: Essex, Connecticut: Lyons Press, [2023] | Includes bibliographical references and index.
Identifiers: LCCN 2023007658 (print) | LCCN 2023007659 (ebook) | ISBN 9781493067718 (cloth) | ISBN 9781493078578 (epub)
Subjects: LCSH: A-10 (Jet attack plane)—History. | Airplanes, Military—United States.
Classification: LCC UG1242.A28 S88 2023 (print) | LCC UG1242.A28 (ebook) | DDC 358.4/2830973—dc23/eng/20230224
LC record available at https://lccn.loc.gov/2023007658
LC ebook record available at https://lccn.loc.gov/2023007659

♾️™ The paper used in this publication meets the minimum requirements of American National Standard for Information Sciences—Permanence of Paper for Printed Library Materials, ANSI/ NISO Z39.48-1992.

for mom, love hal

Contents

Author's Note xi

Part I: Create 1
1: West of the Smoke 3
2: The Redeemer .15
3: The Whiz Kid .27
4: The System 39
5: Simplicate, and Add More Lightness 47
6: The Thud 57
7: Fly Before Buy 69
8: The Military Reformers Assemble 81
9: Owning an Elephant 93
10: Attack, Revise, Re-Attack 103
11: Friction 113

Part II: Destroy **127**
12: "High" Tech 129
13: To Be Seen 139
14: The Joint Strike Fighter 149

Part III: Survive **163**
15: Muck Brown 165
16: The Hammer and the Nail 183

17: Survivable 193
18: The Fathers of the A-10 201
19: Mud 207

Acknowledgments 219
Notes on Sources 225
Bibliography 237
Index 245

This book was made possible by the tremendous generosity and patience of a great many folks, quite a few of whom invited me into their homes, spoke with me for hours on end on numerous occasions, and put up with my follow-up calls, text messages, and emails to confirm details of specific events or further explain particular concepts. Any quotations throughout this book that are not directly attributed to another source are the product of these interviews. Not everyone I interviewed is directly quoted in the book, but every interview was utterly instructive in shaping my understanding of this story.

Author's Note

When I teach writing, I use something called "the Burkean Parlor," named for rhetorician Kenneth Burke. The Burkean Parlor is a thought experiment of sorts, something to help writers understand what it means to participate in an academic conversation. It invites you to consider multiple perspectives, then encourages you to have the conviction to say your part, all while accepting both that your argument will inevitably be challenged *and* that your own views on the subject may one day change, too:

> *Imagine that you enter a parlor. You come late. When you arrive, others have long preceded you, and they are engaged in a heated discussion, a discussion too heated for them to pause and tell you exactly what it is about. In fact, the discussion had already begun long before any of them got there so that no one present is qualified to retrace for you all the steps that had gone before. You listen for a while until you decide that you have caught the tenor of the argument, then you put in your oar. Someone answers; you answer him; another comes to your defense; another aligns himself against you, to either the embarrassment or gratification of your opponent, depending upon the quality of your ally's assistance. However, the discussion is interminable. The hour grows late, you must depart. And you do depart, with the discussion still vigorously in progress.*

As I wrote this book, I returned often to Burke's parlor for reassurance. Though I have been teaching writing for some time now, I've never identified as an academic. Similarly, despite this book's clear ties to military history, I never considered that to be its genre. I always just thought of it as a story and myself as a writer.

Of course, this story is very much one of military history. And military history, I found, is very much an academic subject. By academic I do not mean that military history is stuffy or boring. Rather, it's a subject that is continuously debated, re-examined, and re-interpreted. There's a reason we keep reading new books about the American Civil War and World War II; history of any war refuses to be understood definitively.

So I made some decisions in how to approach this subject. To tell the story of an airplane's design, development, and service life, I chose to focus on a handful of folks. In a sense, I wanted to tell the story of an airplane *through* them, with a particular focus on one character who you will soon meet.

I have never flown an airplane or served in the military. Thus, service members may find something lacking in my perspective. To be honest, I don't even like to fly. In this way I'm writing almost the way a basketball super-fan might write about the sport without ever having played it competitively.

This is not the first book about the A-10 Thunderbolt II attack airplane, nor, I suspect, will it be the last. As Kenneth Burke says, the "discussion is interminable. The hour grows late, you must depart. And you do depart, with the discussion still vigorously in progress." The rigorous and enlightening works already in existence about the A-10, military aviation, and the men who would become known as "The Reformers" were utterly instructive for me. Those books are the conversations that began before I ever thought to enter the parlor, and they can be found in the bibliography.

I hope you find this book to be a worthy addition to the ongoing conversation of the A-10. I tried to write something not unlike the A-10 itself: focused in its purpose and design, and rugged enough to stick around for a long while. I guess we'll see.

PART I

CREATE

I

West of the Smoke

PERCHED ON A ROCKY HILLTOP IN THE MARAH VALLEY OF AFGHANI-
stan, Matt Secor certainly looked the part of U.S. Special Forces. Secor
was built thick like a powerlifter and sported a wooly beard, which he
along with the rest of his twelve-man unit had grown before deployment
because they were told elders in nearby villages held greater respect for
bearded men. Sometimes, Secor intercepted radio communication from
the Taliban referring to Special Forces as "the Bearded Ones."

The late October sun shone on the Bearded Ones, warming Secor's
mug as he sat in the open bed of a "gun truck," a modified Humvee with a
pickup truck bed and a gun turret. He monitored the radio, which crackled with rumors of an ambush. These reports were usually nonsense, but
one could never be sure. For now, there was calm. Down the hillside ran
an arid creek bottom pocked with thickets and low trees the same height
as Secor, six feet. In such moments, Secor remembered, the mundane
could suddenly shift to "violent excitement."

The radio shrieked. The Taliban had begun attacking an observation
post about five hundred meters south of the Bearded Ones' position,
sending blasts from handheld rocket projectiles pluming into the bright
blue sky. Secor grabbed the radio. As a Joint Terminal Attack Controller
(JTAC), it was his job to coordinate any air support that ground units
like his—or the friendlies now taking enemy fire—might need.

What had promised to be a firefight barely registered as a skirmish,
an exchange of gunfire that ended before the air support arrived on scene.
Still, Secor had a hunch this dust-up was a foreshock for a gnarlier battle

3

yet to come. *Be ready in case we need you,* he radioed to the pilots. Sporadic ambushes, after all, were common.

As the sun set, the Bearded Ones spent the evening prepping for a dogfight, loading their weapons and confirming their radios worked. Throughout the night they took turns manning the gun turrets while others slept on the ground, in the truck bed, and under the Humvee, anywhere they could get comfortable. For Secor, the night skies in Afghanistan were incomparable to anything in the United States, completely unpolluted by urban lighting. A collage of shooting stars unlike Secor had ever seen streaked across the inky black sky.

The sun rose without incident, and the Bearded Ones were restless. They'd spent the whole night psyching themselves up for a fight that never came. "It's kind of morbid, in a sense," Secor told me. "We're like 'this kind of sucks, man . . . I thought we were going to get after it, you know?'"

"And then all of a sudden," he remembered, "things just start[ed] going." About a quarter mile across the valley, an allied Army platoon of a few dozen soldiers were taking fire from the Taliban. Secor hopped in back of the gun truck and began lobbing forty-millimeter grenades onto the opposing hillside. The platoon was pinned down. Secor radioed in for the air cavalry; this was now a rescue mission.

The first airplane to answer Secor's call was a B-1B Lancer, a sleek but behemoth bomber nicknamed "the Bone" because of its long, slender frame and wings that sweep back into its fuselage at high speeds. As the Bone's bombs began carpeting the hillside, the Bearded Ones hit the deck behind their gun trucks, desperate not to be killed by their own airplanes. In all, the Bone dropped twenty-five bombs, ranging from five hundred to two thousand pounds. "One of those bombs hit about three hundred meters from the truck," Secor told me, "and I could feel the heat from the bomb hit my face."

Within ten minutes, more coalition allied airplanes showed up: first a set of British Harriers, jack-of-all-trades jets used for both air-to-air and air-to-ground missions and known for their ability to land vertically, like a helicopter; then a few French F-1 Mirages, fighters agile like the Harrier and fast like the Bone. In fact, the Bone could fly 1.2 times the speed of sound, the fastest bomber the U.S. Air Force had to offer. But all the speed of the Bones and Harriers and Mirages was of little use to the Bearded Ones. What they needed was "close-air support," a kind of air cover flown by planes slow and low to the ground so that they could keep an eye on the action and provide continuous fire on the enemy. Each of these airplanes had their own Achilles' heel preventing them from executing perfect close-air support: they either flew too high or too fast or burned too much fuel or were too vulnerable to small-arms fire to stay in the battle area for very long.

All the while, another pair of airplanes piloted by Major Andy Stone and his wingman, Major Reid Rasmussen, were loitering above the action like vultures. Majors Stone and Rasmussen were each flying in A-10 Thunderbolt IIs, airplanes specifically designed for the close-air support the Bearded Ones needed. The A-10 had been built to be shot at, capable of withstanding damage that would render most airplanes good for nothing but scrap metal: its cockpit is cradled by a titanium bathtub to protect the pilot from ground fire, and the plane itself can remain in flight with half of one wing blown off, one engine, and a chunk of its tail missing. All of the A-10's flight controls have a backup: if one part malfunctions, another is there to do the job. If the A-10 loses hydraulic controls, the pilot can fly the airplane using a mechanism called manual reversion, whereby the pilot (A-10 flyers prefer the term "driver") governs the rudders, elevators, and ailerons with a system of pulleys and bell-cranks similar to the Wright Flyer.

Compared with the sleekness of the B-1 "Bone," the A-10 is grotesque: with the fixed wing of a crop duster and the turbofan engines of an aged commercial airliner, it looks like it was assembled by dumping out the pieces from a stack of plastic models and gluing them together at random. And, in a sense, it was. Its designers conceived of the plane entirely around the gun, a 19.5 foot, four-thousand-pound Gatling gun that fires thirty millimeter bullets at a blistering rate. No one calls the A-10 by its official name ("Thunderbolt II"). It is "The Warthog," or simply "The Hog," an affectation borne out of its brutish appearance. Some—referencing the massive cannon that juts from the plane's nose like a pebbled wart—call it "The Flying Gun."

The Bearded Ones had one thing going for them: Major Andy Stone was among the best A-10 drivers in the world, a graduate of the Fighter Weapon's School, the U.S. Air Force's version of "Top Gun." If there was such a thing as earning a PhD in flying the A-10, Major Stone had it (Stone's call sign was "FATTS," meaning "Fatally Allergic to the Sun," and that is how he will be addressed from here). Though the A-10 had not been FATTS's first choice out of flight school—he'd wanted to fly something faster, like the F-16 Fighting Falcon or F-15E Strike Eagle—he'd quickly developed a love for his airplane and its mission supporting the grunts on the ground. "When they get into a really bad situation," FATTS told me, "sometimes they just need you."

Like all A-10 drivers, as part of his training FATTS had attended air-to-ground operations school at Nellis Air Force Base in Las Vegas. There, he'd learned to do Matt Secor's job of directing airplanes from the ground, pointing out targets and clearing the airspace so no allied jets collided above the hectic battlefield. More importantly, FATTS's training allowed him to understand everything going through Secor's mind in this moment, creating a kind of telepathic connection between the two men despite being thousands of feet apart. FATTS understood, for example, that Secor's main difficulty was that he simply could not see very far in any direction, especially down in the grove surrounded by all the high brush. Thus, FATTS was able to "extend a little bit of grace" to Secor. After all, while Secor had spent the night before battle all jacked up, sleeping outside just waiting to be shot at, FATTS had gotten a full night's sleep indoors, eaten a hot breakfast that morning, and was now flying in an air-conditioned cockpit. Secor was in hell, and it was FATTS's job to be his guardian angel.

Prior to entering the airspace, FATTS had been listening into the radio frequency that Secor was using to communicate with the Bone, the Harriers, and the French Mirages. He could sense the struggle between the air and the ground. "I could hear the frustration in the [French Mirage] pilot's voice . . . [and] I could hear the frustration in Matt's voice because he wasn't able to get the Mirage fighter's weapons onto the targets that he needed them to be on," FATTS remembered. Without his training, FATTS could have easily gotten frustrated with Secor, too. *Just tell me where to aim, and I'll blow the spot off the map!*

FATTS remembers Secor was "pretty amped up" by the time they got connected over the radio. The situation was simply too dire and chaotic for Secor to deliver the kind of detailed intel typically required for airplanes to provide effective close-air support and avoid friendly fire. FATTS could see where the enemy was, but he couldn't make out where the friendlies were. *Did Secor have smoke grenades available?* FATTS asked. He did. So did the Army platoon stuck on the hillside. "Tell the unit that you're *not* with to get their smoke out, too," FATTS instructed Secor. "The only way I can do this, the only way I can give you fire right now within the next minute, is you're going to have to pop some smoke."

Both units tossed their grenades, releasing green smoke that streamed into the sky, at which point FATTS and his wingman, Major "Ras" Rasmussen, performed one strafing run, unloading a short burst of thirty-millimeter rounds into the valley. After just one pass from the A-10s, the Taliban scattered; the A-10 had such a lethal reputation that it was common for enemies to flee at even the sight of them. The Bearded Ones were now free to join up with the stranded Army platoon on the hill.

With the ground troops safe for now, FATTS and Ras returned to vulture mode, directing their attention for the next hour to securing the area: there were rescue helicopters who needed to be guided in to pick up the wounded, and nearby an inbound enemy convoy was hauling in supplies and reinforcements. Ras began coordinating with various air operations agencies to bring more airplanes into the area. After a little more than an hour, Secor radioed FATTS again. They needed help, *now.*

Unbeknownst to FATTS, the now-consolidated U.S. forces comprised of the Bearded Ones and the Army platoon had begun moving back across the valley, leaving their position in the high ground and—believing the area to be safe—traversing once again through the grove where the first ambush had occurred. "They were just getting hammered down in the grove of trees," FATTS remembered.

This time the Taliban ambush came from two or three sides—Secor isn't quite sure—sending rockets and heavy caliber machine gun ammunition careening off Humvee walls and obliterating the thickets and trees in the creek bed. The metallic stink of sulfur and gun lubricant hung in the air. "It smelled like chaos, if chaos has a smell," Secor said.

The Taliban were now much closer than before, within a city block's distance, such that from the sky it was almost impossible for FATTS and Ras to distinguish friend from foe. On the ground, dust and smoke clogged the air, and the high brush blocked so much of Secor's view that he was using a 0.50-caliber machine gun to mow down the surrounding trees in a desperate attempt to improve his sightline.

From the video monitor inside his cockpit, FATTS could see various sets of vehicles traveling on a road below. But everyone was close, and the visibility was so poor that both sides had trucks driving on the same roads within minutes without seeing each other. Adding to the chaos was the fact that both sides were actively moving, which meant the data stream of the Bearded Ones' coordinates to FATTS was constantly outdated. "I struggled with the fact that there's stuff all over the battlefield, I could see RPGs flying everywhere," FATTS told me. "You just look down there, and you just see impact after impact after impact."

It was almost the golden hour on that late October afternoon. The sun was now low in the sky and FATTS knew that because Secor was taking fire from the southwest he was staring directly into the sun, yet another impediment to his vision. FATTS called a "timeout," of sorts. He asked Secor to take a drink of water. They needed to reset and reassess their position. Did Secor have more smoke grenades? Indeed he did. During the previous hour, between the first ambush and the second, FATTS had asked Secor to check in with the other vehicles in his unit and make sure they all had their smoke grenades at the ready. Because the mayhem of war magnifies the complexity of even the simplest tasks, during that hour of calm FATTS wanted the guys on the ground to preemptively remove the caps from their smoke grenades so they would go off the moment they were thrown: one less thing to think about, one less thing to do. Thus, what happened next, FATTS said, wasn't an accident, but rather "by thoughtful design." How Secor handled the ensuing action confirmed for FATTS that he was "in the top 5% of JTACs I've ever worked with."

By now the Taliban were within forty meters of Secor's unit, or two-thirds *less* than what the military deems to be a "danger close" situation. Machine gun fire crackled as Secor threw two smoke grenades to mark his team's position. This time, red smoke billowed out of the valley. "Look for the smoke," Secor hollered over the radio. "It's going to be red smoke! It's going to be red smoke!" The tenor of Secor's voice in that instant was not panic, but it was certainly urgent. For context, a thirty-millimeter round is about the size of an ear of corn. If a barrage of them hit a vehicle, they would spawn flaming hot shards of shrapnel like molten confetti. A single round could pulverize a human body. Years later, in fact, Secor would see what a high-explosive thirty-millimeter round could do to a person with a direct hit. "The round folded him in half like a taco shell. . . . There wasn't much left to identify his remains."

FATTS and Ras kept talking to the ground, continually performing risk assessment and mitigation. Could the grunts hide behind a gun truck? Was there a nearby rock for them to take cover? The A-10's Avenger cannon was the most lethal, precise gun in the Air Force arsenal, but it was still a machine gun, and like any machine gun, the further it was from its target, the more widely its bullets sprayed. To limit the dispersion of thirty-millimeter rounds, FATTS and Ras would need to fly as close to the ground as possible, "bottoming out" at just seventy-five feet before pulling up, an altitude FATTS told me A-10 drivers get "uncomfortably comfortable with."

The Taliban were now so close that as the A-10s began their approach from Secor's perspective their Avenger cannons were pointed directly at him. He was staring into the barrel of the weapon that would either take or save his life, a fate that would be determined by fractions of a degree. "West of the smoke!" Secor screamed as the A-10s got closer. "West of the smoke! . . . Keep your fire west of the smoke . . . Keep the fuckin' fire west of the smoke!"

In FATTS's mind, the worst possible outcome would be to kill an allied soldier.[1] As he strafed the valley, he purposefully gave the trigger

---

1. A former A-10 Weapons School Officer, David "Rainman" Stephenson, used to implore young pilots during training: "There's going to be a time at night, in shitty weather with people shooting at you that as a brand new guy you're going to have to be able to put ordnance down inside the

on his joystick just a quick squeeze, unloading enough ammo to dissuade the enemy while also limiting the potential for collateral damage. In case his aim was off, he wanted Ras to be able to correct his attack coordinates before he dove into the valley. But FATTS's aim was perfect, and Ras followed behind him twelve seconds later, reciting the "Fighter Pilot's Prayer" in his head: "Please God don't let me fuck this up."

Over the next twenty-three minutes, FATTS and Ras each made thirteen passes through the valley, staggering their attack runs such that every half-minute an A-10 was sweeping over the battlefield. In all, they unloaded eighteen hundred rounds of thirty-millimeter ammunition; that's three thousand pounds, or the weight of an American bison. If every round they fired was laid end to end, it would stretch 1,575 feet, longer than if you stacked the Statue of Liberty *on top* of the Eiffel Tower.

Secor doesn't remember the sound the A-10s made as they flew overhead. He was too busy manning the gun truck and the radios as the Taliban closed in. Footage recorded from the ground and sky that day reveals the snapping *clack-clack* staccato of AK-47 gunfire and the strange *Brrrrrrttt* noise the A-10's Avenger cannon produces, a guttural, grainy burst, like marbles in a coffee grinder.

Because of the continuous close-air support that Secor had orchestrated with FATTS and Ras, there had been no friendly fire accidents. More than two dozen enemy Taliban were killed, and a "high value target" had been severely wounded. An after-action intelligence report had calculated the Bearded Ones' chance of survival at just 20 percent. To this day, video of the attack collected from FATTS's and Ras's cockpit displays is used to train incoming A-10 drivers on how to provide close-air support. For his efforts, Secor was awarded the Army Commendation Medal with Valor, and FATTS received the Distinguished Flying Cross with Valor for Heroism (he maintains that his wingman, Ras, should have been recognized as well).

It's unusual for troops on the ground to feel so connected with airplanes high above and out of view. The A-10 is the exception. It was

---

minimum safe acceptable distance to friendly forces. And you cannot miss. You cannot miss. If you miss, we would have been way better off had we never taken off . . . I mean, if we're killing our own guys, that's like the cardinal sin. And you can't do it. So you better be good."

moments like those in the valley, connected to a small team, that had compelled Matt Secor to join Special Forces in the first place. Such closeness could only be achieved when extreme danger and purpose were intertwined and shared with others. Radioing with the A-10 pilots on days like that one produced an unusual sensation for Secor.

It was, he said, a kind of "intimate feeling."

Some fifteen years later, far removed from the Marah Valley, Pierre Sprey stood on the flight line of Maryland's Warfield Air National Guard Base, just outside Baltimore, squinting against a harsh sun as an airplane—his airplane—came into view, descending through scattered clouds and sailing over the sun-baked tarmac before twisting into a steep, unhurried climb. Sprey, who developed the design specifications for the A-10 in the late 1960s at the height of the Cold War, had seen this before. Many times. This was a routine demonstration, just the beginning of a tour of the airbase that Sprey had arranged on my behalf. Still, the scene carried with it a reverence.

Sprey didn't much mind his airplane's sluggish pace. He delighted in the soft whistle of its engines, a sharp contrast to the roar of most fighter jets. But he wished the plane had been smaller. And though he loathed most of the Air Force's fleet of sleek aircraft, even he would admit that his creation was an ugly thing.

Sprey's airplane should be retired in an airplane boneyard by now. Yet hundreds of A-10s remain in service, beloved by pilots like FATTS and Ras and ground troops like Matt Secor. While more advanced jets fly into hot war zones, drop their ordnance and bug out, the Warthog has developed the reputation as the plane that sticks around. Because it can sustain so much damage and continue to do its job, the A-10 is what engineers call "survivable."

Despite these attributes the A-10 has been fighting for its life since it was the mere zygote of an idea in Sprey's mind. From the time he recommended the Air Force develop an airplane like the A-10, Sprey's reputation and intellect were relentlessly attacked by military bureaucrats.

Stubbornly, Sprey could not be silenced, and his plane would not be grounded.

The A-10 has achieved a kind of cult status. Hog drivers direct the extraordinary discipline, intellect, and physical excellence required to be a fighter pilot toward something that can't even fly as fast as a regional jet one might take from Cleveland to Chicago. Aircraft engineers flock to the A-10 for the unexpected creativity and innovation required to maintain this Cold War relic. But it all began with Sprey. He had an exceptional analytic mind, one that his close friend, Winslow Wheeler, once characterized as endowed with "immense mental horsepower."

At age fifteen, Sprey enrolled at Yale where he double-majored in mechanical engineering and French literature. He was not yet thirty when he was recruited to join Robert McNamara's Whiz Kids in the Pentagon. With his pedigree, Sprey could have done anything. Instead, at a time when the United States was putting men on the moon and dreaming up airplanes that could fly three times the speed of sound, Sprey chose to go slower and lower. There was no glamor in that.

The results are indisputable. The A-10 may very well be the finest military aircraft ever built—on the cheap, no less—a weapon so well-suited for war that it would expose the insatiability of the military industrial complex. Throughout its tumultuous life, the A-10 became the "Forrest Gump" of airplanes, a singular character whose story coincides with almost every major development in aviation, technology, and military engineering history.

But while the A-10 may represent the Boomer mythology of bootstraps innovation, it also exposes the worst of these qualities in approaches to design. That it endures half a century later is both a testament to the foresight of its creators and an indictment of the waste and groupthink that pervades so much of new product development in a capitalistic marketplace. Sprey would often lament how it was embarrassing that an adequate successor to the A-10 had yet to be developed. In this way, the Hog is an exhibit of duality: a result of humanity's worst and most destructive qualities (the better its design, the more proficient in its killing), but also an artifact of ingenuity containing a remarkable story of survival.

The sophistication of most modern fighter jets promotes a sinister illusion, a high-altitude supersonic view that sterilizes combat's gruesome realities. Meanwhile, every bullet-riddled A-10 fuselage compels the discerning observer to reckon with the moral dilemmas and atrocities of war. The A-10 wasn't designed to hide its purpose or avoid misfortune. It's not stealth or ultra-fast, and because it's so slow it's not what aviators would call "escapable." It was built with the expectation that accidents will happen, that chaos is unavoidable.

It was late July 2021—a sweltering morning—when Pierre Sprey and I watched the A-10s fly by at Warfield Air National Guard Base. For much of the rest of the day I looked on while Sprey held court, recounting to growing crowds of Warthog drivers, maintenance crews, and anyone else who cared to listen about the A-10's origins and Sprey's exploits pissing off high-ranking Pentagon officials.

Sprey was eighty-three years old. In less than a week he would die unexpectedly from a heart attack. His obituary the following month noted that among Sprey's many accomplishments *The Baltimore Sun* once claimed he "may well be the most fascinating person you've never heard of."

But on this day, he seemed in good health, trim and charming. He had a temporary tattoo of a flower on his left forearm, a remnant from the previous night spent out at the bars with Hog drivers.

At the end of the day, the base commanders presented Sprey with a dummy thirty-millimeter ammunition round and a bottle of bourbon engraved with the silhouette of a Warthog, which he accepted graciously. But when they referred to him as "the father of the A-10," Sprey gently corrected them. That distinction, he insisted, belonged to someone else.

So this is where the story of the A-10 Warthog's life begins: in the recesses of the Pentagon with a conscience-stricken colonel seeking redemption.

2

The Redeemer

THOUGH HE HAD SINNED UNWITTINGLY, COLONEL AVERY KAY WAS guilty of deception. Which is why in the late fall of 1966, Colonel Kay stewed inside his office at the Pentagon.

It hadn't always been this way for Kay. In World War II, he was a decorated navigator in the Eighth Air Force, dodging flak inside America's prized long-range bomber, the B-17 "Flying Fortress." Now he was toiling in the office of Air Force Doctrine, Concepts, and Objectives Directorate, a smoke screen moniker for the bureau's true role of preserving—and expanding—the Air Force's lucrative budget. And such was Kay's sin: he had done his job too well.

Less than a year earlier, Kay had been tasked with brokering a deal between the Army and the Air Force.[1] Following orders, Kay helped to convince the Army to trade the bulk of their airplanes in exchange for the Air Force's helicopters, with the added assurance that if Army troops ever needed support from the sky, the Air Force would answer the call. On its face, the deal appeared not only sensible, but equitable, and perhaps even honorable.

In truth, the Air Force was not wholly committed to providing air cover for foot soldiers. This mission, known as "close-air support," contradicted the ideology under which the Air Force had been founded, that a battle could be won largely from the sky. Perhaps officials at the time

---

1. The Johnson-McConnell Agreement of 1966, between U.S. Army Chief of Staff General Harold K. Johnson and U.S. Air Force Chief of Staff General John. P. McConnell.

worried that devoting substantial energy and resources to supporting ground troops would be a tacit acknowledgment that their ideology was flawed.

A crestfallen Kay, whom friends described as deeply ethical, believed he had betrayed his country's infantry, in effect abandoning the grunts on the front lines. Kay's remorse likely swelled as complaints streamed in from the knotted jungles of Vietnam, where pinned-down troops were reportedly waiting upwards of forty minutes to have their prayers for air support met.

The United States war effort could only be described as a mess. One of the United States' main initiatives, "Rolling Thunder," a relentless bombing campaign against the North Vietnamese that began in 1965, was supposed to have swiftly ended the war before too many lives were lost on the ground. But when the Institute for Defense Analysis assessed the strategy, they found the campaign was largely unproductive. In fact, the primary North Vietnamese supply lines had not buckled under incessant American bombing; they had strengthened. Short of unleashing nuclear war—clearly a last resort—success in Vietnam seemed futile.

But how could this be? The United States had bet the farm on developing aerial bombing technology. So, why were the bombers and the bombs they dropped consistently missing the mark?

Throughout World War II, Avery Kay spent much of his time in a B-17 some twenty thousand feet above the battlefield, shuffling among navigation charts from his perch on the flight deck while thick black clouds of eighty-eight-millimeter German artillery burst violently in the sky and hot flak pierced his bomber's thin aluminum skin. From this view, Army Air Corps crews like Kay's spent the war trying to guide millions of tons of bombs over enemy targets of major infrastructure. The tactic, known as interdiction bombing and, later, long-range strategic bombing, had been popularized by an Italian military theorist named Giulio Douhet shortly after the first World War. Douhet believed you defeated an enemy not by attacking its military forces head-on, but rather by "totally [cutting] off the arteries of a functioning army": that is, its supply lines. Disciples of Douhet viewed strategic bombing as the most humane approach to armed conflict—a sudden, demoralizing blow, an amputation of a digit before the infection of bloody ground warfare took the limb.

On a closer look, Douhet sounded less like an ethicist than a madman. In *Command of the Air*, the seminal text of strategic bombing, Douhet argues, "[I]t is not enough to shoot down all birds in flight if you want to wipe out the species; there remain the eggs and the nests. The most effective method would be to destroy the eggs and the nests systematically." Douhet endorsed the use of poison gas on civilians, and he believed in not just attacking supply lines but terrorizing cities. "How could a country go on living and working, oppressed by the nightmare of imminent destruction and death?" he wondered. In response to criticism that high-altitude bombing was often terribly inaccurate, Douhet did not find fault in his theory, the pilots, the planes, or the ordnance. Rather, he blamed the choice of targets:

> *A projectile that falls on a trench may be limited to making a hole in the ground; one that falls on a city will produce an immeasurably greater material and moral destruction. For that reason, the preferred targets of aerial war will necessarily be cities—the largest, most populous, most industrialized, most intellectual cities.*

The veracity of Douhet's claims remained uncertain, though, because just as nations began dropping bombs out of airplanes, World War I came to a close. No definitive argument could be made about the efficacy of strategic bombing[2]: the experiment hadn't yielded results so much as hypotheses in need of further testing. Still, Douhet's theories emboldened airpower advocates around the world to demand independence (and funding) from the ground armies they served.

Douhet's most prominent American devotee was Brigadier General Billy Mitchell. Mitchell bought into the awesome potential of aerial bombing when, during the first World War, he had the opportunity to fly above the trenches with a French pilot. "We could cross the lines of these

---

2. To be fair, the same could be said for close-air support. Really, airpower in general was largely unproven as a weapon.

contending armies in a few minutes in our airplane," Mitchell notes in his memoir. "Whereas the armies had been locked in the struggle, immobile, powerless to advance, for three years." Mitchell would go on to organize the first bombing attacks to great effect, most notably at the Battle of Saint-Mihiel, and ultimately be instrumental in forwarding the bombing doctrine that would shape the U.S. Air Force.[3]

Inspired by Mitchell, Douhet, and others, U.S. airmen made a bid to forge their own military branch, seeking an arrangement much like Great Britain's aviators enjoyed in the Royal Air Force, whose air marshall, Hugh Trenchard, was also a proponent of strategic bombing. While the American government refused this request, the passing of the Air Corps Act of 1926 functioned as a lucrative consolation. The act infused almost 35 percent of the Army's budget into developing airpower over the next five years, resulting in thousands of jobs and expensive new airplanes. During that time, not one new rifle was bought for ground troops. At the Air Corps Tactical School at Maxwell Field in Montgomery, Alabama, new hires studied under instructors who preached much of Douhet's bombing doctrine, devoting almost no time or scholarship to the study of supporting ground troops. After all, Douhet, who died in 1930, believed air warfare could be executed "completely independently from the progress of land and sea operations."

But instructors at Maxwell didn't just blindly follow Douhet's and Mitchell's theories; they advanced them. Aircraft needn't terrorize populated cities with indiscriminate carpet bombing. With enough skill and the right technology, pilots could practice precise bombing during the

---

3. Mitchell's legacy is complicated, to say the least, and one's opinion of it likely hinges on one's views of the merits of strategic bombing. Mitchell received the Distinguished Service Cross for valor and has been called "The Father of the United States Air Force." But in 1925, as a result of his repeated open criticism of the United States military, he was court-martialed for "conduct to the prejudice of good order and military discipline and in a way to bring discredit upon the military service." "Mitchell promoted his ideas with crusading fervor, inside the military bureaucracy, as assistant chief of the Air Service, and outside it, in a stream of books, articles, and public lectures," writes Donald Miller in *Masters of the Air*, later adding, "When Mitchell was opposed by the brass hats of both the Army and the Navy, who saw airpower—power in the third dimension—as a mere adjunct to traditional surface warfare, he attacked them with rancor, alienating the very powers he hoped to persuade."

daytime, in theory crippling an enemy with targeted attacks on industrial factories essential for warfare (ball bearings, steel, and the like).

In 1927, a few years before his death, Douhet noted that "the true combat plane, able to impose its will upon the enemy, has not yet been invented; nor does it seem likely it will be soon." But in less than a decade, the airplane Douhet fantasized about, the tool that would enact the doctrine of the Maxwell instructors, was realized: the B-17 "Flying Fortress." It was a marvel; a sleek, gleaming, four-engine bomber capable of carrying four thousand pounds of ordnance. Equipped with machine guns on each side, in the tail, and in bubble turrets above and below the fuselage, the B-17 was meant to be the bomber in no need of an escort, an offensive and defensive weapon unto itself (later models also featured guns nestled in a chin turret beneath the pilot).

Along with the B-17, the United States invested $1.5 billion (approximately $27.5 billion in 2020) in the Norden Mark 15 bombsight. Accounting for airspeed, wind, altitude, and a bevy of other factors, the Norden—designed by the Swiss engineer Carl Norden—was intended to solve the chronic inaccuracy of bombers. Advertisements embellished the Norden's precision, suggesting it could place a bomb inside a pickle barrel from twenty thousand feet in the air. Years later, the Norden company would lean into the fanciful image when, for an evening in 1943 to celebrate winning an Army-Navy "E" award for excellence in military manufacturing, the company rented out Madison Square Garden and partnered with Ringling Bros. and Barnum & Bailey Circus for the event's entertainment. During one act, a clown dropped a wooden "bomb" into a pickle barrel, sending a pickle flying out.

But prior to combat the Norden received little testing outside of highly controlled military exercises, on clear days with no simulated enemy interference. "It was, at best, an unproven 'therapy,'" the historian Donald Miller notes in his comprehensive account of the Eighth Air Force, *Masters of the Air*. "More than that, it had become dogma, not just untested but unquestioned orthodoxy."

Not everyone bought into the bomber as a panacea to the horrors of war. General Douglas MacArthur worried over the imbalance of airpower in a 1934 annual report, cautioning that an "Army overstrong in

the air would be like an Army overstrong in Cavalry; able to strike suddenly and with great effect, but powerless to hold objectives thus gained."
For their part, Wilbur and Orville Wright had resisted the temptation
that building ever-larger and imposing planes would make small, nimble
aircraft obsolete. "[L]arge airplanes built with the same shape and relative
dimensions as small ones will not have the same relative performance,"
they advised. Nonetheless, funding poured in for lumbering planes and
their long-range bombing efforts.

Early results from Europe should have unnerved military leaders'
faith in high-altitude bombing. A 1941 study found that only one-sixth
of explosives dropped from British bombers landed within a five-mile
radius of their targets. Further, the Battle of Britain demonstrated the
resilience a dedicated population could muster in the face of tremendous
airpower. Though Germany mercilessly bombed England, the British did
not cower as Douhet had theorized decades earlier. They dug in.

Soon after the United States entered combat at the end of 1941, they
suffered the awful consequences of devoting so much energy to sluggish
bombers at the expense of durable, agile fighters that could fly close to
the battlefield. Too often, bombers could not fly in western Europe's
perpetual overcast skies, and those that did were easy targets for German
fighter planes. In a panic, turret gunners would fire recklessly, striking
friendly bombers. Even when smaller aircraft were recognized as viable
tools of war, they were frequently unavailable for supporting soldiers
because they had been called away to escort bombers. Meanwhile, troops
desperate for air assistance sometimes waited as long as three hours for
close-air support; by then, the fight could be long over, the battle lost.

On occasion, heavy bombers flying over the battlefield foretold disaster for American troops. Harried by flak and enemy fighters, bomber
pilots would take evasive action. But these maneuvers disturbed the
gyroscopes of the complex Norden bombsights, rendering them nearly
useless. Poor visibility led to bombers not just missing their targets, but
sometimes hitting their own men. "It makes you feel very helpless,"
Sergeant William Nelson told Thomas Alexander Hughes in his superb
book, *Over Lord*. "It's like a huge sewing machine coming at you, and you
can't get away from it."

Bomber crews experienced a similar sewing machine phenomenon in the sky; once German fighter planes and artillery began chewing into the bombers, pilots could either try to dodge the attacks and sacrifice the accuracy of their bombing run, or simply fly through the firestorm and hope for the best. Bombing had been presented as an antithesis to trench warfare, but in practice it brought the horrors of the trenches into the sky. Despite the B-17's glamorous outward appearance, inside it was a narrow, congested tube. The fuselage's thin walls provided no insulation from extreme temperatures at twenty thousand feet. Where infantry in World War I suffered trench foot, bombardiers endured frostbite. While there was a tube for crew members to relieve themselves mid-flight, it often froze over, so bombardiers took to urinating directly on the cabin floor. Among Avery Kay's duties as a navigator—aside from keeping the flight crew on target—was to make sure no one passed out and died from oxygen deprivation, which was common considering how easily the various life-giving masks and tubes could malfunction. If an inexperienced crew member vomited in their mask, it could quickly freeze and cut off their oxygen supply.

Kay had experienced first-hand how a meticulously planned bombing effort could devolve into chaos. In 1943, he served as the lead navigator on the Schweinfurt Raid, a massive allied bombing assault on a German ball-bearing factory. The Schweinfurt Raid embodied Douhet's philosophy of attacking lines of production: ball bearings were essential to much of Germany's military weaponry. In theory, if their production could be disrupted, the larger German war effort would suffer mightily.

But the raid was a catastrophe. Bad weather prevented many planes from taking off, and nearly a fifth of the bombers that made it off the ground had to reverse course due to mechanical problems. The bombers that did reach the ball-bearing factory had to drop their ordnance through thick cloud cover and were hammered by heavy artillery and German aircraft. The 1st Bomb Wing alone lost thirty-six American bombers and had 352 airmen killed, along with more than a hundred bombers significantly damaged (total losses amounted to sixty bombers and 564 men). The destruction of the factory had been significant, but not devastating.

A second mission followed a few months later, again resulting in extensive casualties for the Allies. Ironically, the Nazi minister of armaments, Albert Speer, believed a third attack from American bombers could have totally destroyed the factories. "Had they continued the attacks with the same energy," Speer said at the time, "we would quickly have been at our last gasp." But the United States did not have enough functioning bombers left for another raid.

Perhaps the most glaring repercussions of America's bomber fixation played out on June 6, 1944. Prior to the D-Day invasion, bombers dropped six million pounds of explosives on Normandy's beaches in hopes of destroying Germany's defenses and clearing the way for the allied assault. The soldiers who stormed Utah Beach benefited from the awesome potential of airpower, taking control of the beach. But the men assigned to Omaha Beach walked into a slaughter. When the Higgins boats carrying allied platoons crossed the choppy surf, neared the beaches, and lowered their ramps, a largely intact German defense network of heavy machine guns nestled in dense concrete bunkers awaited. The bombs had missed Omaha Beach by miles.

If anything, D-Day represented the polarity of bomber theory. When it worked, it could be magnificent in the totality of its destruction. When it failed, it inspired a perverse "tree-falls-in-the-forest" paradox: if hundreds of bombers soar above the battlefield, but most of their bombs miss, were they ever really there?

Long-range bombing was not a total failure, of course. It played an instrumental role in weakening German supply lines. But World War II made it clear the future of warfare could not depend solely on high-altitude airpower. Germany demonstrated that bunkers encased in thick concrete walls could protect equipment and munitions from bombing raids. And the aerial attack approach had not exactly been the clean, humane operation that was promised: more men perished in the Eighth Air Force than the U.S. Marine Corps.

Still, Douhet disciples continued to promote the fallacy of the almighty long-range bomber. After the Air Force's founding in 1947, bombing quickly became its primary focus, the lens through which it viewed war. The growing belief in nuclear warfare as the way of the future further strengthened this conviction. It helped, too, that the Air Force had a near-monopoly on nuclear combat; the only planes that could deliver nuclear weapons were Air Force bombers.

What had been lost in the bomber frenzy was just how effective—and essential—close-air support had been in World War II. Much of the credit for its success is attributed to General Pete Quesada, who made great use of the Republic P-47 Thunderbolt, a bulbous but (given its massive wingspan) highly maneuverable fighter that proved to be remarkably rugged. Unlike the more iconic P-51 Mustang, which had a liquid-cooled engine and was thereby vulnerable to even minimal ground fire that could damage its cooling system, the P-47 was powered by a large radial engine that could take a beating and keep on humming.

Poor communication between air and ground had resulted in costly friendly-fire incidents. Such friendly fire went both ways, as "mistakes were made on the ground, too," notes Hughes in *Over Lord*. "Allied antiaircraft artillery was responsible for nearly as much damage to Quesada's commands as the Luftwaffe and German flak combined." Quesada did his best to rebuild trust between the ground and the air, putting compatible radios in the tanks and airplanes flying close support. He also arranged for an airman to sit in one of the tanks who could clearly communicate the ground's position to airplanes overhead, a necessary move since the "air and ground speak a different language, and what a tank driver might see as a good landmark might be something virtually invisible in the air," Quesada told Hughes. All these efforts enabled Quesada's "armored-column-cover," in which air units loitered above the battlefield and could be called on in an instant to provide ready-made support (much like what Matt Secor had done with FATTS and Ras in the Marah Valley of Afghanistan).

Quesada's greatest achievements came during the Normandy offensive. Where the bombers had come up short, his P-47s slowed the encroaching German Panzer tank divisions enough for U.S. soldiers to reach the cliffsides after landing at the beaches. When the air and ground forces set up headquarters in the French countryside, Quesada performed his most controversial move yet; he pitched his tent directly next to Army General Omar Bradley's, signifying his belief that air and ground were intertwined and need to be in close coordination and cooperation.

After the war and the Air Force's founding, the Air Force recognized Quesada's expertise by naming him head of the Tactical Air Command. But as subsequent changes in defense policy further reduced the importance of non-nuclear airpower, Pete Quesada resigned. Meanwhile, Avery Kay accepted an assignment teaching aviators how to fly bombers from treetop level at night with nothing but maps and compasses to guide their way. These training exercises were preparation for possible nuclear assaults against the Soviet Union, which would necessitate flying bombers beneath enemy radar. Kay also led "spooky missions," in which spies leapt from cargo planes into Eastern Europe. This time, the ordnance was actual human beings who could not risk being caught, so Kay and the other navigators had to be extremely accurate. Despite his rank, Kay insisted on flying these precarious missions. As one of Kay's mentees remembered years later, Kay felt he "needed to share the danger with his students."

Kay's courage and sterling record earned him his spot in the Pentagon, likely on his way to becoming a general. But his crisis of faith in long-range strategic bombing complicated his path to promotion. Many of the airmen who believed airpower should be subservient to the ground had left the service or simply faded into obscurity. By the time Kay realized his accidental sin, how he had only further exacerbated the Air Force's distance from the ground, he had few allies who would empathize with his predicament. He was on his own.

But Kay had problems more pressing than his troubled conscience. So dissatisfied was the Army with the Air Force's woeful close-air support efforts that they had proposed their own tool to do the job, an expensive new helicopter called the AH-56 "Cheyenne." Ultra-fast and technologically far superior to any helicopter in the world, the Cheyenne could carry a bevy of weapons, promising to be for attack helicopters what the B-17 "Flying Fortress" had been for bombers thirty years prior. If Congress approved the proposal—likely, given how easy it would be to illustrate the Air Force's neglect—the funding would come from the very thing it was Kay's job to protect.

Pressure mounted as air combat in Vietnam continued to underwhelm. Pilots flying over North Vietnam received mixed messages for how to drop their ordnance, leading to dispiriting results. *Inflict damage on the enemy*, pilots were told, but at all costs avoid damage to themselves or America's pricey jets. Consequently, fighter-bomber pilots popped in and out of war zones as quick as possible, which limited their effectiveness. One could sympathize with the bomber pilots, some of whom may have found their efforts to be largely futile anyway. It was nearly impossible to make out anything on the ground below, which was capped by a thick jungle canopy. To help with the bombers' accuracy, the Air Force employed pilots to fly aging F-100 Super-Sabre jets in the role of "Forward Air Control," or FAC. In this role, FAC pilots flew low to the ground, spotted possible threats, and fired smoke rockets at the targets. The FAC missions were grueling—often lasting more than four hours— and given the extended exposure to ground fire, extremely dangerous. The fighter-bombers that followed would then drop their ordnance on literal clouds of smoke enveloping the jungle below, like shooting at the suggestion of a ghost in the night. One didn't measure the effectiveness of these sorties so much as guess. All the while, the Vietcong moved through the jungle relatively unscathed.

At the end of yet another meeting filled with bad news, Air Force Chief of Staff John P. McConnell reportedly bowed his head in distress and sighed, "I'm so sick of it . . . I have never been so goddamned frustrated by it all." Amid this desperation, Avery Kay and his superior, Major General Richard Yudkin, conceived of a shrewd proposition. What if the Air Force could design a plane that was both cheaper and more effective than any Army helicopter could ever be? The Air Force was no more passionate about the mission of close support than before. But the solution would preserve their robust budget.[4] More crucially for Kay, the arrangement offered him a shot at redemption.

---

4. The lore behind the plane that would become the A-10 is that it was designed for killing just one thing: not Soviet tanks, but rather, a U.S. Army helicopter.

The Air Force approved Kay's plan but provided little in the way of logistical support. Kay's small design team consisted primarily of former pilots who had flown aging planes in the role of close-air support, but not a single airplane designer. When Kay pinged various offices for available engineers to join his team, he was rebuffed. In this way, the problem Kay now faced was as elegant in its difficulty as his proposed solution had been in its simplicity—to design an airplane without anyone who knew how.

But on that late fall day of 1967, the bureaucratic gods extended Kay an olive branch; it took the form of a controversial memo written by a young staffer with the most peculiar name.

3

The Whiz Kid

In 1967, military strategists predicted that if the Cold War escalated, a Soviet tank army would roll into West Germany through a narrow stretch of rocky terrain known as the Fulda Gap. The Fulda Gap had been where the frostbitten, battered armies of Napoleon Bonaparte retreated after their defeat at the Battle of Leipzig in 1813. A little over a century later, U.S. General George S. Patton traversed the Gap in the Second World War en route to victory. U.S. service members nicknamed the Fulda Gap the "wasp waist of West Germany." More reserved military strategists dispassionately deemed it a "key-terrain feature."

Whatever you called it, this scenario presented a serious problem for the U.S. military because it had no weapon that could halt such a massive tank assault. The constant overcast sky above central Europe would make targeted bombing hit or miss, much as it had been for Colonel Avery Kay in his B-17. For now, the best proposed solution was to have small jets fly at high speeds and low levels beneath the enemy radar to drop nuclear weapons, killing untold numbers of innocent civilians in neighboring towns and propelling the world into a nuclear holocaust.

The document that passed over Avery Kay's desk on that late fall day in 1967 offered an incriminating assessment of the Air Force's current spending. The memo argued that far too much of the United States' military funding was directed toward strategic bombing. The plan to bomb Russian airfields would fail mightily because these airfields were heavily defended by antiaircraft fire. Plus, the Soviets stored their jets in fortified shelters, akin to a trench defense network. Even Giulio Douhet would have disapproved: bombing does you no good against a dug-in enemy.

The memo estimated the United States' current approach would stall a Soviet tank assault for thirty days at most. Given the Soviets' ability to quickly repair their runways, railyards, and bridges, interdiction bombing would have a limited effect. Even if the Air Force tripled its airpower, a long-range bombing strategy would come up short.

Instead of investing in bombers with nuclear capability, or shoe-horning hybridized fighter-bomber aircraft into multiple jobs, the memo argued that the Air Force needed two purpose-built airplanes. First, a small, supremely maneuverable, and lethal fighter plane for dogfighting to protect the skies,[1] and second, an agile yet durable attack plane that could fly beneath the clouds and support troops on the ground while blasting away Soviet Union tanks and enemy infantry. This second airplane is exactly what Kay had been tasked to develop.

The memo, written by a plucky civilian who was not even thirty years old with no military experience, was to be delivered directly to President Lyndon Johnson. The optics were terrible: a young and bold noncombatant ratting out the Air Force's overspending directly to the President. But Colonel Kay did not recoil as so many others had when he finished reading the report. Rather, he saw a potential ally in his maligned crusade.

Pierre Sprey despised bureaucracies. He had no tolerance for their grinding inefficiencies and stubborn hierarchies. As a civilian with no intentions of making a career out of his time in the Pentagon, Sprey was wholly uninterested in the political maneuverings required to get ahead. Phoniness sickened him, and he had little respect for careerists. Impervious to groupthink, he was an empiricist allied with the truth and elegance of numbers, for if calculated and presented honestly, they never lied.

Air Force officials quickly came to resent Sprey. To be fair, he could be abrasive. If our conversations some fifty years later were any indication,

---

1. This would eventually become the F-16.

two of his favorite descriptors were "horse-shit" and "dumb-shit." He spoke freely and had little regard for military ranking. He would joke that the stars on an officer's shoulder were inversely related to their intellect.

Sprey's reluctance to assimilate bore out even in his dress. He bucked the muted business suits of the Pentagon for bright sportcoats paired with turtlenecks. If the occasion called for a tie, he opted for an ascot. But the obstacle most likely in the way of Sprey winning the favor of Air Force officials was not his affect or his language. It was his job: Sprey investigated how the Air Force spent its money.

Born in Nice, France, in 1937, Sprey's family fled the Nazi occupation in 1941, hopping a flight out of Casablanca, "just like the movie," he remembered years later. The family settled in Kew Gardens, Queens. Sprey's father, who had worked with precious metals and refining in France, made jewelry. His mother was a nurse for children with special needs; she was direct and "rock hard," Sprey said, the toughest person in his upbringing. But she also loved her son deeply, and from a young age she taught Sprey how to build model airplanes; Sprey constantly modified the kits to improve their flying ability.

At fifteen, Sprey spurned an acceptance from the Massachusetts Institute of Technology and enrolled at Yale instead, where he double-majored in French literature and mechanical engineering. Judging by the surviving papers in his storage barn a half century later, Sprey was a precocious, albeit distracted student. His work was often late ("A very good analysis," a professor scribbled on one of his essays, "Too bad it was late") or loosely held together ("get some paper clips!" another professor bemoaned). He once lost twelve points simply because of spelling and "sloppy typography." Years later, one can imagine Sprey questioning how something as arbitrary as typography or paper clips could detract from the quality of one's analysis. The inanity of bureaucracy set in early.

Determined to design airplanes, Sprey spent his summers working in Bethpage, Long Island, for the Grumman Aircraft Engineering Corporation. Grumman had built the F4F-Wildcat and F6F-Hellcat, two workhorse Navy aircraft in World War II that eschewed sleek design flourishes in favor of rugged, dependable functionality. Sprey advanced rapidly through Grumman's ranks. In his first summer, he bucked rivets on the production line, before moving into the experimental machine shop and stability and control labs in the following summers.

Near the end of college, Sprey became disillusioned with his dream. He realized it would take twenty years before he would have the autonomy to design his own plane. In what was to be his last summer at Grumman, Sprey took a position in the research department, which focused on probability and statistics. Though Sprey was primed to enter a graduate program at Cornell for aeronautical engineering, he so enjoyed his work in Grumman's research department that he changed course, studying the burgeoning field of operations research and mathematical statistics.

Grumman appreciated—and depended on—Sprey's work enough that they offered to keep him on as a consultant through graduate school. At just twenty-two, he became Grumman's official internal statistical consultant.

In the summer of 1965, Grumman sent Sprey to a convention in San Francisco hosted by the Hudson Institute, a think tank founded by Herman Kahn. Kahn had gained notoriety after the publication of his 1960 book *On Thermonuclear War*, in which he advocated for "deterrence theory." In short, Kahn forwarded the idea that in the horrific event of a nuclear war, the first strike would not necessarily be the last. Rather, what really mattered was how a nation could respond to such an attack. Life could indeed go on after such a horror, Khan argued. Most unusual, though, was Kahn's belief that a nuclear attack could inspire morale among survivors: "It would not surprise me if the overwhelming majority of the survivors devoted themselves with a somewhat fanatic intensity to the task of rebuilding what was destroyed." It is probably worth mentioning that Kahn's work relied on intelligence that overestimated the Soviet weapons arsenal. In the late 1950s, the United States believed the Soviet Union possessed roughly three hundred intercontinental ballistic missiles; in fact, they only had four.

At the convention a representative of Secretary of Defense Robert McNamara's "Whiz Kids," a group of innovative thinkers tasked with reimagining the Department of Defense, approached Sprey and offered him a job at the Pentagon. "We were the only two guys there who thought [this] was all bullshit," Sprey remembered.[2]

Because the Whiz Kids dealt with such highly classified information, the representative could only offer vague descriptors of the type of work Sprey would be doing. Understandably, Sprey was reluctant to accept. He mulled over the proposal for a few months before waking one morning that fall and deciding on a whim that he was headed to the Pentagon.

Sprey officially joined the Whiz Kids in January 1966. He was assigned to the Strategic Transportation Group, which was responsible for assessing all military transportation. He didn't last long.

The group was proud of a strategic deployment model they had recently developed, which was being used to build a hefty new air transport called the C-5 Galaxy. Sprey was not impressed. The model essentially projected military deployment in a linear fashion (the more cargo planes you had, the more troops and weapons you could transport). Sprey had studied linear programs in graduate school and did not believe they were useful for military efforts. Deployment did not happen linearly. There were just too many variables to ever allow for a seamless transition into war: too many unexpected delays and sudden mechanical problems with various vehicles; too much human error.

Upon joining the group, Sprey openly derided the model, unaware of how much pride the team took in their work. In November of that year, Sprey's boss called him into his office and fired him. Years later, Sprey learned he had been fired not for incompetence, but because his ardent criticism of the linear model had been eroding the team's morale. On the whole, Sprey rejected idealized solutions, models, and the abstract moniker of "high tech." He would enthusiastically argue that when it came to winning wars, the most important tool wasn't devastating weapons or sophisticated airplanes; it was trucks, the most basic of instruments that transported soldiers and supplies from point A to point B. As such, Sprey was captivated by the concept that the way to create better spacing on

2. Despite his skepticism, the Hudson Institute tried and failed to recruit Sprey, too.

crowded roads, which had the tendency to "bottleneck," or jam in long stretches, was not to develop better engines, but rather more responsive brakes.

At this point Sprey expected to be kicked out of the Whiz Kids. Instead, he was reassigned to the North Atlantic Treaty Organization group, which oversaw all conventional (read: non-nuclear) weapons throughout Europe. They needed someone to evaluate their data on airpower. Sprey just needed to not piss anyone off. Again, he would fail.

To guide his work, the Whiz Kids gave Sprey three deceptively simple questions: How much money was the Air Force spending? Were they spending the right amount? And were they spending it in the right way?

Sprey spent a year immersed in what he would later recall as "an endless amount of arithmetic." He buried himself in the *Joint Munitions Effectiveness Manual*, a dense totem that listed all possible enemy targets and the United States' available weapons. The data offered calculations for possible attack scenarios with tremendous specificity, down to a target's size, an airplane's angle of attack, its altitude, and the probability it would hit its target given a particular type of ordnance. "I mean that's how detailed this shit was," Sprey told me.

In part, Sprey was not just evaluating current spending, but also helping the Air Force prepare for its next great conflict in the Fulda Gap. Sprey considered low-level nuclear bombing to be a "useless" and "dumb-shit mission." In fact, Sprey was even skeptical of the Fulda Gap's importance. "The nightmare scenario was that they would sweep to the Atlantic, which was, like, utter horse-shit," Sprey said.

At the end of the year, Sprey completed his now-infamous memo. He arrived at his analysis not by projecting an imagined future, but through studying the proven past. "[I got there] basically taking the lessons of what worked in combat, which is how you should design any kind of good weapon, whether it's a good rifle or a good cannon or a good close support airplane," he explained years later. "If you don't base it on the real experience, I mean, the foxhole-level experience of combat . . . [if you] just do it from some technological [and theoretical] perspective, that doesn't get you very far."

To appease the Air Force, the director of the Whiz Kids, Assistant Secretary of Defense Alain Enthoven, drew up a treaty of sorts. If the Air Force could disprove anything in Sprey's memo, it would be amended. At this point, the Air Force set about deconstructing the report and the man responsible for it. They attempted to undermine Sprey's study by running his numbers through an Air Force–endorsed computer program, but Sprey wisely insisted he re-calculate his numbers by hand. Sure enough, one evening two guilt-ridden captains showed up at Sprey's office and confessed they had been directed to botch his data.

Curiously, among the claims the Air Force wanted to dispute was Sprey's confidence that U.S. fighter jets would be effective against Russian MiGs. To discredit Sprey, the Air Force assigned their sharpest tactician, Major John Boyd. A gifted fighter pilot, Boyd earned his nickname—"40-second Boyd"—as an instructor at the Air Force Fighter Weapons School at Nellis Air Force Base in Nevada, where he routinely defeated students in simulated dogfights in forty seconds or less. But Boyd was also a brilliant mind. In 1960, he wrote "Aerial Attack Study," the first (and definitive) dogfighting tactics manual, a meticulous and methodical 150 single-spaced pages that, according to his biographer Robert Coram, became "the bible of air combat."

Boyd's most revolutionary contribution to aviation took the form of the energy-maneuverability (E-M) theory,[3] which completely altered how combat pilots flew their airplanes, and thereby how airplanes were designed and their performance assessed. "After E-M, nothing was ever the same in aviation," Coram writes. "E-M was as clear a line of demarcation between the old and the new as was the shift from the Copernican world to the Newtonian world." Perhaps most impressive, Boyd conceived of his theory when he wasn't even a particularly high-ranking officer, just a major, "a man being bounced from job to job, someone whose job description had nothing to do with computers," writes Coram.

Boyd became obsessed with understanding aircraft performance at a time when there was tremendous emphasis on an airplane's top speed. The high-water mark for speed at that time was Mach 2, twice the speed

---

3. Boyd developed E-M alongside a man named Tom Christie, whom we will meet in later chapters.

of sound, or over fifteen hundred miles per hour. The newest and presumably best fighter planes of the era could fly at or near this speed. However, Boyd insisted that airplane performance—especially when it came to dogfighting—came down to much more than top speed. As perhaps the most skilled fighter pilot of the time, surely he knew. Maneuverability, rather than top speed, was the most important component. And in order to assess an airplane's maneuverability, one had to understand thermodynamics. How maneuverable a fighter jet was depended on the relationship between its thrust, or how much force and power its engine produces, and its drag, or the forces that hamper its aerodynamics. A fighter jet rocketing through the sky is much more complex than just, say, going at the speed that its engines generate power. All those factors of force must be considered along with the factors of drag and gravity. As an airplane executes ever-sharper maneuvers, it pulls what are called "Gs," or forces of gravity. If you're sitting on a chair in your living room reading this book right now, you're "pulling" one G. If you're reading this book on a commercial airliner as it's taking off and feeling the gentle pressure pushing you into your seat, you're pulling a little more than one G. If you were trying to read this book while riding Walt Disney World's Rock 'n' Roller Coaster, you'd be pulling five Gs. The other factor to consider is altitude, as the air is thinner and cooler the higher you go. "Boyd wanted to know how fast a pilot could gain energy when he fire walled the throttle," Coram explains. "At a given altitude, given speed, and pulling a given amount of Gs, how much *ooomph* did he have in reserve?"

To derive this answer, Boyd had to consider not merely the total energy an airplane had, but rather its *specific* energy, which is a factor of its total energy divided by the overall weight of the airplane. The more Gs an airplane pulls, the more drag it accumulates, slowing the airplane down. But slowing down wasn't necessarily a bad thing. Boyd recognized that change of speed—in either direction—was of equal value to an aviator in a dogfight. "The E-M theory, at its simplest, is a method to determine the specific energy rate of an aircraft," Coram writes. "This is what every fighter pilot wants to know. If I am at 30,000 feet and 450 knots and pull six Gs, how fast am I gaining or losing energy? Can my adversary gain or lose energy faster than I can?"

Boyd could empathize with the bureaucracy's harassment of Sprey, too. He'd had to navigate accusations of "stealing" valuable computer time from the Air Force to develop his E-M theory. And he knew how it felt to be the odd man out amid bureaucrats enthralled by technological advances. One of Boyd's primary causes was advocating for the value of machine guns in fighter jets. Increasingly, jets were being equipped primarily with missiles and bombs, but not guns, which were viewed as crude weapons of the past. As Boyd began developing a new fighter for the Air Force called the F-X,[4] one of his chief requirements was that it carry a gun. Not only did Boyd think a machine gun in the nose or wing of an airplane could be a devastating weapon, but it had already proven to be of essential use in Vietnam, where fighter pilots were not allowed to engage a foe with missiles until they had confirmed an aircraft belonged to the enemy. These stipulations put American pilots in a tough spot: to identify the enemy they would need to fly too close to fire their missiles without damaging their own airplane. Consequently, a pilot wanting to down a MiG would need to do an awkward dance of flitting back and forth from the target before engaging. Frustration among pilots mounted, spawning the phrase "IT TAKES A FIGHTER WITH A GUN TO KILL A MIG-21."

While the military industrial complex guided bureaucrats' thinking to the future, Boyd had been obsessively re-examining every instance of air-to-air combat in the Korean War. The U.S. success in downing North Korean MiG fighter jets had led officials to believe in a kind of American exceptionalism when it came to dogfighting, that U.S. pilots had better training and better minds that could overcome any potential deficiencies in their aircraft. It wasn't the American way to complain about the tools, only to get the job done. Boyd didn't subscribe to this line of thinking. He believed the U.S. approach to air combat could dramatically improve, and he wanted to understand the science of aviation.

Like Sprey, Boyd was stubborn. He could not be blindly directed to prove something he did not believe in. Still, the Air Force arranged for Boyd to meet with Sprey, hoping Boyd would quickly dismiss Sprey's

---

4. This became the F-15.

findings and put the memo to rest. Within fifteen minutes of their meeting, though, Sprey and Boyd began talking about World War II dogfighting. Just like Boyd, Sprey had studied aerial combat with enthusiasm. Sprey's interests and intellect intrigued Boyd, who recognized Sprey's math background as a possible asset as he refined his theories. In the coming years, Boyd would entrust Sprey to review his specifications for the F-X, knowing that Sprey would not allow any error in logic or calculation to slip through. Boyd called these evaluative sessions the "Pierre Sprey buzz saw."

Despite his dedication to elegant design and calculation, Boyd remained a fighter pilot at heart. While he didn't believe that American exceptionalism should preclude the United States from designing better airplanes, he did boast to Sprey that, "They give us shit to fly and we win anyhow."

In another failed effort to invalidate Sprey, the Air Force arranged for him to spend the day with Lieutenant Vasily Ilyich Epatko, a Soviet Union defector. Epatko's recent defection had caused quite a stir: he had stolen a Russian fighter jet one night and flew a hundred feet above ground, below American radar, before crash landing in a Bavarian meadow. U.S. officials were alarmed that Epatko had made it a hundred miles inside the boundaries of West Germany without being detected.

Though Epatko remained largely unknown, the jet he flew the night of his escape—a MiG-17—had become a thorn in the Air Force's side. The MiG-17 entered service just after the Korean War and was now already considered outdated (a decade in aviation innovation, especially at the height of the Cold War, was an eternity). At a time when Air Force and Navy jets could reach maximum speeds of nearly twice the speed of sound, the MiG-17 hummed along at a subsonic pace. But as John Boyd discovered, a maximum top speed was far from the most important attribute for a fighter jet to have. Flying at high speeds burned a tremendous amount of fuel, and powerful engines were of little use in a dogfight if a jet had poor maneuverability. During one bombing mission just south of Hanoi, American airmen were stunned when MiG-17s from

North Vietnam's almost comically small fleet of thirty-six jets downed two U.S. F-105 Thunderchiefs, which were weighed down by their six-thousand-pound bomb loads. The F-105, nicknamed "The Thud," embodied the U.S. aircraft philosophy of the time—a big, expensive, powerful jet that compensated for its weight with overwhelming thrust. Upon learning of this embarrassment, Air Force Chief of Staff John McConnell was, according to *Time* magazine, "hopping mad."

The Central Intelligence Agency had stashed Epatko at a safe house on the Eastern Shore of the Chesapeake, with a gourmet Russian chef on staff. Intelligence officials drove Sprey out to meet Epatko, and the two ate borscht and stuffed cabbage and spent the day analyzing air-to-air tactics and the Soviet's airpower strategy. As they spoke, Epatko lit up. Stuck in the safe house, Epatko had been isolated from humanity aside from his chef and the American intelligence officials who repeatedly questioned him about Russian nuclear strategy and weapon placement, information he would not have known as a lowly lieutenant. But he could talk airplanes, and Sprey could, too.

The meeting was supposed to discourage Sprey by illustrating the rigorous training of Russian pilots. If anything, the day's conversation proved the opposite. It soon became apparent to Sprey that the Soviet Union's air training was shockingly primitive relative to the United States', even by World War II standards. Soviet pilots did not fly often, maybe a couple times a week, and flying sessions were short because their jets guzzled fuel.

The intelligence officials who accompanied Sprey were so impressed with how he extracted information from Epatko that they became convinced he was a spy. On the car ride home, one of them turned to Sprey and asked, "Who did you study interrogation with?"

Upon finding Sprey, who was busily preparing to defend his memo, Kay shared his desperation. "I'm dead in the water," Sprey recalled Kay saying. Then Kay offered Sprey a job.

Given Sprey's position with the Whiz Kids, teaming up with the Air Force marked a clear conflict of interest. But Kay was giving Sprey a chance to fulfill a lifelong dream: to design an airplane. And not just any airplane, the exact plane Sprey's study called for, a rugged, agile attack plane.

Because the project was so undesired, Sprey would be working on a small team with little oversight, gifted with the kind of autonomy he thought he would have to wait decades, if ever, to earn when he was at Grumman. Sprey also appreciated Kay's open-mindedness: though Kay had been raised in the tradition of bombers, he was not blinded from considering alternative solutions to a problem as complex as air-to-ground warfare. Oozing humility, the decorated colonel freely admitted that he was stuck and needed help, from a civilian no less.

"So of course, with an appeal like that I had to say yes," Sprey recalled. "How could you turn a guy like that down?"

4

The System

From the end of World War II up to Pierre Sprey's first day in the Pentagon, military aviation evolved at an astonishing rate. The United States went from flying prop-driven B-17s to almost other-worldly prototypes like the XB-70 Valkyrie, a bomber powered by six afterburner engines designed to fly three times the speed of sound (or "Mach 3") at seventy-five thousand feet in the sky, all while hauling fifty thousand pounds of bombs. So advanced was the Valkyrie that it could actually "ride" its own supersonic shockwave thanks to variable wingtips that angled downward.

During this period of unprecedented innovation, a field of study called "systems analysis" gained notoriety. Systems analysis, which Sprey studied in graduate school at Cornell, looked at the world through the lens of systems. Anything with an elaborate set of variables and moving parts that resists seemingly straightforward, linear understanding can be thought of as a system: think major metropolitan traffic patterns, energy usage, and, as their name suggests, ecosystems.

War is an incredibly complex system. Consider all the planning required to transport troops and equipment to the battlefield, all the unpredictable factors of weather and disease and terrain and miscommunication and fear and terror and human error. Designing an airplane is a complex system, a process accountable for innumerable variables pertaining to weight, size, thrust, aerodynamics, payload, and cost. Working in the Pentagon would have been a complex system: all those bureaucratic processes and red tape and egos and political maneuverings. Such complex systems required innovative ways of thinking and analyses to navigate them. "The central feature of the systems approach, and the one which distinguishes it from earlier methods and requires a truly multi-disciplinary attack, is the concept of treating problems as a whole rather than piecemeal," Harry J. White and Selmo Tauber explain in *Systems Analysis*. Central to this interdisciplinary approach is a background in math. To properly study systems analysis, White and Tauber recommend a solid footing in vector analysis and differential equations, among other subjects. During the time Sprey was studying systems analysis at Cornell, the field would have been in its relative infancy, "still seen only dimly as compared to traditional disciplines such as physics, mathematics, and engineering," White and Stauber note, adding however that this systems approach could be tied back to the Greeks and Romans, as well as René Descartes' *Rules for Direction of the Mind*, a lengthy treatise espousing the systems approach first written in 1628 (but only later published in 1701).

More recent systems analysis methods were borne out of World War II with a practice called "operations research." Operations research took scientists, thinkers, and mathematicians and mushed all their brainpower together to optimize how war was planned and fought. If anyone wondered why civilian mathematicians like Pierre Sprey could be so central to fighting wars and building weapons, the answer was clear: mathematicians just looked differently at the world.

In 1943, the Army Air Corps sought the expertise of Abraham Wald, a professor of statistics at Columbia University. Wald was working for the Statistical Research Group, which was "something like the Manhattan Project, except the weapons being developed were equations, not explosives," mathematician Jordan Ellenberg writes in *How Not to Be Wrong: The Power of Mathematical Thinking*. The U.S. military wanted to better understand how to armor their airplanes against ground fire. The answer wasn't as simple as covering the entire airplane in armor. That would be much too heavy. They would have to be more selective. To inform their analysis, the U.S. military wanted to use the existing data they had on airplanes that had survived combat. This data took the form of battered airplanes chock full of bullet holes. Because the airplanes seemed to be taking the most damage in the fuselage, it was suspected that that area should get even more armored. A mathematician like Abraham Wald approached the problem in a way others did not.

"The armor, said Wald, doesn't go where the bullet holes are," Ellenberg writes. "It goes where the bullet holes aren't: on the engines." The sample size provided to Wald was of the airplanes that *survived* combat. Thus, it indicated that the airplanes could survive while being hit in the fuselage. But the airplanes that had been hit in their engines had presumably been lost in action. In hindsight, this might seem obvious. "Why did Wald see what the officers, who had vastly more knowledge and understanding of aerial combat, couldn't?" Ellenberg asks. "It comes back to his math-trained habits of thought. A mathematician is always asking, 'What assumptions are you making? And are they justified?' . . . In this case, the officers were making an assumption unwittingly: that the planes that came back were a random sample of all the planes." But the sample of planes wasn't random: they were the lucky ones to go into battle and make it home.

Such mathematical approaches to analyzing problems guided the field of operations research. Mathematicians and scientists across all disciplines, from physics to zoology, applied their thinking to the science of war. Because while there had been many innovations during the Second World War, implementing them was almost as challenging as inventing them. "Someone had to devise new techniques for these weapons, new methods of assessing their effectiveness and the most efficient way to use them," writes Fred Kaplan in *The Wizards of Armageddon*. "It was a task that fell to the scientists."

One such precocious mind was Robert Strange McNamara, the future secretary of defense under John F. Kennedy. McNamara was the youngest assistant professor in Harvard's history before he directed his analytical brilliance to aerial bombing. While serving in the Army Air Corps' Statistical Control Office (an outgrowth of the Harvard Business School), McNamara's insights contributed to reducing the "abort rate" of bombers, which (understandably) were often finding excuses to avoid flying over their targets for fear of being killed.

Serving under General Curtis LeMay, McNamara's analysis pushed LeMay to order massive fleets of B-29 bombers—originally designed to drop their ordnance from some twenty-five thousand to thirty thousand feet feet—to fly at attacking altitudes of a mere five thousand feet. The resulting changes led to far more accurate bombing and also extreme tragedy. "I was on the island of Guam, in his command, in March of 1945," a pained McNamara tells Errol Morris in the acclaimed documentary *The Fog of War*. "In that single night, we burned to death 100,000 Japanese civilians in Tokyo. Men, women, and children."

After the war, McNamara and a small cohort of operational researchers joined the Ford Motor Company, transforming the manufacturer's middling finances and reputation. McNamara was instrumental in the production and promotion of the compact Ford Falcon, and through intensive analyses of car accidents, McNamara and the "Whiz Kids," as they'd come to be known, developed safer cars with such innovations as padded instrument panels, steering wheels that wouldn't impale drivers (a leading cause of death in accidents), and, most controversially, seatbelts.

McNamara became the first non-Ford family member to be selected as president of the Ford Motor Company, a position he quit just five weeks later to serve as secretary of defense for John F. Kennedy. A stout negotiator, McNamara only accepted the post after being granted the power to appoint every single senior official. McNamara was forty-four, then the youngest secretary of defense.

During his presidential run, Kennedy was advised by members of the RAND Corporation, a think tank made up of operations research analysts who had gone into defense consulting after World War II. "McNamara was coldly clinical, abrupt, almost brutally determined to keep emotional influences out of the inputs and cognitive processes that determined his judgements and decisions," Kaplan explains. "It was only natural, then, that when Robert S. McNamara met the RAND Corporation, the effect was like love at first sight."

No one likes to be audited, and McNamara was the lead auditor for the U.S. military. Among his exacting accounting methods was to directly compare and evaluate military spending across all branches together, which was unprecedented at the time. How did a battleship compare with a tank? How did an attack helicopter for the Army compare with a close-air support airplane for the Air Force? McNamara wanted these answers, and he wanted to make decisions based on the cold calculus of cost-effectiveness.

It was the Air Force that seemed to bear the brunt of McNamara's new approach. "During the first couple of years of the Kennedy Administration, the Air Force could not win a single battle with McNamara," Kaplan writes. "And all the blame fell on the Whiz Kids, who, except for the relatively low-keyed and gentlemanly Charlie Hitch, practically shoved their victories and their youthful civilian power in the military's face." McNamara's right-hand man, Alain Enthoven, took the position of deputy assistant secretary for systems analysis when he was only thirty years old, where he was effectively Pierre Sprey's boss.

One can imagine the tense dynamic between the Whiz Kids and the military brass as akin to the one that boiled over four decades later between professional baseball scouts and sabermetrics analysts in the "moneyball" era of sports: the nerds who assessed winning with equations versus the jocks who actually fought the battles with blood and grit on the field (of war). In this way, it's possible to even sympathize with the military's frustration with oversight, especially with the Air Force. The Air Force had fought for independence for forty years, and when it was finally granted it resulted in slightly over a decade of relatively unchecked expansion that yielded profound (albeit not always practical) innovations. It must have been jarring for this independence to be so suddenly curbed. Worse, the leader of this new auditing effort was the dashing man with the distinguished part in his hair and the irritating habit of answering questions with a cocksure grin who cultivated such unsavory nicknames as con-man, dictator, and "Mr. I have all the answers McNamara."

By the time Pierre Sprey entered the Pentagon, the Whiz Kids' reputation was particularly strained. Vietnam was a disaster. On October 21, 1967, as Sprey was preparing to defend his controversial memo, twenty thousand Americans marched on the Pentagon to protest the war effort. Soon thereafter, McMamara submitted his own memo directly to President Lyndon Johnson urging that the United States absolutely must change course in Vietnam. On February 29, 1968, McNamara resigned from his position as secretary of defense.

Adding to Sprey's unfavorable reputation was that he didn't particularly align himself with any segment of the bureaucracy. He neither subscribed to the Whiz Kids' thinking and projections nor to the military's more brash approach to combat. Sprey's outcast status could be attributed in part to his perception of war and its relationship to innovation. Weapons were often developed in the interest of almost sterilizing the awfulness of war. Aside from nuclear missile technology, nowhere was this mindset more prevalent than in the realm of military aviation. Then, as now, aviation attracts and showcases the most unique concentration of humankind's intellect, innovation, and creativity; all that brainpower directed into the majesty of making man fly.

Sprey was never seduced by projections and theories that war could be lessened by more destructive weapons of bombing or nuclear missiles or faster airplanes equipped with ever-more sophisticated technology. If war was indeed a fundamental, yet grisly, quality of humanity's coexistence, then one could not mask its ugliness; doing so only further perpetuated the horrors of war. The most ethical manner in which to plan for war was to confront it honestly for what it was, not for what we hoped it one day might become. As such, Sprey argued throughout his life the best resources for gaining insights on war were the first-hand accounts of those who had served, whether by directly speaking with surviving soldiers and airmen or reading the voluminous post-war memoirs penned by infantrymen and pilots. He was an empiricist, believing that past experience was far and above the most accurate indicator for what the future would hold. Though I never heard him profess an allegiance to a particular mode of thinking, Sprey's ethos fit comfortably within the paradigm of human-centered design, the now widely popular design philosophy in which technology should be built with its users in mind[1]—easy to use and in service of an existing problem rooted in historical evidence.

---

1. Hog driver Tom "TC" Norris would later reflect on the design process of the A-10:
"I think the most impressive thing to me is the amount of time that the designers spent with the end-users, and I'm not just talking about the pilots . . . [who fought in] Vietnam, because that was a very, very important group to consult with as well. But also they spent a tremendous amount of time

He had the mind of a McNamara and the mouth of a fighter pilot. Because he was unwavering in both his morals and his analysis, he never found himself in the position of cozying up to a particular side. Consequently, he was often isolated. One can imagine how discouraging it would have felt to spend months or years working on a new project only for Sprey to pop in, poke a hole in its logic, and send all of the optimism streaming out. It's no wonder that when he eventually found his clique, of sorts, they were all outcasts of a similar kind, champions of practicality and authenticity amid the muck of pseudo-optimism. Sprey's longtime friend, the defense journalist Andrew Cockburn, put it simply: "He was uncompromising for the truth."

[asking], 'What does the customer [i.e., the soldiers being supported on the ground] want? It really started with a very detailed list of requirements of what the customer wants, and then kind of . . . treating that as the target and then going backwards. . . . I mean to really take the time and energy to really understand what it's like from the guy on the ground's perspective . . . and how will I shape the design of the aircraft to fulfill those needs? . . . When you start with that level of research and go backward, that's why I think the airplane is as good as it is. Because they not only researched and paid attention and asked good questions to thoroughly understand it, but they applied it."

5

Simplicate, and Add More Lightness

"I think the Russians are clever enough to make use of my experience. In the field of combating tanks alone, which must play a part in any future war, my instruction may prove disadvantageous for the enemy."

–HANS ULRICH RUDEL, *STUKA PILOT*

SPREY'S CONVICTION, INTELLIGENCE, AND STUBBORNNESS NO DOUBT made him a frustrating employee within the Pentagon. "I kind of measured my success by the opposition I got," he told me. In a very real sense, he behaved as if he had nothing to lose. "I wasn't trying to become Secretary of Defense or something," he said. But if his disposition rankled superiors, it also fostered admiration among his contemporaries.

"I never myself thought of Pierre as 'arrogant,' but I am sure some people who were on the receiving end of his rebuttals might use that, or a similar term, to describe him," said Sprey's former colleague, Bob Speir. Instead of attacking the opposition, Sprey would meticulously deconstruct their logic, challenging whatever fundamental assumptions they might have. "But he could say it in a very polite way," Speir added. "You know, unless you were an antagonist and then he'd just rip you to shreds."

Despite Sprey's unwillingness to play bureaucratic ball, he continued to get promoted, where various offices sought out his honest, exacting analysis. In a September 9, 1969, memo to the Department of Defense's testing and evaluation division, Sprey recommended that two of the latest fighter jet projects (what would become the F-15 Eagle and F-14 Tomcat) be cancelled. His memo concluded with a forthright declaration that embodied his philosophy—he would walk if he was ever forced to compromise his analysis:

> *Unfortunately, my conscience does not permit me to write the kind of material that could be accepted as the DoD input. Therefore, I recommend that you find someone with more flexible views to write the . . . paper, if it remans necessary to produce such a paper.*

A month later, after visiting Wright Patterson Air Force Base in Dayton, Ohio, to further examine the F-15, Sprey again offered blunt assessment:

> *After two relatively enjoyable days spent with Col. Bellis and the SPO "experts," my findings on the F-15 are as follows: 1. The aircraft is still shockingly gold-plated . . . There is a strong mood at Wright-Patterson of defending the form on the remaining mountain of "goodies." 2. No attempt has been made to use this opportunity to improve performance by cutting the weight. . . . In a room full of USAF officers I found myself in the curious position of being the only person advocating higher performance. . . . The USAF is very inclined to postpone any contractor redirection on additional cuts until after a contract is signed. Since I've never heard of anything being removed from an aircraft after contract signature, I'm rather leery of this approach. 4. The USAF model contract is a complete disaster and was presented with great hedging, evasiveness and fuzziness. Their contract is so inflexible in quantities and schedules as to force the USAF into bed even with a contractor who is performing badly—just like the C-5 option mess.*

Sprey's frankness occupied a curious position within the Pentagon. He freely critiqued not just the Air Force, but the Navy and Army, too. In fact, he didn't feel particularly aligned with the Whiz Kids either, who had a reputation for dreaming up "solutions" that were efficient and effective in theory, but unworkable in the turmoil of war.

Thus, Sprey's new assignment with Avery Kay wasn't exactly a secret: he still reported to the Pentagon for work, and the secretary of defense knew of Sprey's involvement with the A-X project. But given the stir caused by his presidential draft memo, all parties thought it best not to publicize Sprey's involvement in an already maligned project. So each day at 5:00 p.m., Sprey quietly left the Pentagon and made the twenty-minute drive east to Falls Church, Virginia, where Avery Kay had carved out space in a small office on the ground floor of a nondescript building belonging to the government think tank Analytic Services, Inc. There, Sprey worked on the A-X each evening until midnight or so. The added responsibility and hours came with no extra pay, which Sprey did not mind. He thought of the arrangement as a privilege, and in the following decades he would echo a familiar refrain, "The reason I came to Washington was because I believed the country needed a much better defense than it had and that we were paying way too much for what we had."

Sprey now inherited Avery Kay's puzzle of conceiving an airplane without any actual airplane designers on staff. He would have to work with what he had.

Among Sprey's best resources were the experiences of members from his design team who had flown the Douglas A-1 Skyraider in Vietnam.[1] Reminiscent of the P-47s that General Pete Quesada used to such great effect in World War II, the Skyraider was hardwearing and propeller-driven, with a bubble canopy and a fat radial engine. The Skyraider belonged to a different era, first conceived in the waning years of World War II as a "bomber-torpedo" to protect naval aircraft carriers from submarine attacks. But the war was over before the Skyraider could enter service. High-speed jets soon ruled the sky.

In Vietnam, most of the United States' air fleet were simply too fast or too fragile to fly close-air support for troops on the ground. Zipping over the jungle canopy at high speeds on moonless nights made spotting

---

1. Lieutenant Colonel Bob Winger and Major Tom Pulham.

enemies extremely difficult. The seemingly outdated A-1, however, was ideally suited for flying low to support troops. Its radial engine could take hits from ground fire and keep running, and the A-1's long wingspan made it highly maneuverable even at slow speeds.

"We seldom got over 1,000 feet above the ground," said Paul Gray, who flew A-1s in the Korean War, to Rosario Rausa in *Skyraider: The Douglas A-1 "Flying Dump Truck."* On one harrowing occasion, Gray's A-1 sustained more than fifty bullet holes. Other pilots reported taking up to two hundred hits, some leaving holes large enough to fit a basketball or even an entire person through.

During a series of tactical exercises with the Air Defense Command, U.S. radar operators tried to detect A-1s simulating an enemy attack on American soil. The A-1s could fly so close to the ground that they couldn't be detected, since terrain like trees, hills, and canyon walls—of which the A-1 flew low enough to weave through—confused radars. The "outdated" A-1 was effectively a stealth airplane decades before an official stealth airframe would ever take flight. "In the entire history of these exercises," James Fallows writes in his book *National Defense*, "from the late forties to the early sixties, the radars from the Air Defense Command never tracked the A-1s, and the interceptors never caught them."

Nothing flammable (hydraulics or fuel) was placed anywhere near the cockpit, so pilots did not have to worry about catching fire like they did in other jets of the time. And the cockpit was highly user-friendly. A-1 designers found that a pilot's head was typically two feet away from the instrument panels, so they adjusted the gauges to be easily read at that distance.

The A-1 contained one more crucial, if oft-overlooked, tool: its radio. "You can give up on almost anything in the airplane," the A-1 drivers told Sprey as they developed the A-X, "but you can't give up the FM radio that talks to the Army." As Pete Quesada and others had learned in World War II, close-air support was best coordinated not through intermediaries, but rather directly between the pilot and the ground, as any delays or miscommunication could be fatal; war happens fast. All told, A-1 pilots proved they could quickly and clearly communicate with ground troops, which literally saved lives: A-1s facilitated the rescue of approximately a thousand downed pilots in Vietnam.

At the heart of the A-1's dependability and versatility was Ed Heinemann, whom Sprey called the "single designer I have the deepest respect for." Like Sprey, Heinemann was precocious, but unpretentious. He "never completed a formal degree as an engineer," notes writer and engineer John Golan, but he "rose through the ranks, first as a draftsman, then as an apprentice to and colleague of other legendary aircraft designers—Donald Douglas, Jack Northrop and Howard Hughes among them—before finally becoming Douglas Aircraft's design engineering chief." Most importantly for Sprey, Heinemann was a "tiger on weight control," consistently delivering airplanes lighter than expected, which is practically unheard of in aircraft design because of the urge to always add extra (often heavy) features to a plane (what Sprey called "gold-plating"). Heinemann adhered to the motto of Gordon Hooton, a designer for the Ford Motor Company in the 1920s: "Simplicate, and add more lightness."

Heinemann kept his airplanes light by rejecting fads. One such fad was "swing-wing" technology, in which wings extended outward for takeoff to improve lift, and then swept back once the airplane was in flight and traveling at high speeds. Swing-wings appealed to the Navy as a way to save space: a plane that could sweep back its wings dramatically reduced its wingspan, which made it easier to stow on a crowded aircraft carrier.

When Heinemann was tasked with building a new jet for the Navy called the A-4 Skyhawk, he didn't bother with the complexities and inevitable maintenance problems that came with swing wings (namely, that the joints on which the wings swept back and forth often wore down). Instead, he utilized a simple delta-wing design. There were no unnecessary moving parts, no added complexity, no extra opportunities for something to break. The delta-wing design shaved off about two hundred pounds on the A-4's overall weight, and Heinemann cut an additional fifty-eight pounds by ordering an entirely new ejection seat. Like the A-1, the A-4 had an extremely user-friendly cockpit. It was so simple, in fact, that pilots found it disarming. "It scared me to death for the first half hour," a pilot told *Aviation History Magazine* of the first time he flew an A-4. "I kept looking around the cockpit for something to do."

With Ed Heinemann and the A-1 Skyraider in mind, Sprey and his team determined a few things. For one, their airplane would need to be extremely durable *and* maneuverable so that it could fly low to the ground, dodge small arms fire, and keep flying even if it got hit. This meant it would need a big wingspan. It also needed to have a bubble canopy so pilots could easily see their surroundings. And it would have *two* radios, in case one broke.

In essence, Sprey had learned what an airplane needed to withstand damage. But what did it need to *inflict* damage, especially on heavy Soviet tanks that might roll through the Fulda Gap at any moment? For this, Sprey turned to an unlikely source.

With a young boy's foolish aspirations of flight, at ten years old Hans Ulrich Rudel jumped from a windowsill with an umbrella in hand and broke his leg. Undismayed by this failure, Rudel decided in that moment that he would become a pilot. The naive child grew to be the greatest tank-busting airman in history, ultimately destroying more than five hundred tanks in World War II fighting for the German Axis forces against the Russian army on the eastern front.

Growing up, Pierre Sprey had read Rudel's autobiography, *Stuka Pilot*, and he now required his design team to read it, too. The book's title refers to the airplane Rudel used to kill so many tanks, the Junkers Ju-87G dive-bomber, more commonly known as the "Stuka." Not a glamorous airplane, the Stuka was slow and clumsy and ugly. It had a long narrow nose like an opossum, and gangly landing gear that didn't retract after takeoff.

The Stuka had not been Rudel's first choice out of flight school. But he was a slow learner, the last in his squadron to pass his training. Never a serious scholar, Rudel spent his off-hours playing sports or hiking in the nearby mountains of the Steiermark province. But he was rigorous when it came to his own physical fitness. He skied and pole-vaulted in primary school and found solace in long runs. The health-obsessed Rudel made no drinking buddies, either: he never drank beer, only milk.[2]

At first Rudel resented being relegated to the Stuka. In training, however, he proved to be an exceptionally accurate dive-bomber and gunner. During strafing runs, he learned to utilize the Stuka's diving breaks to violently slow down and improve the accuracy of his attack run. The maneuver made him easier to hit, but Rudel didn't care. He frequently disobeyed conventions, dropping bombs at nine hundred feet that were supposed to be released from three thousand feet, risking damage to his own airplane and only pulling out of dives at the last instant to avoid hitting the ground. His commanding officer thought Rudel was "crazy" because he "generally dive[s] to too low a level in order to make sure of hitting the target and not to waste ammunition."

Still, Rudel's technique for killing tanks was masterful. He would fly out of range of enemy flak cannons, about twenty-four hundred feet in the sky, and then "scream down in a steep dive, weaving violently." Years later, he would describe his flying style as "almost like a drunken man," wobbling and twisting his airplane arrhythmically, only to straighten out for 1 to 1.5 seconds to aim and fire, hoping to "hit a particular spot (i.e. petrol or ammunition) with incendiary or explosive stuff." Rudel's effectiveness is all the more impressive considering his cannons could only fire a single shot each per pass. If he missed, he would have to begin the whole risky process again.

If there was a secret to Rudel's mindset, it was that the mission took priority over everything, including personal safety. "Skill is often the result of getting hurt," he writes. His true superpower was his tolerance for excruciating pain. Once, after being shot down behind enemy lines, he hiked sixty kilometers in Russia's bitter cold without winter clothing

---

2. "It cannot be said that I am a rapid learner. . . . It takes a long time to ring the bell, too long to please my squadron leader," Rudel writes. "I catch on so slowly that he ceases to believe that it'll ever ring at all. The fact that I spend my leisure hours in the mountains, or at sport, rather than in the officers' mess, and that on the rare occasions when I put in an appearance there my only beverage is milk does not make my position any easier."

Later, Rudel notes how he sticks out in "the pleasure-seeking atmosphere of France," where his "clean-living, [his] addiction to sport and [his] everlasting habit of drinking milk are more conspicuous than ever."

or shoes. During another crash, he wrecked his shoulder and the skin on his feet was stripped clean. Still, he flew. "Every pressure on the citrons involves acute pain," he writes of flying after the injury. "I have to be carried to my aircraft."

After another battle wound forced him to have his leg amputated, Rudel lamented that "the only catastrophe is that I cannot fly for weeks." Rudel believed hunting for tanks required a "sixth sense," one that could only be acquired by flying every day. For Rudel, time off wasn't recuperative; it was deadly. And so, with one leg Rudel flew his Stuka, alternating between pressing the rudder bars with his remaining foot like one does with the clutch and gas pedals in a manual drive car. Eventually, he had an artificial limb constructed, which made flying easier, but irritated what remained of his amputated leg:

> [W]ith every pressure upon it, that is to say when I have to kick the right rudder-bar, the skin at the bottom of the stump which was doing its best to heal is rubbed sore. The wound is reopened again with violent bleeding. Especially in aerial combat when I have to bank extremely to the right I am hampered by the wound and sometimes my mechanic has to wipe the blood-spattered engine parts clean.

Rudel's near-lunacy fueled the fanatic devotion to flight he began cultivating when he jumped from that window with umbrella in hand. It was as though he didn't trust the ground beneath his feet, like it was the ground that broke his leg, not his foolhardiness. It was on the ground where superiors called him crazy, where fellow soldiers ridiculed him for drinking milk instead of beer. But in the sky, he wasn't crazy; he was a god. He often slept under his airplane for just four hours a night, and routinely flew twelve-mission days; once, he flew seventeen missions in a single day.

There is a kind of perverse irony in Sprey utilizing Rudel's experiences to build what would become a distinctly American plane. After the war, Rudel was a Neo-Nazi activist, whereas Sprey's family had come to the United States after fleeing the Nazi occupation of France. Even more strange, then, are the similarities that can be drawn between Sprey and Rudel. Here were two stubborn men who disdained bureaucracy, slept very little, and channeled their conviction toward achieving a clear purpose.

So confident—or perhaps self-righteous—was Rudel that on numerous occasions he disobeyed direct orders from his superiors, including Adolf Hitler, in the service of flying the Stuka. When Hitler wanted to pull Rudel from the battlefield and use him as a propaganda mascot, Rudel refused. "To disobey an order is, I know, unforgivable," Rudel writes, "but the determination to save my comrades is stronger than my sense of duty."

For all the technical lessons to be learned from Rudel, perhaps the most valuable lesson Sprey and the A-X designers could glean from *Stuka Pilot* was the mindset of a close-support airman: a selfless devotion to the mission. By extension, Rudel's insights informed what an airplane like the A-X had to have to foster such commitment: it would need to be so dependable, so unshakeable that a pilot could endure barrages of enemy gunfire and not think twice.

Rudel remained a loyal German soldier to the end. When it came time to surrender, he ordered his squadron to crash- land their Stukas, sheering off their landing gear as they collided with the ground, rendering them unflyable. During interrogations with U.S. officials, Rudel balked at their fascination with new weapons technology. "They boast of their rockets which I already know about and which can be fired from the fastest aircraft; they do not like to be told that their accuracy is small in comparison with my cannon."

6

The Thud

"Many of the more agonizing aspects of fighter combat are the direct results of the failure of the simplest systems."
—COLONEL JACK BOUGHTON, *THUD RIDGE*

ON JUNE 6, 1950, THE GRADUATING CADETS OF THE U.S. MILITARY Academy at West Point considered a monumental question: what would the next war look like? Only six years removed from the Normandy D-Day invasion, the very idea of warfare had fundamentally changed. Or so it seemed. No longer would the United States fight interminable wars that relied on masses of infantrymen hauling gear through the muck. Instead, wars would be decided with specialized combat troops brandishing sophisticated weapons and supersonic jets delivering nuclear bombs in swift, destructive blows.

To reflect this changing landscape, West Point cadets now took an extra year of English, along with classes in public speaking, leadership, geopolitics, and psychology. "The academy curriculum . . . now prepares its graduates to fight a cold as well as a hot war," *The New York Times* noted the following day.

In his address to the graduating class, Secretary of the Army Frank C. Pace, Jr., made another bold proclamation, one marking a paradigmatic shift in the understanding of war. With innovations such as the bazooka along with rocket and missile technology, Pace argued, "[I]t may well be that tank warfare as we have known it will soon be obsolete." To be clear,

Pace did not discredit the very real danger tanks still posed. A Soviet tank army invading Western Europe was just as much the threat-du-jour in the early stages of the Cold War as it would be fifteen years later when Pierre Sprey entered the Pentagon. Rather, Pace believed that the countermeasures for killing tanks would be much different in future wars.

"The best way to prevent such a catastrophe is to be prepared to meet these masses of heavily mechanized ground forces with similar numbers of highly scientific ground troops equipped with revolutionary new weapons," Pace said. While war would always be brutal, it could at least be shorter: triumphs of annihilation rather than attrition.

Like the airplane that would ultimately be designed to destroy it, the tank has had the peculiar quality of endurance. As we know them, tanks came into use during the First World War. Their development was fueled by the same grisly impetus that expedited airpower: trench warfare. Hunkered in trenches lined with barbed wire, soldiers were locked in siege. If infantrymen poked their heads above the trench's rim, they became easy targets for riflemen in an opposing trench. Heavy artillery guns, which could fire punishing rounds and puncture enemy defenses, were among the best tools infantry could use to make forward progress. But this artillery had to be hauled by men and animals, and traversing the disputed ground between trenches (a.k.a. "No Man's Land") was suicide. Even if the artillery made it to the opposing trench, their progress stalled as they struggled to make it past the barbed wire lining the trenches and bridge the wide gaps between the trench walls. If the infantry couldn't move, their artillery couldn't either, effectively rendering the technology useless.

It was French Colonel J. E. Estienne who encouraged the use of what we now know as a tank. Indeed, he believed it would decide the outcome of World War I. According to Richard Ogorkiewicz's book *Tanks: 100 Years of Evolution*, "after only a few days of operations" Estienne "is reputed to have told the officers of his regiment that victory would belong to whoever of the belligerents was the first to mount a 75 mm gun on a vehicle capable of moving over all types of terrain."

Inevitably, early tanks were ill-suited for war. They had a range of less than twenty-five miles and a top speed of under four miles per hour. Mechanical issues abounded. But as the war progressed, tanks showed promise, especially as mobile artillery that could move behind troops and shell the enemy at a distance, clearing the way for foot soldiers. Though tanks weren't invulnerable—even as their engines and track technology evolved, they were still prone to breaking down—they became a staple of a modern army.

In the coming decades, the tank's importance only grew, particularly in the Soviet Union. Already a defining feature of its army in World War II, the Soviet Union doubled their tank divisions (from thirty-five to seventy) while the United States shrunk their tank army down to just a single division. Just three weeks after Secretary Pace's address at West Point the world would be reminded that the tank's time as a decisive weapon was not yet past when North Korea invaded South Korea with 140 Soviet Union tanks. By the time the A-X began development, the most fearsome Soviet Union tank was the T-62, which carried a revolutionary 115-millimeter "smoothbore" barrel, as opposed to a grooved rifle barrel enabling it to fire advanced armor-piercing rounds that were longer and more narrow than traditional cannon rounds. With its new gun, the T-62 could hit targets a thousand yards away, penetrating armor more than a foot thick (the T-62 was itself shielded by armor more than three-quarters of a foot thick). The T-62 could even create its own "smoke screen" by pushing extra diesel into its engine, and if the occasion called for it, the tank could be affixed with a snorkel so that it could (briefly) travel underwater.

As Pierre Sprey and his team developed the design specifications for the A-X, they needed to determine what weapon could most effectively (and efficiently) kill such heavily armored tanks. Hans Rudel had had great success killing Russian tanks with the thirty-seven-millimeter cannons under his Stuka's wings. But Rudel's guns only carried twelve rounds each, for a total of twenty-four bullets. If the A-X was going to provide the hours of close-air support required of it, its gun would need to fire much more than two dozen rounds; it would need to fire a thousand.

For now, the United States had no such gun in development. They believed missiles were the way of the future. But missiles were expensive, and no airplane could carry more than a handful. As of late, it had been a fight to even get guns of any kind into their newest airplanes. So, yet again, Sprey would need to look to history for a solution. He would find it in a century's-old piece of technology, a relic from the Civil War.

Like many an enterprising businessman whose industry happened to be death, Richard Gatling professed humanitarian aims. The staggering body counts and gruesomeness of the American Civil War horrified Gatling. But these horrors also inspired in him the capacity for invention:

> *It occurred to me that if I could invent a machine—a gun—that would by its rapidity of fire enable one man to do as much battle duty as a hundred, that it would to a great extent, supersede the necessity of large armies, and consequently exposure to battle and disease would be greatly diminished.*

It was a familiar refrain, one that would be echoed the following century by proponents of strategic bombing and nuclear warfare. But Gatling had an additional motive. "[Gatling's] records make clear that he was driven by profits," C. J. Chivers notes in *The Gun,* his masterwork about the proliferation of the AK-47 assault rifle. Still Gatling, Chivers adds, "never ceased claiming that compassion urged him on at the start."

What Gatling strived to create was a mobile, reliable gun that could be manned by just a few soldiers and fire bullets at an astounding rate. He succeeded. Featuring six barrels that rotated on a center axis, it was powered by a hand crank and "shared design elements with a cotton planter and rotary cultivator," Chivers explains, "except that it directed evenly spaced bullets, not seed, where the handlers intended them to go."

It wasn't until 1946 that something like the Gatling gun found its way into airplanes with the U.S. Army Air Corps' "Project Vulcan." The Vulcan contract was awarded to General Electric, who presented a Gatling-style design that had numerous benefits over the current crop of airplane-mounted guns. For one, airplane guns of the time were single barreled, which meant that every bullet fired went through the same barrel. Firing bullets heats up a gun barrel and wears down the barrel's lining and walls. A Gatling gun's barrels, on the other hand, rotated such that each barrel shared the burden of firing ammo. Put simply, firing six bullets through a one-barrel gun led to six rounds' worth of wear and tear on the barrel, or perhaps even more as the barrel heated up with each round fired in quick succession. Firing six bullets through a Gatling gun effectively caused just one rounds' worth of damage on each barrel.

A Gatling-style gun could also fire much faster than other guns, which made it more accurate as there was less time between each bullet's discharge and therefore less variation in its placement on the target. An airplane firing a Gatling gun wouldn't shower a target with bullets in a wide swath; it would hit one distinct spot repeatedly. Each of these qualities would later prove perfectly suited for penetrating even the most formidable tank armor.

After testing for Project Vulcan ended, Vulcan cannons became the standard for jets (that is, if they had a gun at all). A Vulcan cannon, however, would not work for the A-X. Vulcans fired twenty-millimeter rounds, which were about the size of small garden-variety carrots. To penetrate tank armor and cause meaningful damage, the A-X would need a round closer to the size of an ear of corn, about thirty millimeters.

Gun size grows dramatically with even small increases to its ammunition, and Vulcan cannons had already proved difficult to fit onto existing airplanes. If Sprey and company were going to require the A-X to carry a Gatling-style gun that fired thirty-millimeter rounds, it couldn't just be attached to the airplane after the fact. Rather, the A-X would need to be built *around* the gun.

"We said the gun is at the center of this airplane," Sprey recalled. "If we didn't have that gun, I couldn't have backed the airplane."

In mid-November 1970, a request for proposals for this new massive gun went out to manufacturers.

While guns had become an afterthought in aircraft design, a new vision of aerial attack had taken hold: high-speed, low-level nuclear bombing. Skimming the trees, a jet would theoretically fly below enemy radar, drop its bomb, and bug out before being devoured by the nuclear blast. Who needed a gun when you had a nuke?

For this purpose, a variety of airplanes[1] were built, none in greater numbers than the F-105 Thunderchief, nicknamed "The Thud." The Thud was a hulking jet, about as big as a World War II–era bomber, though it carried just one pilot (later models had two seats). It could fly nearly twice the speed of sound and haul almost double the bomb load of the B-17 Flying Fortress.

But the Thud was designed to carry just one thing: a nuclear bomb. These were "one-way missions": the trip would be so long and the Thud guzzled so much fuel that a pilot would not be able to fly home after dropping his bomb. Instead, he was directed to fly past the target and bail out over neutral (or at least less-hostile) territory as he unleashed World War III in his wake.

The Thud never did the job for which it was designed. Instead, as the Vietnam War began, Thuds were relegated to conventional bombing, where they suffered catastrophic losses. Weighed down with bombs, Thuds were juicy targets for enemy MiG jets and surface-to-air missiles. Of the more than eight hundred Thuds built, nearly half were lost in combat.

The blame for the Thud's dreadful loss rate could be partly attributed to the United States' puzzling restrictions for attacking enemy defenses over Vietnam. U.S. officials feared that bombing any airstrip or munitions headquarters that might be housing Soviet representatives could provoke an all-out war with Russia. "MiGs could and did take off and land directly beneath the bomb sights of our aircraft, and the rule forbade their destruction until they were airborne," Jack Broughton, an F-105 driver, explains in his memoir *Thud Ridge*, a core text for fighter and

---

1. Such as Ed Heinemann's A-4 Skyhawk. "He was a guy," Sprey said of Heinemann, "that had this amazing ability to take a special occasion for a dumb-shit mission like low-level nuclear attack and design an airplane that actually turned out to be a great and useful airplane, even though the mission was useless."

attack pilots. "The result was inevitable: military and psychological stulti-fication, and an increasing pilot and aircraft loss rate as Moscow helped Hanoi to establish the most sophisticated air defense system ever tested in war—a far-flung complex of missiles, ground guns, interceptors, radar, and communications and control centers." Because of these restrictions Thuds never benefited from the element of surprise. They flew the same routes at the same time of day, over and over. Enemy air defenses adjusted accordingly, and Thuds routinely flew into a slaughter.

It's difficult, then, to chalk up the Thud's losses to poor design. With better tactics and planning, perhaps it would have had more success. Undeterred by flying a bombing mission for which it wasn't designed, Thud pilots like Jack Broughton developed an affinity for their jet, in particular its roomy cockpit and straight-forward flying mechanics:

> [T]he Thud would show in most people's books as a loser . . . but . . . the Thud was getting to North Vietnam as nothing else could. Nobody could keep up with the Thud as it flew at high speed on the deck, at treetop level. Nobody could carry that load and penetrate those defenses except the Thud. Sure we lost a bundle of them and lost oh so many superior people along with the machines, but we were the only people doing the job, and we had been doing it from the start.

Still, it would be the Thud's shortcomings that proved most instructive for Sprey and his team. Most notably, Thuds were demonstrating a puz-zling pattern; they kept exploding in mid-air.

Why did the Thud catch fire so easily? The question was of particular interest to Franklin "Chuck" Spinney, a young second lieutenant stationed at Wright-Patterson Air Force Base in Dayton, Ohio. Spinney was a military brat, a mechanical engineer whose father had been a test engi-neer for the Army Air Corps in World War II. As such, he felt a strong sense of duty to his country. While many of Spinney's colleagues seemed more interested in building the next great fighter plane—working in the theoretical and imagined arenas of future war, rather than the harsh reality of the present—Spinney wanted to fix the jets they already had.

"We were in the middle of a war," Spinney said years later. "I felt like I should be working in some way related to that . . . working in wind tunnels [. . . and] looking at nose cones and stuff, you just didn't get that feeling."

Spinney managed to get himself transferred to another office where he could focus on remedying the Thud's vulnerabilities. Quite simply, the Thud's fire problems stemmed from the dissonance between its design and its use. As a low-level nuclear bomber, it may have excelled. As a traditional bomber, it was a design disaster.

Airplanes often store fuel in their wings, but the Thud's wings were much too thin. What the Thud did have was a bloated belly fuselage, intended to house its singular nuclear bomb. This belly had since been repurposed as a bladder for fuel tanks. When these tanks emptied, they contained flammable vapors that the Thud had no way of purging. In a sense, this empty fuel bladder became a bomb, one the Thud couldn't drop. The bladder was also highly vulnerable to ground fire. One high-powered enemy round could cause fatal explosions.

Fuel itself posed huge problems for Thud. It did not have "self-sealing fuel tanks," or fuel tanks coated with a rubber mixture that expanded if the tank was punctured and acted like a sponge to soak up the now-leaking fuel. Self-sealing fuel tanks had been around since before World War II, but they were bulkier than integral tanks built into the airframe and had thus become less popular in the supersonic jet age, where everything needed to be streamlined for aerodynamic effect. There was such widespread belief in missiles as the primary weapon of war, too, that the thinking was if a missile completely obliterated a jet, it really didn't matter if there was a fuel leak anyway. Because the Thud's non-self-sealing belly fuel tanks were also wrapped around its engine, if a tank caught fire, the engine soon followed. "Basically," Spinney remembered, "if you had a fuel leak in a 105, you had a problem."

It got worse. Just like its fuel tanks, the Thud's already fragile hydraulic systems were housed around its engine. If they leaked, a fire could easily start. And while the Thud had multiple sets of hydraulic lines, they ran a mere half-inch apart from each other. A well-placed 0.50-caliber round could punch through the Thud's belly and disable all the lines. Without hydraulic power the Thud went into a "tumble": the jet's nose pitched violently up and then down, sending the plane hurtling to the ground.

"This was the curse of the Thud," Broughton corroborates in *Thud Ridge*. "She would go like a dingbat on the deck and she would haul a huge load, but she was prone to loss of control when the hydraulic system took even the smallest of hits. There is just no way to steer her once the fluid goes out, and I can tell you from bitter experience that you can lose two of the three hydraulic systems that run all of your flight controls by the time you realize you have been hit."

Even if a pilot managed to survive a Thud's "tumble" and eject, it meant doing so over enemy territory, resulting in either death or a torturous stay as a prisoner of war. But Chuck Spinney's colleagues had learned that if they could keep a Thud pilot in the air for five additional minutes after being hit, the probability of saving that pilot skyrocketed (a few minutes of flying time add up quick in a jet traveling six hundred miles an hour).

Much of this work predated Spinney, but he read up on it in earnest. The current problem facing Thuds and other combat aircraft of the time was that there simply wasn't enough hard data available to make informed inferences for how to best protect them. This would be Spinney's task: to develop a curriculum for training engineers to travel to Vietnam to study damaged airplanes and report back on where and how they had been hit. Like Pierre Sprey, Spinney was interested in solving problems based on mounds of hard data, lessons from history, and a bit of common sense.

It would be some years yet before Spinney's path would cross with Sprey's, but eventually they would become close friends and allies in their fight against a burgeoning military industrial complex. For now, they were working together without even knowing it.

In March 1968, Sprey and his team drafted a Concept Formulation Packet for the A-X: a list of parameters, must-haves, and non-negotiables. The A-X would need a long loiter time, meaning it had to be able to fly circles above the battlefield for two hours while fully loaded. It needed to be both fuel-efficient and safe. And it needed to be slow. Speed may have been the apple of many a designer's eye, but when it came to close-air support, speed was a hindrance. To a pilot flying at high speeds, the ground was a child's watercolor painting, all smudges and splotches and smears. Flying slow, the ground wasn't exactly a photorealistic master-piece, but at least it was legible. Since the A-X was to remain over the battlefield as much as possible, it needed to have a tight turning radius. High-speed jets can turn tightly, but it puts tremendous Gs on the pilot. Pulling off these turns would be much more feasible for a pilot flying in a slow airplane. The idea was to build something akin to a vulture, some-thing that could drift laconically in tight circles such that it never left the battle area, yet could strike the moment a threat was identified.

From this basic idea, the remaining specifications followed. To be maneuverable, the A-X needed a big wing. To prevent fires like those that had crippled so many Thuds over Vietnam, the A-X's fuel had to be placed away from the engines and the cockpit and stored in self-sealing fuel tanks so that even if they were hit they wouldn't explode. All this time over the battlefield would make the pilot extremely vulnerable to ground fire, so he needed to be cradled by a titanium bathtub to protect him from the inevitable hits to his airframe.[2] Lastly, if the A-X lost hydraulic controls, it could not be at risk of "tumbling" like the Thud. Instead, it would have an old-school backup flight control method called "manual reversion," a system of cables and pulleys that the pilot could use to control the airplane.

Sprey also felt it extremely important for the pilot to be able to see over the nose and to the rear of the airplane. Any fighter plane that had metal blocking the rear view was a sign that the designers "were ignor-ing the pilot, they were ignoring real air combat. . . . So we demanded a

---

2. One early airplane with an "armored bathtub" was the Russian Ilyushin-2 Sturmovik, which Joseph Stalin held in the highest regard. When production of the Il-2 slowed, Stalin admonished one factory: "You have let down our country and our Red Army," Stalin said according to The Smithsonian's National Air and Space Museum. "You have the nerve not to manufacture Il-2s until now. Our Red Army now needs Il-2 aircraft like the air it breathes, like the bread it eats. [This plant] now produces one Il-2 a day. . . . It is a mockery of the Red Army. . . . I ask you not to try the gov-ernment's patience, and demand that you manufacture more Il-2s. This is my final warning. Stalin."

very extreme bubble canopy," Sprey said, one that would actually bubble *beyond* the width of the fuselage.

Chiefly, the A-X would be far more lethal than anything in the current Air Force arsenal. In a study on close-air support that Sprey produced for the Air Force Scientific Advisory Board in April 1968, he boasted, in his characteristic manner of teasing a supposed weakness of his argument before adamantly squashing it, that the A-X "will have 3–6 times the destructive capability of the F-4/A-7 except against tanks where its advantage increases to 8–10; it will destroy [close-air-support] targets at 1/4 to 1/5 the cost per target except against tanks where it will be almost 10 times cheaper in terms of direct 10 year costs including munitions and attrition." All this promised capability would be achieved with technology that had been around for decades, if not longer: Gatling guns and self-sealing fuel tanks and manual-reversion backup flight controls. The A-X was shaping up to be the antithesis of nuclear air warfare: a dumb, slow airplane with a big gun.

7

Fly Before Buy

"Nobody had ever designed an airplane to be accurate at shooting at the ground."

−Pierre Sprey

In the late 1960s, buying a new airplane was not so different from ordering off the prix fixe menu. The Pentagon would pay a large up-front sum to a contractor, and then leave it to that contractor to conceive the entire airplane. "Total package procurement," as it was called, had been implemented by Robert McNamara when he became secretary of defense. In theory, total package procurement was supposed to keep costs down: one contractor supplying everything would streamline the production process. In reality, it created bloat. "Design teams grew to two thousand people then three thousand," notes the historian Robert Coram. "And the cost of developing a new fighter rose to around $1 billion." Seduced by potential, the government awarded contracts based largely on theoretical models of what the yet-to-be-built airplane was *projected* to do, rather than a real, physical prototype that could be seen and touched and actually flown. Unsurprisingly, this led to some production debacles, including the C-5A Galaxy, a cargo plane the size of a football field that had gone two billion dollars over its projected cost.

To sidestep such pitfalls, Sprey's team insisted on a different method of defense procurement, colloquially known as "fly before buy." Instead of theoretical models, they required fully armed prototypes and a competitive fly-off between airplane manufacturers, a then-unheard-of arrangement. "They had never had a head-to-head competition between two airplanes armed with weapons, and to see which one could use the weapons better, and which one could survive," Sprey said.

Defense contractors balked at the competitive fly-off idea; a prototype that didn't perform well meant the end of a fat government contract. Defense analysts argued that expenses would actually be *higher* since the upfront costs required to build a physical prototype were far greater than producing theoretical calculations. In fact, why did the United States even need the A-X? In 1968, the Senate Armed Services Committee called for an audit of the military's airpower spending, specifically its attack airplanes designed to bomb and strafe the ground. In the current arsenal were Ed Heinemann's A-4 Skyhawk, along with the Grumman A-6 Intruder and the Vought A-7 Crusader. Did the U.S. military really need *another* attack airplane? What's more, the Marine Corps was working on acquiring the AV-8B Harrier airplane, renowned for its ability to take off from short airstrips and land vertically like a helicopter. In the coming years, the A-X project would face scrutiny as the entire fleet of attack aircraft—both existing and in development—came under review.

Further complicating Sprey's hopes for a competitive fly-off was the A-X's original nemesis, the Cheyenne helicopter, though not for the reasons you might think. Now grossly more expensive than originally proposed, the Cheyenne's problems kept mounting. Just before noon on March 12, 1969, a Cheyenne prototype exploded mid-flight along the coast of southern California, killing its test pilot, thirty-two-year-old David A. Beil. In another incident a year prior, a Cheyenne's rotors went off kilter, colliding into the canopy.

Like so many "groundbreaking" designs, Sprey thought little of the Cheyenne. "It was a horrible, really screwed up design, grossly gold plated," he said. On the whole, Sprey turned a skeptical eye toward attack helicopters. Sure, they could get low to the ground, but they couldn't survive worth a damn, he felt. One couldn't simply add extra armor to a helicopter, either, since any added weight was especially taxing on the chopper's engine, which provided most all of its lift (as opposed to an airplane's wings that work in concert with its engines). What Sprey cared for the least was the Cheyenne's high-end top speed, reported at more than 240 miles per hour, faster even than the AH-64 Apache attack helicopter in use today. To provide close support or hunt tanks like Hans Rudel, one needed to be able to not just fly low, but to be able to turn tightly at slow speeds, such that the pilot could always keep their eyes on target. "We did a lot of the geometry in order to set what we what we really needed," Sprey explained. He'd found that to be able to successfully hunt tanks that were hidden under trees and rocks, a pilot had to be able to turn and stay within a quarter mile of the battle area. Any further than a quarter mile and a pilot would lose sight of the target and have to begin the whole arduous process of spotting tanks over again.

In a way, the Cheyenne's failures posed just as much a threat to the A-X as a fully formed helicopter prototype would have. If the Cheyenne failed to come to fruition, then any sense of urgency created by its impending production would dissipate. Sprey believed the "Air Force would have been perfectly happy to design the A-10, have a beautiful briefing, go to the Congress . . . and the moment the Cheyenne helicopter died, that briefing would have gone right in the trash bag, and there wouldn't have been a nickel put behind it."

Coinciding with the Cheyenne's struggles were what Sprey called a series of "happy accidents" in pushing the A-X through development. "The accident that gave us the money [for prototyping] was the advent of Dave Packard." Packard, who co-founded the technology company Hewlett-Packard in his garage, had been appointed the deputy secretary of defense by President Richard Nixon, and it just so happened that Packard believed in prototyping when others doubted it. "He felt we had to do lots of prototypes before you can ever figure out what you really needed," Sprey remembered. "So that got us at least into a hardware airplane instead of a paper plane."

Merely building prototypes, though, isn't what set Sprey's demands apart from other airplanes; prototypes abounded for fanciful airplanes dreamt up by overly ambitious designers hoping to conceive of the next hot jet or terrorizing bomber. What made Sprey different was that he wanted these prototypes tested *competitively* against one another, fully armed and in realistic combat scenarios. Which leads us to the second happy accident that befell the A-X. At the time, John McLucas was serving as under secretary of the Air Force (the position of secretary of the Air Force was vacant), "and by dumb-ass luck," Sprey said, "he thought well of close support. So he really had very little connection with all of this down-in-the-mud stuff we were doing. But he was amenable to prototyping." If Sprey ever had trouble dealing with the Air Force, he sought out McLucas, who offered a "sympathetic ear" and in the case of competitive prototyping "rammed it down their throat."

With competitive prototyping approved, the A-X development team set the ground rules for the competition. After soliciting proposals from possible contractors, Sprey's group would narrow the list down to two candidates, each of whom would deliver three functional prototypes. Two of these prototypes would be used for flying tests, and they would need to be fully weapons capable, not simply glorified high-performance models. There would be gunnery competitions, bombing competitions, and even maintenance competitions. "And if your airplane breaks too often it's going to count against you," Sprey remembered. "Even though it's a prototype, we know you haven't refined it, we better make sure this thing's pretty maintainable right from the start." In the interest of limiting as many variables as possible, Sprey insisted that the same group of pilots fly both prototypes, and that they be *tactical* pilots with real combat experience rather than *test* pilots. He wanted pilots for whom bombing and strafing were "like second nature."

The third working prototype that each candidate delivered would be tested for *survivability*. That is, rather than theorize how an airplane *might* survive against enemy defenses using projections and calculations, the A-X prototypes would be blasted with live enemy rounds. The prototypes were to be delivered in pieces, each fully loaded with fuel or hydraulic fluid so that they could be shot with Russian weapons.

As with so much of what Sprey did at the Pentagon, his methods bucked the trends. Typically, engineers tested survivability using a computer modeling program called shot-line analysis, which basically projected how a round would affect an airframe from hundreds of different angles. For example, the shot-line analysis could determine if a round fired from one angle would only scrape an airplane's fuselage or, if fired from another, would pierce a fuel tank and set the airplane ablaze. Sprey, as always, remained skeptical of the computer modeling, in large part because he suspected the results could always be distorted to favor a particular side. Furthermore, an airplane is such a complex system with so many moving parts that it's extremely difficult to project how a bullet might impact an airplane when that airplane did not even physically exist.

"That's where the rub was," Sprey explained. "First of all, the calculations were very inexact, they didn't really know how well these bullets could go through a spar [i.e., the backbone of the wing], because nobody had ever shot at spars, they'd shot blanks at aluminum. Aluminum is different than a riveted spar, it's a different structure. So even the structural stuff was very shaky." Sprey felt there were simply too many variables to account for, too many different kinds of bullets and missiles and angles of attack. How could you know if a bullet that pierced a fuel tank would light it on fire unless you did it?

"So there's no way we're going to use shot line analysis to analyze anything to do with survivability," Sprey declared. "We're going to bring pieces of the airplane and we're going to shoot it with real weapons." Consistent with his view that no simulation could match up to the real thing, he was staunchly opposed to the idea of using "surrogate" Russian weapons. "I said, 'No, we're gonna buy them on the black market. And they're gonna be exactly what the Russians shoot.'"

The stipulations for the live-fire survivability testing caused the most trouble. Sprey knew they couldn't just fire rounds at, say, a wing loaded with fuel sitting stationary on a range; this would eliminate the crucial variable of wind, since air and fire behave much differently when the air is static compared to when it's moving at hundreds of miles per hour. Sprey's critics argued that the prospect of shooting live ammunition at airplane parts loaded up with highly flammable fluids *indoors* didn't sound like such a great idea. How could you possibly build a wind tunnel big enough to accommodate such an egregious fire hazard? And even if you could build such a tunnel, the expenses would be colossal. But Sprey's critics were missing the point. They didn't need a wind tunnel, he argued. They just needed *wind*.

"It's so much simpler," Sprey remembers telling them. "Of course, we're going to shoot outdoors . . . and you guys are at Wright Patterson [Air Force Base] and I know you have at least 50 bomber engines from World War Two. And they all swing 15-foot props. There will be huge radial engines from the B 29. They had them out there, I know about them. And . . . I guarantee you, they will blow wind more than 200 miles an hour because the bomber went faster than 200 miles [per hour]." Ever the pragmatist, Sprey said the only equipment needed was a concrete base to elevate the bomber engine off the ground and blow wind over the prototype pieces.

Unbeknownst to Sprey, Chuck Spinney was working on the Thud's fire problems over at Wright-Patterson Air Force Base, where Spinney remembers seeing a rudimentary vertical wind tunnel being built. This tunnel blew wind upwards through a cylinder, over top of which a piece of an airplane could then be placed and shot at with live rounds safely outdoors. Years later when Spinney and Sprey started working together, Spinney told Sprey about this "innovation."

"He said those sons of bitches six months later published a paper . . . about how they invented the ballistic wind tunnel," Sprey said, though he claimed to be unbothered by this discovery. When pressed on if he invented this technology, Sprey told me, "It's an act of huge arrogance to call it the ballistic wind tunnel. I invented a bomber engine on a concrete pillar swinging a prop. I mean, what's to invent?"

In May 1970, a request for A-X design proposals went out to twelve contractors. These proposals needed to be "design to cost," meaning that contractors were given a fixed cost for their design: they needed to present a working prototype that could be produced at $1.5 million per airplane. The design-to-cost philosophy sought to protect the government from overspending by preventing defense contractors from adding features that might improve an airplane's capability, like flying at night or in bad weather, but also exponentially increase their cost. Sprey called non-essential add-ons "gold-plating," and though he never expressed to me any strong opinions about the design-to-cost philosophy, he often shared how he believed airplane design was (and still is) quite gold-plated. Whatever capability gained by "gold-plating" came at the cost of extra weight, which decreased an airplane's aerodynamic performance or fuel efficiency. As Ed Heinemann had repeatedly emphasized: simplicate and add more lightness.

By December 1970, the list of candidates winnowed down to two companies: Northrop and Fairchild-Republic. They would have just over two years to design and build their prototypes. Northrop, founded in 1939, counted among its creations the F-5 Freedom Fighter, a no-frills, high-performing jet that was one of the few planes Sprey actually deemed to be both well-designed and a good use of taxpayer money. Fairchild-Republic was formed after the 1964 merger between the Fairchild Hiller Corporation and the Republic Aviation Corporation, the latter of which had a particularly rich history in airplane design. Republic's origins began in 1931 with Alexander de Seversky, a Russian naval aviator in World War I who lost a leg on his very first combat mission. He'd been shot down, and the bombs still attached to his airplane detonated on the crash. While Russia prohibited Seversky from flying, he rebelled, participating in an airshow soon after to prove it was possible to fly a plane with a prosthetic leg (much like Hans Rudel would two decades later). Though Seversky was arrested, he was later permitted to fly, becoming the top "ace" in Russia's navy by shooting down thirteen enemy airplanes over the course of the war.

Seversky's career in aviation and weapons design inspired awe. He received the first patent for air-to-air refueling and helped invent the first bombsight to be stabilized by a gyroscope, a predecessor to the Norden bombsight—the same bombsight used by so many bombers, including the B-17. In 1931 Seversky founded the Seversky Aircraft Corporation. But after just eight years, he was fired as president and replaced by Wallace Kellet. The struggling company changed its name to the Republic Aviation Corporation and would go on to build the P-47 Thunderbolt, used masterfully by Pete Quesada in World War II for close-air support, and the infamous F-105 Thunderchief.

As the finalists for the A-X project were announced, Pierre Sprey unexpectedly resigned from the Pentagon. His resignation letter, sent

October 23, 1970, was just one sentence, streamlined and to the point, like the airplanes he admired and strived to build: "This letter is to inform you that I would like to resign, effective December 1, 1970." Years later, Sprey elaborated on his reason for quitting with an equally efficient sentence: "Because my boss was a total horse's ass and totally a tool of the industry."

Sprey's superiors clearly thought more highly of him. In response to his resignation, they wrote to Sprey, praising his "keen conceptual skills and perceived analytical abilities," which had earned Sprey "a well-deserved reputation as one of the very best systems analysts." As such, the Pentagon offered to keep Sprey on as a consultant so that he could stay involved with the A-X and whatever else might benefit from his expertise. Sprey accepted. Thus began the remainder of his off-beat career in the defense industry, one in which he maintained a minimal "official" profile but managed to seemingly participate in just about everything of consequence. The Whiz Kid was now untethered and ubiquitous.

Sprey's new gig was in environmental consulting with Richard Hallock, whom Sprey had met when he joined the Pentagon. (At the time Hallock was developing the M-16 assault rifle.) Soon Hallock became Sprey's primary mentor on ground warfare, a mentorship that proved essential in Sprey's understanding of close-air support.

It was Hallock who implored Sprey to understand how hard it was for pilots to see the ground; he knew because he'd experienced it first-hand. In World War II, Hallock had been a paratrooper, and he was captured behind enemy lines. While being transported with other American prisoners of war in a truck convoy, the trucks suddenly pulled off the side of the road, barely concealing themselves under a sparse clump of trees. Then a flight of P-47s whizzed past, just above the treeline. "They didn't see a single truck and all they were was under trees," Sprey remembered Hallock telling him, later adding, "I've always kept that lesson with me." In the coming years, Sprey would emphasize the importance of actually training pilots for the amount of focus and discernment needed to *look at the ground* in an intentional and useful way. "One of the things that nobody thinks about [is] just training them to see . . . the most important thing they can be trained for is how *hard* it is to see."

Miraculously, Hallock soon escaped his captors. "The Germans couldn't hold him more than three weeks [before] he got away," Sprey recalled. Much like how Sprey's design idol Ed Heinemann approached building airplanes, Hallock took a historical approach to examining any task. When assigned to work with a new organization, the first thing he did was read everything possible about its history to understand its context. "He was a guerilla insurrectionist against the bureaucracy," Sprey explained. "When he took on a bureaucracy he studied everything about their background."

In the coming years, Hallock would play a crucial role in getting the A-X project into production. For now, he and Sprey continued their environmental consulting work, and Sprey kept a toe dipped in the Pentagon pool.

Northrop and Fairchild-Republic began work on their respective designs. Northrop's design team was headed by Walt Fellers, who had studied under Edgar Schmued, the designer of the P-51 Mustang. Fairchild-Republic, meanwhile, was guided by Robert Sanator, top executive and then-president, and project engineer Vincent Tizio.

Among the top priorities for both teams was deciding on an engine. Sprey's group hadn't specified what type of engine the A-X needed to carry, only what it needed to do: provide enough fuel economy for it to fly long hours and just enough thrust so the attack plane wasn't a sitting duck over enemy territory. Propeller-driven engines like the one that powered Ed Heinemann's A-1 Skyraider were initially considered but ultimately deemed too cumbersome. On the other hand, jet engines would be of little use to the A-X since they could be wildly fuel inefficient and would make the airplane much too fast. The A-X didn't need to fly hot and fast; it needed to fly long, cool, and slow. What did seem promising, however, was the turbofan engine, the same kind of engine powering commercial airliners. Turbofan engines didn't offer great acceleration, but they were more propulsive than a comparable propeller-driven engine, and they didn't burn near as much fuel as jets.

In October 1972, Northrop and Fairchild Republic unveiled their competing designs at Edwards Air Force Base in the desert of southern California, where the competitive fly-off testing would take place. Both designs had much to recommend: ultra-survivable fuel tanks, cockpits swaddled in a titanium bathtub to protect the pilot, bubble canopies for enhanced visibility while flying, and a manual-reversion backup flight control mechanism. No gold-plating. What's more, both designs featured "interchangeable parts," whereby the hardware on the left and right sides of the airplane could easily be exchanged with each other and across other airframes: you could take a right wing panel from one airplane and put it on the left wing of another airplane of the same model.

Of the two designs, Northrop's A-9 looked much more the part of a contemporary airplane. Its two engines were nested into a slender fuselage, enhancing its streamlined appearance. Northrop's A-9 engines also had the benefit of being low enough to the ground that maintainers could easily access them without needing to climb up on ladders. By comparison, Fairchild-Republic's A-10 was grotesque. But its grotesquery was the product of an ingenious design concept. If the A-X was supposed to be above all *survivable*, that meant, among other things, protecting its engines.[1] As such, the Fairchild-Republic group decided to mount the plane's turbofan engines high above and behind the wings, on the tail of the airplane. This decision resulted in an awkward, clunky look, but it afforded some remarkable benefits.

For one, the wings functioned as a shield from ground fire. And given how far apart the engines were spaced, if one engine was hit it was less likely the other engine would be damaged, too. With the turbofans—which already ran cooler than traditional jet engines—situated up by the tails, it further reduced the amount of exhaust that could be detected from the ground. The high-engine placement also enabled the A-10 to take off from even the cruddiest airfields. Debris can easily be sucked up from engine intakes that are close to the ground, so the A-10's high-mounted engines made it much less susceptible to accidentally ingesting rocks or dirt or whatever else may have found its way onto the tarmac.

---

1. Recall the mathematician Abraham Wald's lesson from World War II, that what mattered in examining the surviving bombers was where the bullet holes *weren't*: the engines.

Though maintainers did have to climb up on ladders to reach the A-10's engines, they still found them relatively easy to repair, especially since they could do so without tinkering too much with the rest of the plane. Like much of the rest of the A-10's parts, its engines were to be the first "unhanded" engines in Air Force history (either engine could be placed on the left or right side of the aircraft).

Over the next two months, both airframes were tested for survivability, maintainability, and lethality. (Because the thirty-millimeter cannon that was going to be the airplane's signature feature was still in development, each competitor instead used a twenty-millimeter cannon.) While Northrop's A-9 put forth a competitive showing, the A-10 ultimately won due to its easier maintenance, ability to carry more weapons, and its simple design. Test pilots also favored the A-10 to the A-9 as it proved more survivable in outdoor wind tunnel gun testing.

Survivability would come to be the A-10's calling card. Its self-sealing fuel tanks were placed throughout the airplane and away from the fuselage, so even if one fuel tank suffered damage it would not cause a catastrophic failure. The cannon's ammo drum was shielded with "trigger plates" that would activate if an enemy round penetrated the airframe, essentially exploding the round before it could get to the ammo drum itself (a similar technology existed in tanks of the time). Fairchild-Republic overengineered the A-10 to such a degree that internal structural components that were essential in other airplanes could be disconnected or disabled in an A-10 and it could still remain in flight. The result was a practically unkillable airplane, one that could remain in flight with half the tail and wing blown off, just one functioning engine, and no hydraulic controls.

In another wise move, the folks at Fairchild-Republic decided to have the A-10's landing gear retract only partially into the airframe, in bulbous external wing pods. Sure, the wing pods contributed to the A-10's funny look, but they actually allowed the airplane to be smaller since there didn't need to be extra internal space in the fuselage to stow the landing gear. For pilots, the landing gear arrangement provided another practical benefit: the wheels always remained exposed, so if the A-10's landing gear ever failed to lower it could still effectively "crash-land" without crashing or damaging too much of the airplane; indeed, in later years

A-10s and their pilots would survive doing just that. Fairchild-Republic clearly conceived of the landing gear with disaster in mind: since the gear retracts forward rather than backward, if the gear ever malfunctioned mid-extension, the incoming airstream would literally *push* the wheels down into place.

No doubt, the A-10 was far from perfect, and it failed to meet Pierre Sprey's exacting standards. "I was appalled at how big it was," he said. "When they rolled it out I said, 'Oh my god, it's a fucking bomber.'" Sprey lamented the A-10's overly complex manual reversion mechanism, and pilots wished the airplane had more technological sophistication to aid in deploying weapons. Nonetheless, working within the constraints of the design-to-cost philosophy, Fairchild-Republic had produced a durable and highly capable airplane.[2]

How *lethal* the A-10 would be remained uncertain because its thirty-millimeter cannon was still in development. And just because a prototype had been selected did not guarantee the A-10 would enter full-scale production. It would have to clear a few more bureaucratic hurdles before it became a reality.

"By the end of the fly-off," Sprey remembered, "building the A-10 was by no means a done-deal."

---

2. Years later, Brigadier General Michael "Johnny Bravo" Drowley described the plane as so user-friendly for the pilot that it "makes you feel like you're wearing the plane, you know, versus flying the plane."

Jeff "Bones" Bonner, another A-10 driver who flew both Hogs and Harrier jets, noted that it was so easy to learn to fly he deployed to Kandahar in 2010 with less than one hundred hours of total flying time in the Hog, compared to the months and months it can take to learn to fly other airframes.

8

The Military Reformers Assemble

"The thing is, people like us find each other."

—RAY LEOPOLD

AS FOR THE MATTER OF THE A-10'S DEFINING FEATURE, IN JUNE 1971, the two finalists to develop the A-10's gun were announced: Philco-Ford (from a merger between Philco Electronics and Ford Motors), and the massive conglomerate General Electric (GE), which had already built the Gatling-style twenty-millimeter Vulcan cannon. Both companies were now tasked with constructing a weapon of immense destruction, capable of obliterating tanks, artillery, bunkers, and armored troop transports.

To help in selecting the winner of the gun competition, the program's manager, Sam Kishlein, sought counsel from Tom Christie who, despite his rather late entry into our story, would prove to be among the most important figures in getting the A-10 and its gun into production. Christie was a kind of Danny Ocean figure who would assemble a small team of stubborn, brilliant non-bureaucrats to take on the military industrial complex. To tell the story of the A-10's development and that of its gun is to tell Tom Christie's and his team's story, too.

History is overly complex with too many events happening concurrently for it to be told linearly. So at this juncture, in the early 1970s, just as the A-10 has been green-lit for production, we must travel back forty years, to the Florida panhandle.

There is no sugarcoating it. Tom Christie's childhood in Pensacola was traumatic. His family suffered extreme poverty. His father was a violent alcoholic. "I grew up . . . having to defend my mother, I can remember, with a baseball bat," Christie told me. "Oh my gosh, we were very poor." He went to a Catholic high school, for which he received a scholarship, and like Pierre Sprey, he graduated early.

But Christie hated school, and he didn't particularly want to go to college. Both his math teacher and high school principal, however, insisted the clearly bright Christie get his degree, helping him earn a scholarship to Spring Hill College in Mobile, Alabama. Like Sprey and Chuck Spinney and all with whom he would align in the Pentagon, Christie found his way into military defense development because he, too, was sickened by how the United States' misguided defense spending contributed to the killing of so many young soldiers. After college, he hitchhiked fifty miles to Eglin Air Force Base in the western Florida panhandle for a job interview. Though he interviewed well, he wasn't offered a job because he was "draft-bait" for Vietnam. Christie would later be deemed ineligible for the draft after being diagnosed with rheumatic fever, and he eventually landed a job at Eglin, where he paired up with John Boyd as they developed the revolutionary energy-maneuverability (E-M) theory; Christie, a superb mathematician, did the calculations for Boyd's theory.

Before Christie ever connected with Pierre Sprey, they were linked. It was Christie who put together the *Joint Munitions Effectiveness Manual,* which outlined all the weapons' effectiveness statistics that Sprey used to develop his controversial presidential draft memo. And while Sprey was finding his footing with the Whiz Kids, Christie was stationed in the Armament Laboratory at Eglin, studying airplane vulnerability, as Chuck Spinney would later do as well. In that work, Christie and his team modeled enemy air defenses to predict where airplanes might be most vulnerable and what weapons an airplane needed to most effectively attack targets.

"So there were two aspects of that survivability," Christie said. "One of which was of course the basic vulnerability of the aircraft—you know the F-105 was horrible in that context, you know, just took a hit or two with small weapons and they came down. So we began to get into not just analyzing the design . . . of air-to-ground weapons, but the survivability of the aircraft that is delivering them, and the ease with which the pilot could operate the aircraft and use the weapons. . . . And that's where I met Pierre."

As Sprey was developing the design specifications for the A-X, he traveled to Eglin, hoping to learn more about Christie's work on air-to-ground weapons. At the time, there was a big push to promote a new missile called the "Maverick," of which Sprey was (unsurprisingly) not a fan. "Missiles miss more often than you might think," Sprey once told me. Through all of their testing, Christie's team found that the Maverick's main issue was time: before it could launch it simply took too long to lock onto its target, all while flying straight and level, which of course meant the airplane was an easy target—not much different than B-17s flying steady into flak-filled skies. Given its electro-optical workings, the Maverick depended on a contrast between the target and the rest of the area. Such contrast rarely manifested in the canopy jungles of Vietnam and overcast skies of Europe. In the panhandle, Mavericks were being tested in pine scrub and swamps, a much denser and cluttered area than the testing being conducted in the arid Nevada desert, where the air was dry and clear.

In any event, Sprey got clearance to visit Christie and his team at Eglin, "And I'll never forget," Christie remembered, "we got his clearance . . . and my boss . . . called me up one day and he said, 'Hey, who is this guy Pierre Sprey?' And I acted dumb because I knew the Air Force was out to get him." It wasn't just Pierre. The Whiz Kids inspired resentment for their auditing ways, and according to Christie they were viewed as "anathema to the Air Force. . . . They were the enemy."

The same day that Sprey arrived at Eglin, Christie got a call from Wright-Patterson Air Force Base, warning Christie about Sprey. "Nobody knows I'm here," Christie remembered Sprey saying. "How's that happen?" But the caller had made a crucial error: he had mixed the two up, thinking Christie was the "enemy," not Sprey. So the caller asked for Sprey, who took the phone and just listened while the voice on the other end proceeded to tell him all the strategies they were going to use to "stop" him from discrediting the Maverick missile. Christie happily played along with the mix-up, and over the next few years whenever he traveled to the Pentagon he made sure to connect with Sprey. "Pierre was always there late," Christie remembered.

"Tom was a great, great, great bureaucratic gamester," Chuck Spinney said. Despite so often backing the work that Sprey and others were doing, the kind of work that aroused resentment among Pentagon officials, Christie somehow managed to keep getting promoted. Spinney, for one, held Christie in such high regard because of his work with John Boyd on the E-M theory. "I mean, I damn near had an orgasm when I first read their report," Spinney told me. "It was just brilliant. It was simple, succinct, beautifully written . . . I mean, it literally revolutionized the way airplanes, fighter airplanes, were designed."

Christie inspired such intense admiration and loyalty from the folks who worked for him, but none of them could quite articulate what made him special. "Somehow, saying he is extraordinarily intelligent, quietly charismatic, stuck up for his people, was a good office athlete, and organized outrageous and famous parties still doesn't quite capture it," Bob Speir, another Christie disciple, said. "It also doesn't describe well why he always had around him a small group of non-sycophantic people who were dedicated to him. Leadership and integrity goes a long way, but does not quite get there either. . . . Plus, he's just flat goddamn brilliant."

When Speir arrived at Eglin, some lieutenants suggested he work for Christie because "he has a little group of people and a crazy ass major [John Boyd] who apparently has contacts all over the Air Force. And nobody knows what they really do. But they have more fun than anybody else on the base." Indeed, when Christie interviewed Speir, they only briefly reviewed his resume. Mostly, Christie wanted to talk sports. "It's football season," Christie told Speir. "Go get your stuff, we're playing at noon." To make it look like Speir was doing actual work, Christie threw a pile of random files on his desk. Then they went outside to play.

But Christie was more than just a good time. He was a selfless leader who encouraged his colleagues to take courses in continuing education and professional development. When he could, Christie would attend the classes, too. "And he would come in, sit down, knock off a two hour test in 15 minutes and walk out the door," Speir said. All the more impressive was that the subject material—graduate-level courses in advanced physics and space dynamics—were things Christie hadn't formally studied. It's no wonder, then, that Christie and Sprey hit it off. Like Sprey, Christie was promoting intellectual work with the E-M theory that ran counter to the Air Force's current thinking, and he emboldened his team to remain steadfast in their analysis, no matter how controversial their findings. "We're kind of like a bunch of little puppy dogs, following this guy who was feeding us to some extent, but none of us knew anything or had any shame about it," Speir said. "He was our hero. . . . The people he pissed off were the people who were either out for themselves or they're out for their favorite contractor, regardless of what the product was."

In 1973, Christie moved his family from Florida up to Virginia, where he accepted a full-time position in the Pentagon. Christie's ability to curb misguided military spending was desperately needed. A few years prior, he had led a study that resulted in the end of the much-maligned Cheyenne helicopter program, and by extension pushed the A-10 forward into production. Now, he began recruiting: first, John Boyd, and then, in an informal capacity, Pierre Sprey, who was still consulting with Richard Hallock.

At this time, Chuck Spinney was twenty-seven years old and consulting with the Air Force inspector general doing what he felt was inane work reorganizing the Air Force's budget. "He had this thing so tightened down," Spinney said, "you literally couldn't move an ashtray in a command support plane without approval of the Chief of Staff of the Air Force." Spinney wholly endorsed the responsible use of taxpayer money, but this was overkill he thought.

Spinney got himself transferred to the mailroom, where he took on another thankless job gathering all the "inserts for the record," which were additional clarifications to questions that had not been sufficiently answered in congressional hearings. "Well, you know, doing these inserts for the record was a royal pain in the ass . . . basically I was the messenger that they could all shoot," Spinney said. If you were an officer in the Pentagon and Spinney came knocking on your door on a Friday afternoon, it meant your weekend was toast. "So people saw me coming and, you know, I was like Lucifer."

Spinney's inserts for the record assignment did have advantages, though. The records spanned all of the Air Force, which morphed what could have been a mindless task into what Spinney called "an intensified training program in the Air Force research and development program." As it happened, Spinney's boss reported to John Boyd. Working under Boyd was a man named Ray Leopold, who like Spinney was young and already pretty well disillusioned with the Pentagon. Leopold would be Spinney's ticket out of the mailroom.

Ray Leopold grew up in a working-class family in Chicago. He was a smart kid, but an undedicated student. Through his first two years of high school, he had a 2.35 GPA. After a come-to-Jesus discussion with his father, Leopold committed himself to his schoolwork. Between the summer of his sophomore and junior years of high school, he designed and built his first computer, and as a first semester junior in high school he scored a 798 out of 800 on the SAT math and a 640 on the physics achievement test, despite having never taken a physics course before.[1]

After meeting Spinney, Leopold said he'd put in a good word with John Boyd. Boyd asked Spinney to lunch in the cafeteria, where the de facto job interview began with the boilerplate stuff: Spinney's resume, where he went to school, and the like. Then the conversation turned to Squadron Officer School, the training program for all officers that both Spinney and Boyd had attended. What did Spinney think of that, Boyd wondered?

"I gotta be honest with you, Colonel," Spinney told Boyd. "I thought it was the stupidest fucking thing I ever did." This was the right answer; Boyd felt the exact same way and moved Spinney up to his office that week. "I thought I better be honest, you know, and I'm gonna be honest with him," Spinney said. "He's got to know me for what I am."

---

1. Leopold turned around his academic record to such a startling degree that he was accepted into the Air Force Academy. In later years, he would help create the very first Iridium Satellite Constellation.

A team was assembling: the bureaucratic gamester, Tom Christie; the hot-headed fighter pilot, John Boyd; the brainy Chicago kid, Ray Leopold; the irascible Chuck Spinney; and Pierre, the renegade. Soon, they would be known by a different name.

In the first half of the twentieth century, the folks who believed in Giulio Douhet's philosophy of long-range strategic bombing as the ultimate decider in any war were called the "Bomber Mafia." Pierre Sprey, Tom Christie, John Boyd, and a small group of others had all been part of the "Fighter Mafia,"[2] which in essence stood for the opposite. Adding Chuck Spinney, Ray Leopold, and few more allies along the way, this outgrowth of the Fighter Mafia would eventually come to be known as "the Military Reformers."[3] If the Bomber Mafia believed in spending money and manpower to build a few highly sophisticated, enormous airplanes suited for the wars of the future, the Fighter Mafia argued for the inverse: spending less money in order to acquire *more* airplanes that were smaller, lighter, less complicated, and more reliable. Critics argued the Reformers were "anti-technology" and against innovation. In actuality, they believed in developing technology that responded to a proven need. And they wanted this technology relentlessly tested to be sure it worked. The A-10 aligned perfectly with their values: a cheap, reliable airplane designed for a close-air support mission that had proven vital to success in war.

While so many others in the Pentagon seemed to drag their feet or look lost in the eyes, the Reformers behaved like a small rambunctious clique. "And I think the difference was we had clear consciences, we were doing good work," Ray Leopold explained. "And we were having fun doing it and doing it together." In fact, they seemed to actually *revel* in the backlash they received from higher-ups. On occasion, Chuck Spinney remembers John Boyd calling him and Leopold into his office and saying, "I've been getting complaints about you again, turn up the heat."

---

2. Including Chuck Myers, Harry Hillaker, and Colonel Everest Riccioni.
3. While development on the A-10 began before the "Military Reformers" earned their moniker, for purposes of clarity, I am referring to the key figures involved as such from here on out since not all of the "Reformers" were members of the "Fighter Mafia," and vice versa.

Now the Reformers set about exposing the latest Bomber Mafia jewel: the B-1 bomber. In theory, the B-1 was a wonder of innovative design. It could fly faster than the speed of sound, haul an enormous bomb load, and featured a variable "swing wing" design, such that the wings would extend out horizontally on takeoff to improve lift, and then sweep back when the bomber was in flight to improve its aerodynamics at high speeds. If a plane could be designed to directly oppose what the Reformers stood for, it was the B-1.

The B-1 emerged just as the U.S. military was shrinking. Coming out of the Vietnam War, the United States started investing in fewer, but more expensive, weapons; in other words, they were spending more for less. All that sophistication was costly to maintain, though, and these weapons of future wars siphoned funding for routine maintenance of the weapons being actively used, creating "readiness" problems. On paper, the United States looked like it had a formidable military force structure, but they were not nearly as ready to fight as it seemed.

John Boyd suspected the Air Force was lying about the cost of the B-1, so he assigned Ray Leopold to investigate. "Boyd tells me to figure out what the real cost of the B-1 bomber is," Leopold remembered. "He said basically airplanes cost about $1,000 per pound, and their avionics [electrical equipment] cost about $10,000 per pound, and each engine costs about a half million dollars." Boyd warned Leopold that whatever he found would likely upset the Bomber Mafia. "So whatever you do," Boyd told him, "if you have to make a value judgement on something, make the value judgement in the direction of the lower cost, so that when they dig into it, the numbers only get worse." "And that's exactly what I did," Leopold said.

The Air Force was reporting that the B-1 cost around twenty-five million dollars per airplane, a figure based on the roughly 240 bombers they planned to buy. After his investigation, Leopold uncovered a much different estimate: sixty-eight million dollars per airplane, the most expensive Air Force project at the time. Leopold filed his report, then flew home to Chicago to visit his mother. When he walked in the door, he found his mother exasperated: the phone had been ringing all day.

"And the first person I call is Boyd," Leopold said, "And Boyd said, 'Yeah, you kind of blew the roof off this place.'"

Leopold returned to the Pentagon to have his data vetted. "When they did their own review of my analysis, and they were told by their superiors, 'Just dig into it, find out where he made his mistakes and come back and tell him' . . . things only got worse for them. So [Boyd] gave me good advice."

The B-1 emblematized the larger problems with weapons procurement: ballooning costs resulted in fewer weapons and a less prepared military. As the B-1's price kept rising (by 1974 it climbed to one hundred million dollars per airplane), the Air Force couldn't afford to buy as many as they'd planned. Meanwhile, the ultra-cheap A-10 (roughly three million dollars per airplane) was still struggling to get into production. Here, Tom Christie and the Reformers showcased their resourcefulness.

In 1973, Secretary of Defense James Schlesinger yearned to leave a lasting legacy on the military. He sought the counsel of Pierre Sprey's mentor on ground warfare, Richard Hallock, who by Sprey's estimate started pulling eighteen-hour days developing a plan for Schlesinger. Wisely, Hallock delegated the airplane component of the plan to Sprey. "I said, if you want to leave a legacy, get the A-10 and F-16 into production," Sprey said. "And we already had both into prototype phase . . . we weren't talking about paper airplanes; we were talking real stuff." It was Tom Christie and another Reformer, Chuck Myers, who figured out how to put the plan into action.

How could you convince the Air Force, or any organization for that matter, to agree to spending less money? "The key was to offer them the opportunity to grow their forces," Christie told me. Christie effectively gave the Air Force an ultimatum: "The only way you're going to be able to grow your force is to go for aircraft like these two relatively cheap, but in our view, effective, [airplanes]," Christie said.

Until now, the Air Force operated under a "fixed-force structure," meaning the size of its arsenal stayed constant. Christie sold the Air Force on the possibility of actually *growing* their force structure with something called a "high-low" mix. Rather than pooling all of their money into just a few expensive B-1s and F-15s, the Air Force could still buy some of its expensive bombers and fighters as long as they allocated money for A-10s and F-16s at a fraction of the cost. Essentially, by accepting the A-10 and other cheaper airplanes into the force structure, it allowed the Air Force to have its cake and eat it, too. It was a graceful workaround that managed to appease the Air Force while guiding the A-10 through another bureaucratic hoop.

A hoop remained. This force restructuring occurred just as Congress had cut back on the initial buy of A-10s. Congress wanted yet *another* fly-off, this time between the A-10 and the A-7 Corsair II, an attack plane built by the Ling-Temco-Vought corporation out of Texas. The A-7 had been a relatively reliable and affordable Navy attack plane in Vietnam, and it was still in service. Why couldn't the United States just keeping using them? A-7 skeptics wondered if the fly-off was politically motivated to keep manufacturing jobs in Texas, but to be fair, similar arguments were made for the A-10 with Fairchild-Republic stationed out of New York.

In April 1974, the A-10 flew off against the A-7 at Fort Riley in Kansas. The A-10 won handily, with pilots testifying in June to the House Armed Services committee their unanimous support for the plane. But Fairchild-Republic had other troubles; they were struggling to meet the manufacturing order, and in late 1974, the Air Force criticized Fairchild-Republic for its lack of preparedness. As former Hog driver Douglas Campbell notes in his book, *Warthog*, Fairchild-Republic's equipment was old, their most experienced workers were retiring, and it had been over a decade since the company had built its last notable airframe, the F-105 Thunderchief. While the original design-to-cost stipulation for the A-10 had been $1.7 million, it now cost upwards of four million dollars (albeit still much cheaper than the other current crop of airplanes).

By 1975 the prospects for the Reformers looked grim, too. In November, President Gerald Ford fired Reformer ally James Schlesinger as secretary of defense. Then John Boyd retired, which meant Chuck Spinney's time in the Pentagon was over, too. "I knew that having Boyd's name on my efficiency report, no matter how good the efficiency report was, and it was very good, was the kiss of death because the Air Force hated Boyd," Spinney said. Spinney's last day was June 30, 1975. "And I just said, 'I gotta change my life.' I'm never going to work in the Pentagon again."

In a few years' time, the Reformers would reassemble in full, but for now, they kept a low profile. Meanwhile, across the country in the arid Nevada desert, a few informal additions to the Reformers would discover just how devastating the A-10's gun could be.

9

Owning an Elephant

"The airplane would have been a failure without him." –Pierre Sprey *on Colonel Bob Dilger*

To oversee testing of the gun, now designated the GAU-8 Avenger, the A-10 program office brought in Colonel Bob Dilger, a stubborn fighter pilot who'd flown more than 160 missions in F-4 Phantoms over Vietnam. A fearless and crafty airman, Dilger once found himself in a dogfight with an enemy MiG-17 in which his missiles failed to fire; dancing in flight with the MiG, Dilger fooled him into crashing into a mountain. Though Dilger had no formal training or knowledge in the study of close-air support, he'd developed a keen interest in the mission in recent years. "And boy did [they] ever pick the right guy," Sprey said. "Holy shit."

With equal rigor, Dilger pursued that which interested him and ignored that which did not. "Dilger was the worst guy at meeting schedule," said Chuck Spinney, who met Dilger while doing the dreaded inserts-for-the-record assignment in the Pentagon. "Dilger had a way of operating that basically was if it wasn't important, he said, 'Fuck it.' And so those things [that] were important that he was working on were always done first class, and he's a really bright guy, and he did fabulous work on things he was interested in. But he wasn't interested in [my stuff] so Dilger was a pain in the ass . . . He'd say, 'Oh, I'll do better next time.' But he wouldn't. He just left a trail of craziness behind on things he didn't care about. He just didn't give a shit." As a lowly captain, Spinney couldn't simply order around the higher-ranking Dilger, a lieutenant colonel at the time. As a last resort, Spinney confronted Dilger in a way he might understand, through the vulgar vernacular of a fighter pilot. "'You're a Lt. Col., I'm a captain. Get fucked.' That's literally what I said," Spinney recalled. "After that we were buddies."

Like the rest of the Reformers, Dilger responded to authenticity, no matter how abrasive. He was motivated to complete tasks that had a clear purpose, and he harbored a resentment for the Bomber Mafia ethos. In an early meeting with Dilger, Pierre Sprey wondered aloud about the popularity of bombers across all air militaries: "What's the inherent mechanism that in every air force, U.S. Air Force, RAF [Royal Air Force, of the U.K.], Israeli Air Force, bomber generals rise to the top? . . . I don't understand how that's inherent to any air force." Sprey remembered Dilger turned toward him and "looked at me like I was stupid." "Have you ever flown a bomber?" Dilger asked. Sprey hadn't. "It's fucking boring," Dilger said. "It's hours and hours of droning along on autopilot and doing nothing. So [they] got all this time to think about how to get themselves promoted."

Dilger's stubbornness and conviction had a dual effect: he got results, but often with plenty of collateral damage. "Having a guy like Dilger working for you, it's great, it's great," Sprey recalled one of Dilger's superiors telling him. "It's like owning an elephant. You have the elephant, you have a big stone wall in front of you. You tell the elephant 'knock that wall down.' And the elephant just charges and down goes the wall. The only problem is once he's through that wall you've got to go behind him with a really big shovel."

The stone wall now in Dilger's path was the bureaucratic stipulations for testing the GAU-8 Avenger cannon and its new thirty-millimeter armor-piercing ammunition, which was made of depleted uranium, or DU. DU, which had been around for decades, basically functioned like a more powerful magnesium, which made it almost impossible to extinguish once it caught fire. As such, a DU round did its most damage *after* impact, when it penetrated its target and splintered into white-hot fragments, burning anything in their path. Moreover, DU cost just an eighth the price of tungsten, then the standard for armor-piercing rounds at the time.

As its name indicates, DU itself is not radioactive. It is what's left over after the radioactive U-235 uranium has been harvested for uses in atomic weapons. "[C]arrying a pound in your pocket is less hazardous than wearing a watch with a radium dial, Pentagon technologists say," reported Charles D. Sherman for the *International Herald Tribune* in 1979.[1]

---

1. Though the long-term effects of being exposed to DU have been hotly debated. With respect to health concerns regarding DU exposure, the International Atomic Energy Agency (IAEA) notes that the "general medical and scientific consensus is that in cases of high intake, uranium is likely to become a chemical toxicology problem before it is a radiological problem." As a chemical toxicology problem, "uranium that is ingested or inhaled . . . [can] depress renal function (i.e., affect the kidneys). High concentrations in the kidney can cause damage and, in extreme cases, renal failure." However, they add, "Like any radioactive material, there is a risk of developing cancer from exposure to radiation emitted by natural and depleted uranium."

Referencing studies on veterans of the Gulf War, the IAEA says that a "small number of Gulf war veterans have inoperable fragments of DU embedded in their bodies. . . . These veterans show elevated excretion levels of DU in urine but, so far, there have been no observable health effects due to DU in this group. There have also been epidemiological studies of the health of military personnel who saw action in conflicts where DU was used, comparing them with the health of personnel who were not in the war zones. The results of these studies have been published and the main conclusion is that the war veterans do show a small (i.e., not statistically significant) increase in mortality rates, but this excess is due to accidents rather than disease. This cannot be linked to any exposures to DU."

With regard to the environmental impact of areas where DU munitions have been fired, the IAEA says that "most of the DU aerosols created by the impact of penetrators against an armoured target settle within a short time (minutes) of the impact and in close proximity to the target site," however the "smaller particles may be carried to a distance of several hundred metres by the wind" and the "potential risk from inhalation will be associated with material that is re-suspended from the ground by the action of the wind or by human activities, such as ploughing." The IAEA also notes that "DU projectiles lying on the ground or buried under the surface will corrode with time, slowly converting the metallic uranium of the DU penetrators into uranium oxides. The specific soil characteristics will determine the rate and chemical form of the oxidation and the rate of migration and solubility of the depleted uranium. This environmental pathway may result in the long term (in the order of several years) in enhanced levels of depleted uranium being dissolved in ground water and drinking water." Since "[c]onsumption of water and food is a potential long term route of intake of DU," the IAEA suggests that "monitoring of water sources may be a useful means to assess the potential for intake via ingestion. If the levels were considered unacceptable, some form of filtration/ion exchange system could be implemented to reduce levels of DU."

On March 26, 2023, White House National Security Council Spokesman John Kirby was asked on *Face the Nation* why Russian President Vladimir Putin was threatening to put nuclear weapons in Belarus. "You'd have to ask Mr. Putin, I can't speak to that. I think in some of the Russian media reports they linked it to claims that the United Kingdom was going to provide depleted uranium rounds," Kirby replied, adding, "there is no radioactive threat from depleted uranium rounds, they're common on the battlefield, even Russia uses similar rounds, so if that is in fact the justification it's a stake through a straw-man, there's no radioactivity concerns with that."

As it stood, the plan was to test DU rounds by firing the Avenger cannon on a concrete block and monitoring for any jams or malfunctions. When Dilger heard this plan, he was "horrified" according to Sprey. "Are you fucking kidding me?" Sprey remembered Dilger saying. "A gun sitting on a concrete block is [not] the same as a gun in an airplane going 300 miles an hour, vibrating and twisting and bouncing through turbulence and all that."

Dilger was wise to insist on a more stringent and realistic method for evaluating the gun. Prior testing had already uncovered hidden problems with the gun, such as how when it fired, a blinding smoke engulfed the bubble canopy. What good was a gun if the pilot couldn't see what they were shooting? These tests had also found that gas from the gun was getting sucked into the A-10's turbofans, causing compressor stalls that disabled the engines (this problem was fixed by using a different propellant and changing the ammunition rings from copper to plastic for a tighter seal, along with constructing a muzzle deflector to divert the gun gases in a different direction). To more accurately evaluate the gun and its ammunition, Dilger created the Lot Acceptance Verification Program, a series of realistic tests to gauge the reliability and lethality of the A-10's brutal weapons system.

"I think the gun ended up being even more effective than we were predicting back then," Tom Christie told me. Indeed, on the whole the GAU-8 was a destructive weapon, nearly twenty feet long and more than four thousand pounds. A one-second squeeze of the trigger unleashed fifty thirty-millimeter rounds (because the Gatling actually takes a half-second to rotate up to full speed, its true one-second fire-rate is closer to seventy rounds).

The real jewel of the Lot Acceptance Verification Program, however, was its method for evaluating how well the A-10 could kill tanks. Just how lethal were its thirty-millimeter armor-piercing rounds? Dilger and his group didn't want to simply waste bullets on paper targets scattered across the ground; instead, they amassed a mighty tank army out in the Nevada desert.

To organize and run these tests, Dilger enlisted the help of an enterprising and assiduous fighter pilot named Lon Ratley. Ratley, whose father served in the Army Air Corps in World War II, moved around a lot as a kid, and in the late 1940s and early 1950s he lived in Germany, where he developed what became a lifelong passion for German culture and history. In Sprey's inimitable words, Ratley "was an Air Force fighter pug with extraordinary command of German and most unusual interest in history and in ground warfare."

In Vietnam, Ratley flew F-105s and F-4s, including the first—and extravagantly dangerous—"Wild Weasel" missions in which he trolled for fire in areas infested with surface-to-air missiles, essentially asking to be shot at so that the enemy would expose their position. Ratley also flew rescue missions in the A-7 Corsair II (the second attack plane the A-10 had to fly-off against before it went into production). For these missions, Ratley flew alongside helicopters searching for downed airmen. When the airmen were spotted, the helicopter began its descent as Ratley flew tight circles around the area to provide extra support. "What we found out was you have to keep the helicopter in sight," Ratley said, adding, "So he's flying in here, maybe doing maybe 120 knots or something like that. And then you're flying an A-7, which is all loaded up with munitions because that's what you do. And so you had to be in about a constant three-and-a-half, four-G turn making these big ovals, elipses . . . to keep the helicopter in sight . . . you're supposed to be protecting this guy. You have to keep him in sight . . . pulling three and half, four Gs constantly. That's exhausting."

After the war, Ratley enrolled at the Naval Postgraduate School in Monterey, California. There, he found a mentor in Rusell Stolfi, a professor emeritus who specialized in analyzing damaged and destroyed tanks. Sprey knew Stolfi to be "meticulously honest," adding, "I mean, it takes a certain kind of anal personality to do autopsies of dead tanks in the first place, right?"

Ratley was an insatiable student, not content with merely earning a passing grade. "We had an option of writing a thesis for the program and . . . I said, you know, since I'm here, I might as well do something worthwhile," Ratley told me. He chose to study Germany's tactics in

World War II, particularly their Blitzkrieg and anti-tank strategies. He felt this historical perspective could inform how the United States and NATO would fare against the feared Russian tank invasion through the Fulda Gap. "Well my argument was, let's use the experiences that the Germans had in World War II and see if we can apply that to our pending deployment of the A-10s to Europe . . . so we won't have to make mistakes again." In particular, Germany had performed exceptionally well in battles against Russia's massive tank army despite being wholly outmanned. "And the [battles] right after Stalingrad," Ratley remarked, "Christ, they're unbelievable."

Of course, Ratley was especially interested in speaking with the Stuka pilot Hans Rudel. But when Ratley arrived in Germany he learned via Rudel's housekeeper that the Stuka pilot had suffered a stroke and was actually now in the United States, Chicago specifically, where he was receiving medical treatment. When Ratley finished his other interviews, he returned stateside and arranged to meet Rudel in Chicago. During this meeting, Rudel shared with Ratley how the battlefield was often in such a state of chaos that the only way Rudel could distinguish between friendly and enemy soldiers was "by making an extremely low pass (5–10 meters) above the ground and look[ing] for the distinctive silhouette of the German helmet."

Probably most informative for the A-10's ammo testing, Rudel shared how stringent the requirements had been for a tank to be deemed a "kill." The tank had to be witnessed to explode and burn *and* another pilot had to confirm these observations. Based on what Dilger, Ratley, and Stolfi later discovered about how tanks burn, this meant that Rudel likely killed three times the number of tanks (519) for which he had been credited. Once again, Rudel had influenced the A-10. It would not be the last time.

The ammunition testing took place on the Nellis Range, approximately one million government-owned acres in the desolate Nevada desert, where the air was clear and dry and temperatures could rise to 130 degrees. Like Dilger, Ratley insisted on realistic testing methods. He studied Russian tactics so he could set up arrays of tanks that mimicked real battle formations. Most importantly, if they were going to test the effectiveness of the gun on Soviet tanks they needed, well, *Soviet tanks.* "I got a [Russian] T-62 tank, and I don't feel comfortable telling you how I got it," Ratley said. With the T-62 in their possession, they filled it up with gas, fully stocked it with ammunition, and placed mannequins inside the compartment. "What we found out was the very first firing that we had against that T-62 . . . the guy came in, he made one pass, which was all we wanted him to do, and he destroyed the tank."

The results weren't obvious at first. From the outside, the tank didn't appear to have sustained much damage at all. "I said, 'Oh Christ, this is terrible,'" Ratley recalled. A few minutes passed. Then Ratley noticed smoke billowing out of the tank: the rounds had penetrated the tank and set it on fire from the inside out. "The [DU] round goes in there and it's still kind of this heavy mass that goes in and then penetrates the fighting compartment, and then it splinters up and all these really red hot fragments . . . go in and they torch off the ammunition that's in the tank," Ratley explained.

It wasn't possible for Ratley to assemble a whole Russian tank army for target practice in the desert, so he got the next best thing. After World War II, the United States had sent a fleet of M46 tanks to allies in Europe. While the M46 was more primitive than the T-62, it boasted a comparable armor structure to that of contemporary Russian tanks. Plus, as Ratley notes, "because we actually fired at a Russian tank . . . we knew that our munitions would go through there and kill it."

Next, Ratley learned that the U.S. Navy was sending transport ships to Europe as part of the Cold War stand-off with Russia. He saw an opportunity. "So the ships go over there, they're full of stuff, munitions and whatever, they come back and they're empty. Hmm . . . So I talked to the Navy, say, 'Hey, look, can you guys bring [these tanks] back?'" It was a win-win. The allies were looking to get rid of these old tanks anyway, since it was more expensive to demilitarize and deconstruct them than it was to simply give them away, and the Navy didn't mind having the tanks loaded up on their otherwise empty ships. "So we didn't pay anybody for anything," Ratley explained. "I don't remember, but we were also able to get them somehow shipped to Nellis for free as well. So we had quite a good size number of tanks, I don't know, three or four hundred or something like that."

Ratley even found a way to earn some extra funding for his testing office. The armament laboratory where Tom Christie had gotten his start down at Eglin Air Force Base in Florida wanted a few tanks for their own tests. "I said, 'Oh okay, I'll give you guys 49 tanks. . . . But you have to pay for the transport, 10K apiece, which I also got the Army to ship the tanks for free.'" Ratley and the gun program were now in the green an extra half-million bucks. "The point is," Ratley said, "you can do these things if you want to, you just have to be a little innovative sometimes."

Hundreds of tanks were trucked into Nellis and distributed across the range in attack formations. The tests began offering the kind of realistic and practical information that simply couldn't be guessed at. On every attack run, test pilots recorded their observations, and Ratley and his team plotted the data on printed drawings of tanks, marking in pencil where each round hit and the extent of its damage. From this information, they were able to deduce what hits would have "killed" the tank, rendering it immobile and its crew dead, or merely disabled the tank (where, perhaps, its gun turret was destroyed but the tank itself could still drive). Inside the tanks, cameras recorded the internal damage; the footage allowed Ratley's group to assess what happened at the moment of impact, specifically the pyrophoric effects of DU and how it might, say, ignite the grease from the sump pump beneath the diesel engine before setting the whole compartment ablaze. Scrupulous in his data collection like his mentor, Russell Stolfi, Ratley was a perfect complement to Bob Dilger's elephant persona.

An October 1978 memo from founding Fighter Mafia member E. E. Riccioni hailed the live-fire testing, while deriding the issues with the electro-optical Maverick missile against tanks nestled in the wooded areas of New York State. "To their dismay," Riccioni wrote, "they had trouble locking up Maverick in days of beatiful(sic) daylight, visibility, and sunshine. Somehow, the missile dislikes the task of separating the contrast of green (tanks) from green (foliage). Even the tank shadows get lost." In another series of tests "simulating European weather conditions," there had been 190 planned launches of Maverick missiles, of which only 117 fired. Of those 117 missiles, just twenty-five locked on to their target. The primary issue with missiles—aside from how long it could take to lock on to a target, sometimes as much as fifteen seconds—was how inefficient it was to use a high-priced missile to kill just one tank. The findings for the thirty-millimeter rounds, however, were glowing. Riccioni noted that the latest tanks may in fact be "*more* vulnerable to the 30MM(sic) DU round than the medium tanks," particularly in the rear, where they were much less armored. "The evidence is tending to imply that the 30MM cannon is not only the best weapon, air to ground; it looks like the *only* practical weapon, air-to-ground."

"What were the findings from all these tests?" Ratley asked rhetorically. "I can tell you, it's really simple. A kill is a function of the number of hits on the tank, [the] number of hits on the tank is a function of slant range, i.e., hit density. So, the closer you are to the tank when you fire, [the] higher probability of kill. But you got to hit the tank." On each pass, pilots shot about thirty rounds, or a little less than a one-second trigger squeeze on the Avenger cannon. If about 10 percent of the rounds hit the tank, that was deemed a good hit-rate. The GAU-8 and its thirty-millimeter rounds were proving to be so effective that they didn't even need to be fired at a perfect angle to penetrate a tank's heavy armor and cause significant damage.

If Bob Dilger could be said to have a superpower, Sprey believed it was "unbelievable common sense." Dilger flexed his superpower by asking something so obvious it might not even occur to most folks, including you reading this chapter. That is, how the hell do you efficiently load over a thousand thirty-millimeter rounds into an A-10?

"If you did that manually, the way we used to do with machine gun bullets or even manually cranking a belt or something, that would take forever," Sprey noted. Instead, Dilger worked with a contractor to design a specialized ammo loader on wheels that would fit into a cargo plane without much trouble. "The whole idea of this . . . was to minimize the amount of ground support equipment," Sprey explained. "Following the

[Hans] Rudel idea that you're always in the wrong place and you need to be able to move overnight to a new base." Dilger's foresight with the ammo loader offered an important lesson in design: a sophisticated tool was only as good as the systems in place to support it.

Dilger's final lasting mark on the A-10 involved making the ammunition cheaper. Much cheaper. At the time, the estimated cost of thirty-millimeter ammunition was quoted at about eighty-three dollars per round. At that figure, to fully load a single A-10 would cost one hundred thousand dollars, an untenable expense for what had otherwise been marketed as an economical tool. Dilger, however, managed to whittle the cost-per-round down to just thirteen dollars. He did this by having two ammunition manufacturers constantly competing every year for the contract, and he structured the contract in such a way that even the losing manufacturer would still get a small slice of the production order, and thus give them a chance to best their competitor the following year. "He awarded enough to the loser . . . [to] make it uneconomical to shut down the production line, but not make the big bucks," Sprey explained. It was yet another example of relentless competitive testing to reduce cost (the ammo team also replaced the thirty-millimeter ammo's brass cases with a far cheaper aluminum). Dilger's practicality continues to influence the entire U.S. military up to the present day. For Sprey and the Reformers, Dilger's live-fire testing "became the model for the legislation that we passed . . . in the early '80s, that to this day dictates that the Pentagon has to do live-firing against any platform that carries American uniformed people."

Dilger finished his military career as a decorated officer; he received an Air Medal, a Purple Heart, three Silver Stars, and four Distinguished Flying Crosses. He passed away on August 18, 2022. "Well, Dilger is one of the real unsung heroes of the reform movement," Chuck Spinney told me. "You know . . . getting all that ammunition is, you know, just a super achievement, given the kind of way the Pentagon operates. Monitor cost ahead of schedule, turning money back in. I mean, how many times does that happen?"

10

Attack, Revise, Re-Attack

"When searching for hidden tanks, speed is poison."

–HANS RUDEL

IN MAY 1978, THE REFORMERS AND THEIR ALLIES, BOB DILGER AND Lon Ratley among them, convened in a hotel conference room in Springfield, Virginia. The spartan accommodations played host to a seminar on anti-tank air warfare. Among the speakers presenting was the greatest tank killer of them all: Hans Rudel.

Rudel, speaking through a translator, expounded on the insights he had shared in his memoir, *Stuka Pilot*, and offered his assessment on the United States' new anti-tank weapon. He reiterated that hunting tanks required tremendous focus given how (surprisingly) easy they were to hide. "They could be looking and looking a little more closely at the houses [along the ground] and suddenly they would notice that one of the houses would have this long rod sticking out the window," Rudel's translator explained. The tanks were hiding *inside* the houses, which Rudel was only able to notice because he was flying not just low, but extremely *slow*.

While Rudel felt there was much to recommend about the A-10, he believed it to be much too fast. He also lamented that it could not accommodate two pilots; he would have preferred the A-10 had a second rear-facing seat equipped with a gun (this had been the arrangement in

Rudel's Stuka). In Rudel's mind, a pilot straining to spot tanks couldn't expend energy worrying if an enemy was attacking from his tail.[1]

Probably Rudel's most important insight pertained to what conditions a close-air support airplane like the A-10 could be most effective. He recounted a time when, in May 1943, he was attacking Russian forces heavily dug-in with well-fortified defenses. By Rudel's estimation they didn't kill a single tank. "That day we discovered the limits of the cannon-equipped Stuka," Rudel said, "and we realized that when you attack static [i.e., non-moving] defenses, static positions, you cannot have success." A-10s, then, would be most effective on moving battlefields where allies or enemies were either retreating or advancing.

Rudel's perspective on anti-tank air combat was generally informed by the limited technology of his era. Specifically, he found that his Stuka was not as maneuverable as he would have liked. But it was a sacrifice he accepted because, as the moderator noted, "They were willing to take all these disadvantages and a really poor handling aircraft just to have the gun."

Pierre Sprey believed no such compromise should have to be made. While the A-10 was still just in the infancy of its production, Sprey was already thinking of its successor. At the seminar, Sprey heavily criticized the A-10 in his talk, "Countering a Warsaw Pact Blitz." To those unfamiliar with Sprey, the move may have come as a surprise—was Sprey really deriding his brainchild, the airplane he had fought to get in the air?

Among Sprey's cohort, however, such a stance would have been expected. Much as he would over the next forty years, Sprey emphasized that the A-10 was not perfect. In fact, neither he nor any members of the Reformers professed a devotion to a particular airframe or piece of technology. Their only allegiance was to the technology that best suited the mission for which it was designed.

The A-10 was already too expensive and much too big, Sprey said. And while it didn't need to be fast, it needed better acceleration. He wanted an airplane one-third the size, if not smaller. Despite its high

---

1. One two-seat version of the A-10, the YA-10B was built, but never received a full production run.

maneuverability, he felt the A-10 could be *more* maneuverable, especially at the very slow speeds Rudel urged.

Sprey recalled the ammo tests in Nevada being conducted by Bob Dilger and Lon Ratley. One particular test measured how quickly two A-10s could knock out ten tanks. It was an exercise in timing how fast A-10s could re-attack a target after making their first pass. "Now, what does it take to re-attack fast?" Sprey asked rhetorically. "To re-attack fast, it takes a very high level of maneuvering components at moderate speed." Sprey focused in particular on a maneuver called the "button hook turn," which required the pilot to turn while simultaneously decelerating rapidly and pulling a high amount of Gs, allowing for a smaller turning radius and thereby a faster re-attack time. The button hook turn just wasn't possible with faster, less-agile jets, which needed to fly as far as miles before turning around to re-attack their target. Already, the A-10 could execute this button hook turn. Still, Sprey felt it could be better.

Sprey *did* praise the remarkable results of the GAU-8 Avenger cannon, which had shown that "at over a thousand yards . . . will give us the total destruction of the tank almost half the time and will give us mobility kill of the tank over three-quarters of the time." The next step, Sprey felt, was to enable the pilot to switch between different kinds of ammunition, from DU to standard, not unlike ballpoint pens housing multiple ink cartridges of different colors that can be switched with click of the thumb.

Sprey wanted something like his initial A-X proposal on steroids: a supremely small, markedly agile attack plane that could be produced on the cheap. In Vietnam, the air response time had been approximately forty-five minutes, "which is practically an order of magnitude too large for emergency situations on the ground," Sprey claimed. Sprey wanted a *five-minute* response time, which he believed "is really needed if you are talking about airplanes reinforcing a unit that is suddenly surprised and about to be overrun." The only way to achieve such a quick response time was to have airplanes constantly swarming in the air, so these airplanes needed to be easily maintainable such that they could land and very quickly get right back up in the sky.

There did exist one airplane that embodied many of the extremes to which Sprey was willing to go to have his vision realized. It was a British creation called the "Gnat," just one-fifth the size of the current A-10. It cost less than two million dollars and could be reloaded and refueled with its engines still running (meaning it could immediately take right back off again). The Gnat wasn't the solution, but it was a model for the kind of new airplane that could take over for the A-10. Sprey ended his talk with a sermon of sorts on design:

> *Finally, and this is in a sense the point of today's session . . . the critical thing is that we base the design and our discussion on things that are associated with hard combat experience, and not on the promises of the R&D cartel and those endless conversations about how great it is going to be tomorrow.*

Pierre Sprey wasn't the only one interested in developing a follow-on to the A-10. The subject caught the interest of Chuck Spinney, who after a few years away had been lured back to the Pentagon by Tom Christie. Recently, Spinney had written a short paper noting the strengths and weaknesses of the current A-10, which began making the rounds. "And Pierre took a bit of an interest in it," Spinney said. Despite the interconnectedness of this group, Spinney and Sprey had not formally met until now. An adjustment period followed. "When I first met Pierre," Spinney said, "I had a hard time working with him." Conversely, Spinney had instantly gotten along with the more philosophical John Boyd, who utilized analogies and thought experiments to make sense of the world.

Boyd's philosophical approach had been showcased in two famous papers, "Destruction and Creation" and "Patterns of Conflict." Borne out of Boyd's quest to understand how he came up with the Energy-Maneuverability Theory, "Destruction and Creation" reads as a philosophical proof. In it, he describes how we "destroy and create" the "mental patterns or concepts of meaning" that we use to "comprehend and cope with our environment." He argues that this pattern of destruction and creation is unavoidable and necessary, a process of constantly "generating both disorder and order." The whole process dictates how much (or how little) people cooperate with others. For example, if a group finds themselves within a system that no longer shares their same goals, "the alienated members may dissolve their relationship and remain independent, form a group of their own, or join another collective body in order to improve their capacity for independent action." In a sense, Boyd's paper explains how the Military Reformers coalesced; they had all been alienated to varying degrees in their previous offices before finding each other.

"Destruction and Creation" demonstrates Boyd's keen interest in understanding how we think and make sense of our environments, particularly when we're under pressure. He describes this as a process of developing "mental concepts of observed reality, as we perceive it," and then having the capacity to "change these concepts as reality itself appears to change." In other words, one has to be able to both develop a sound plan and also be able to adapt when one's expectations or plan don't match up with the reality of the situation. To do so, one is always making these "mental concepts," through a process of going from the "general-to-specific, or from the specific-to-general." What Boyd illustrates here is a fundamental mode of academic thinking. In education, we refer to this as the hermeneutic circle, a conundrum of sorts that argues our understanding of something is formed by both our comprehension of its individual parts and the collective whole. The only way to remedy the conundrum is to scrutinize the situation multiple times. When your professors in college asked you to "close-read" a text, they were asking you to practice this mode of thinking, to consider how individual components (words, phrases, patterns) influence our understanding of the whole text, and conversely how the context of the whole text shapes how we understand those individual components.

Whether you're close-reading Heathcliff's characterization in *Wuthering Heights* or the Department of Defense's insistence on building more B-1 bombers, the further you break things down in your mind, the more you deconstruct the system, you're eventually left "swimming around in a sea of anarchy." Where there was once "meaning and order," there is now "uncertainty and disorder." Boyd calls this "unstructuring" a "destructive deduction." From destructive deduction, creation blooms, allowing you to identify "some common qualities, attributes, or operations among some or many of these constituents swimming in this sea of anarchy." In piecing them together, you get something new. This is how the A-10 came to be, after all: the notion of an attack airplane was deconstructed down to its fundamental pieces; from those pieces, the most essential element (the gun) was identified; the airplane was then rebuilt around this most essential element.

"Clearly, such a synthesis would indicate we have generated something new and different from what previously existed," Boyd writes. "Going back to our idea chain, it follows that creativity is related to induction, synthesis, and integration since we proceeded from unstructured bits and pieces to a new general pattern or concept." To achieve this creation, you first have to destroy or break apart the previous structure, what Boyd calls the "separation of the particulars from their previous domains. . . . Without this unstructuring the creation of a new structure cannot proceed—since the bits and pieces are still tied together as meaning within unchallenged domains or concepts." Without destruction, Boyd argues, there can be no creation.

The cycle repeats continually, "[b]ack and forth, over and over again, we use observations to sharpen a concept and a concept to sharpen observations." Just as an idea or concept seems to be perfected, a flaw emerges, the idea's foundation torn down and rebuilt (this is exactly what Sprey was doing when he started proposing a follow-on to the A-10). Boyd's insightful—albeit dense—brief showcases the breadth of his intellectual ambitions: he references Werner Heisenberg (of the Heisenberg uncertainty principle), the second law of thermodynamics, and entropy, the latter of which explains how any system "is moving irreversibly toward a higher, yet unknown, state of confusion and disorder." The struggle to achieve order in the world, to get an idea to "match-up with reality," is what Boyd calls a "dialectic cycle." Fueling this cycle is a "dialectic engine," the mechanism that allows for individuals to assess their environments "in an effort to improve their capacity for independent action."

Boyd's treatise explains the motives and methods of the Reformers, along with why it was inevitable for them to cause such a stir in the

Pentagon. "In this context, when acting within a rigid or essentially a closed system, the goal seeking effort of individuals and societies to improve their capacity for independent action tends to produce disorder towards randomness and death," Boyd writes. That is, as change-makers seek to develop new and innovative things, they can't help but challenge the bureaucratic system in place trying to keep everything under control. Sprey, Boyd, Spinney, Christie, and all their allies were the "Dialectic Engine," embracing chaos rather than running from it.

Boyd would build on these arguments in his next paper, "Patterns of Conflict," which evolved over the next decade and eventually took twelve hours to present in full. "The Brief," as it came to be known, "begins with what was to become Boyd's most famous—and least understood—legacy," Boyd's biographer Robert Coram writes: the OODA Loop (Observe, Orient, Decide, Act). The OODA Loop is a paradigm for instigating chaos in one's enemy—the more quickly one can make it through these four stages, from observation to action, the better, because if one can do so fast enough they can actually anticipate or manipulate the enemy's journey through the same four stages, causing as much confusion as possible. Of the utmost importance to the loop is the second "O," orient. "Orienting" one's self isn't merely about looking around; it's about "bringing to bear the cultural traditions, genetic heritage, new information, previous experiences, and analysis/synthesis process of the person doing the orienting—a complex integration that each person does differently," Coram explains. In effect, this is what Sprey's mentor, Richard Hallock, also imparted to Sprey, that to work within a system you had to have a deep working knowledge of its origins. Inside the Pentagon, the Reformers were constantly cycling through the OODA Loops of their neighboring offices, developing tactics to push their ideas through.

Notably, Boyd's philosophical approach clashed in some ways with Sprey's. "Pierre thinks in a different pathway," Spinney said. "That's why he and Boyd were so effective. He analyzed things differently than [Boyd] did, and they complemented each other." Spinney thought of Sprey as "the ultimate empiricist. . . . He's like a guy like Darwin, you know, where basically he just looks at things and tries to understand them, and then his theory comes out of that. John is more like Einstein. He thought in analogies and he sort of wandered all over the map. And as he zeroed in on something, [it] really drove Pierre nuts." On one occasion, Spinney remembers Sprey venting to him about Boyd's thinking, specifically his reliance on analogies. "[T]hat's a horrible way to reason," Sprey told Spinney. Sprey wasn't wrong, Spinney adds. "[A]nalogy captures your imagination, you just go off the cliff, you got to be really careful." But it was these very competing thought processes that made Sprey and Boyd such a winning pair, functioning in essence as a check and balance on each other's analyses. "John and Pierre basically reinforced each other in a very powerful way," Spinney said.

Spinney awed at Sprey's conviction, as well as how often it bore true. "Pierre isn't in doubt of anything he talks about usually, right? I mean, occasionally, I've seen a few times when he has been wrong, and he can be wrong on a colossal scale, but it's rare. You know, he's almost not mortal in that regard of being right," Spinney said. Together, the Reformers enhanced each other: the poised Tom Christie functioned as the group's forward-facing representative, helping them operate within the bureaucracy; Sprey the empiricist and Boyd the philosopher bounced around controversial big ideas; and Spinney, by his own assessment, was the group's "wrecking ball." They were, Spinney said, "an accretion taking place from different vectors . . . the technology vector, the wrecking ball vector, and the strategy and tactics vector."

On the whole, this group seemed to succeed simply because they found a way to enjoy, rather than loathe, the frustrations of bureaucracy. "I've seen people who were very, very brave in Vietnam combat cower before going before a general who had a bad reputation of beating up on people because they were so afraid of destroying their career," Spinney said. "That's why a guy like Dilger on the A-10 was so interesting: he didn't give a shit." When it came to careerism, none of the Reformers really gave a shit either. Spinney remembered how Sprey in particular relished dealing with Pentagon conflict. "Pierre's eyes would start dreaming," Spinney said. "And his whole physical mannerisms would become much more focused and pointed at John [Boyd]. John would be laughing and hilarious. Pierre actually underwent physical change."

In the same vein, it's also understandable how folks could resent the Reformers. Not everyone enjoyed the creative freedom they possessed thanks to Tom Christie's ability to smooth things over. Lon Ratley recounted a time he overheard an exchange between a general and his staff who recommended they consult John Boyd for a lecture on how to help with a particular problem. The general reportedly said, "Why do I want to invite somebody into my command who is going to tell me how stupid I am?"

The Reformers evaluated their own ideas the same way they evaluated technology, by testing them relentlessly. When a member of the group came up with a new concept or presentation, they "would give it to anyone that [would] listen," Spinney said. They would start by presenting their ideas to the lowest-ranking folks, who according to Spinney "are always the people that know the most about the subject; the generals don't know fuck-all, or the senior civilians, with exception."

Over and over the Reformers delivered their lectures, some of which stretched as long as six hours, begging to be challenged and critiqued. "You'd set it up as a dialog," Spinney said. "You just didn't get up there and lecture a bunch of dummies; you want people hosing you, basically. And so by the time we got to the high levels, these [lectures] were air-tight."

Like a professor delivering a popular lecture for the third decade in a row, the Reformers studied the body language and facial expressions of their audience, altering their presentations to meet attendees' interests and doubts. "And if you knew some guy was kind of gonna jump on here for something, you could sort of warp what you were saying in such a way to get him in deeper and deeper and set the hook in," Spinney said. "And we would just give it and take the heat and give it again. . . . And so these things grew over time in complexity and insightfulness." If one read arrogance in the Reformers' general affect, demeanor, and rhetoric, there was also a great humility in their willingness to continually be challenged and criticized. This unorthodox humility stemmed from John Boyd, whom Spinney noted was "obsessed . . . with the idea of how come he, a dumb fighter pilot with a marginal education in aeronautical engineering" and only a basic training in mathematics conceived of the Energy-Maneuverability Theory before anyone else.

As the 1970s came to a close and the A-10's production ramped up, the Reformers' notoriety seeped out from the Pentagon. What they were arguing for was simply too controversial and important to be contained. Their work, Spinney said, "became sort of the main wrecking ball to bring the Pentagon's credibility into question."

11

Friction

"It is the duty of machines and those who design them to understand people."
—Don Norman, The Design of Everyday Things

In late 1977, Chuck Spinney began developing a John Boyd–style briefing of his own called "Defense Facts of Life." Over the next few years, he delivered it constantly, tweaking, reshaping, and ultimately perfecting it. In final form, it was four hours long, and he had it memorized.

With "Defense Facts of Life," Spinney sought to diagnose the problem around the U.S. military's budget: that is, why was the United States spending so much money and still having what were called "readiness problems," or a lack of readily available weapons should a war break out the next day. It was a problem exacerbated by technology that had become more expensive to maintain, thereby making it more difficult to actually *use*. "In a general sense," Spinney argued, "this pattern reflects a tendency to reduce our current readiness to fight in order to modernize for the future; however, because of rising operating costs, the price of even low readiness is rising inexorably over the long-term." This phenomenon resulted in spending substantially more on a military to have considerably fewer weapons for immediate protection. "By ignoring the real world, we have evolved a self-reinforcing—yet scientifically unsupportable—faith in the military usefulness of ever-increasing technological complexity."

Innovating toward the sophisticated and idealistic was so enticing, Spinney said, because it encouraged a kicking-the-can-down-the-road mindset, one where ambitious ideas would be conceived and built, but rarely tested. He cautioned: "We tolerate an imperfect present because we perceive a bright future."

The Reformers had long been opposed to innovating based on an imagined future. Rather, they all shared the value that history—proven experiences—should inform how and what was innovated. It's why they could all get behind developing a tool for a mission like close-air support; over and over close-air support had proven essential in combat. What Spinney's briefing argued for was that *presence*—a piece of tech simply being available, no matter how primitive—was much more valuable than that technology's *lethality*. Theoretically, a given bomb or missile might be more lethal, more capable of destruction, than a less sophisticated weapon. However, if that weapon couldn't fly because of bad weather or lock onto its target because of muddled jungle canopy, what use was it?

Spinney's insights grew out of what Sprey and his team had been cultivating with the design of the A-10, arguing not merely for simplicity, but also for a realistic view of war, a view that accepted war is chaotic. To illustrate this chaos, Spinney recalled the concept of "friction" as it was furthered by Prussian General Carl von Clausewitz, who posited: "Everything in war is very simple, but the simplest thing is difficult. The difficulties accumulate and end by producing a kind of friction that is inconceivable unless one has experienced war." Friction, Spinney added, included "bad weather during the Battle of the Bulge" and "contagious panic in France in 1940," among any other unpredictable factors that might crop up. To counter such pandemonium, a well-worn phrase was repeated throughout World War II: "Keep it simple, stupid."

Among the problems with highly complex and expensive systems is that they can severely inhibit their user's decision-making, giving them a kind of cognitive overload where they can't adapt to changing circumstances. "[I]ncreasing complexity increases our rigidity in a game where survival of the fittest makes flexibility a paramount virtue," Spinney cautioned. Complex technology entices because it can present as a panacea to the inherent friction of war. But it was Boyd who had gotten interested not just in reducing friction, but *heightening it* for the enemy. "In Boyd's perspective," Spinney wrote, "the idea of decreasing complexity to diminish our friction and free up our operations gives us the opportunity to magnify our enemy friction and impede his operations." In other words, one of the ways to ensure you cycled through your OODA Loop faster than your enemy was to have technology that was easier to use.

With his lecture, Spinney debunked what he felt were false conceptions of the Reformers' ethos. While their approach had "been interpreted as an argument for smaller budgets, or as an argument against advanced technology," in point of fact, "[t]his view is totally incorrect." Indeed, the Reformers *wanted* to fund the military, but they wanted to fund it responsibly. Just because something was complex did not actually mean it was better. And yet too often, highly complex systems were developed without their users in mind. Just as presence was more important than lethality, one could argue ease of use was more important than a weapon's potential for destruction.

One can imagine why Spinney's arguments rankled Pentagon officials and then the defense industry. As he delivered his briefing to various offices and audiences within the Pentagon, he was effectively admonishing them: "Consequently, everybody is at fault and nobody is at fault," he argued. Though some folks may have left his briefings inspired, others undoubtedly were discouraged. Spinney was critiquing what some people had devoted the bulk of their professional lives to, arguing those projects needed to be radically overhauled, if not scrapped and started over. He may have been speaking truth, but he and the Reformers were not winning any bureaucratic popularity contests.

Spinney's briefing, along with the rest of the work of the Reformers, caught the attention of a young journalist named James Fallows, who in October 1979, wrote a cover story for *The Atlantic* called "Musclebound Superpower," later expanded into the book *National Defense*, a 1982 finalist for the National Book Awards for General Nonfiction. Fallows gave the Reformers' arguments a wider platform, noting among other things that Spinney's "Defense Facts of Life" was "one of the most significant documents in Modern American Defense." Discerning readers could detect the Reformers' influence on Fallows' work, especially that of Sprey.

In fact, when Fallows first met Sprey, he was so struck by his demeanor that it raised suspicion. "Is he for real?" Fallows asked Spinney.

Spinney continued delivering his briefing to higher ranking offices, including the secretary of defense. He made enough noise that his boyish mug appeared on the March 7, 1983, issue of *Time* magazine, under the headline "U.S. Defense Spending: Are Billions Being Wasted?" The cover included a note identifying him as "Pentagon Maverick Franklin C. Spinney."

As Spinney's briefings made the rounds, work on an A-10 successor gained steam. In May 1981, E. E., Riccioni, a founding member of the "Fighter Mafia" that preceded the Reformers, gave a briefing to interested parties called "The Blitzfighter Concept of a New Air-to-Ground Aircraft." Riccioni began the presentation with a disclaimer: these ideas were not his. "This is my best effort to simulate the inimitable Pierre." Even if Riccioni had not proffered the disclosure, it would have been easy to recognize Sprey's voice infused throughout the briefing. While lamenting the seventy-five billion dollars per year being spent on non-nuclear airpower, Riccioni said, "Except for 3 A-10 wings, Soviet armor will get a free ride at high noon." Building off Sprey's earlier concept regarding an airplane like the Gnat, Riccioni noted that the United States needed cheap, tiny, agile airplanes in the thousands to be able to constantly patrol the skies while flying very slow (150 knots) and low (five hundred feet above the ground). He expounded on how the already exceptional GAU-8 Avenger could be made more accurate and lethal, namely by having the Gatling barrels spin up to full speed faster (as it stood, the Gatling took a second to get going, so its fire rate was slower in the first quarter to half second of operation). "Above all," Riccioni-as-Sprey argued, they "need[ed] minimum re-attack time," in the neighborhood of thirty-five seconds.

In typical Pierre Sprey fashion, the presentation derided many contemporary weapons systems, arguing that the lethality of enemy air defenses had "not increased since WWII," and that in some ways had gotten worse ("gun variety and density has decreased"). Riccioni promised that an airplane like the proposed Blitzfighter would be able to fly three missions a day, meaning a fully armed force of Blitzfighters would equal out to six thousand daily missions. Ultimately, the U.S. military had a choice: a swarming, seemingly never-ending amount of two thousand Blitzfighters or a mere 125 F-15E Strike Eagles for the same price.

Aside from arguing for cheaper and smaller, Sprey's emphasis on *slower* was noteworthy. Sprey believed an airplane's top speed was *dramatically* overrated relative to its actual practical application. This argument had been reinforced by Riccioni a few years prior, when he examined the flying experience of fighter jets in Vietnam in a 1978 paper. Riccioni found that airplanes that could fly up to twice the speed of sound (Mach 2) had flown more than one hundred thousand missions during Vietnam. And yet *not once* had they actually flown that fast in combat. In fact, they barely even flew at Mach 1.6 (the combined total was a matter of seconds). For the most part, these highly capable airplanes renowned for their speed had spent much of their time right around Mach 1, less than half of their top speed.

Just as Sprey first began exploring the concept of an A-10 successor, another Air Force colonel, Jim Burton, took an interest in the subject. An ally of Sprey's and Spinney's, Burton went on to publish the iconic book *The Pentagon Wars*, which explored the Reformers' efforts inside the Pentagon, particularly throughout the 1980s.

Burton's early concept for an A-10 successor looked a lot like Sprey's, no frills, with no radar or infrared missiles. One difference, however, was that it featured a four-barrel Gatling gun as opposed to a six-barrel. Burton had actually briefed the elephant, Bob Dilger, on his idea, and it was Dilger who then connected Burton with Sprey. By this point, the Military Reformers officially came to be known by this name, and began leading the "Reform Movement," as it was called, calling for major changes in how the Pentagon operated. Soon enough, the Reformers developed a sense of paranoia. Wary of being watched, they reported to being spied on during happy hour gatherings. Allegedly, high-ranking officials had developed a "Wheel of Satan," which featured Tom Christie, Chuck Spinney, and Sprey. "We wore that like a badge of honor," Sprey recalled, saying of the man responsible for the "wheel," "We love[d] that guy." Suspicious that their phone lines might be tapped, they adopted codenames when placing calls. Sprey's identity was "Mr. Grau."

In 1983, Sprey and Spinney identified a possible manufacturer for their A-10 successor. They had attended a lecture at the Smithsonian Air and Space Museum, where another colleague, Roland Smith, connected them with the famed airplane designer Burt Rutan, who is perhaps best known for designing the first airplane to fly nonstop around the world without needing to refuel. The plan—to build a tiny plane with a huge gun—intrigued Rutan. "And Burt is like, he's a lot like Pierre," Spinney told me. "He loves simplicity and elegance. And if anything, [he's] more extreme than Pierre, if that's possible."

Rutan set to work on the design, going so far as to fund the project himself when his company was sold. "Burt got his beginning building these home-built light planes," Spinney said. "And he's a real genius airplane designer. But he loves simplicity. And basically, an engine is sort of an afterthought for Burt. The wing does all the work. That plane that flew around the world was the epitome of his ethos." But the Reformers were looking for "an overpowered dragster," Spinney said. What Rutan came back with was, well, extreme. It weighed a mere six thousand pounds, less than half of what the Reformers had originally targeted, about a sixth the weight of the A-10. It was even smaller than the World War II P-51 Mustang fighter. "This plane was so small," Spinney said. "You couldn't see it. It was stealthy. You couldn't hear it."

The problem? Rutan had built the airplane around a twenty-five-millimeter gun, not the requisite thirty-millimeter tank-killing cannon. Ultimately, his prototype would not be purchased, but the process still yielded some worthy insights. For one, Rutan solved a problem the original A-10 had faced during testing with the gun gases being sucked into the engines: he placed the gun muzzle on one side of the fuselage and the air intake on the opposite. It was an unusual design since one would think placing the gun off center would make it less accurate (indeed, the A-10's gun-firing barrel is placed directly on the airplane's centerline).

But Rutan worked around this problem by altering the design such that extra drag created on the opposite side of the airplane stabilized the recoil of the gun. Years later, Pierre Sprey marveled at Rutan's ingenuity: "Who else in the world would solve a gun-gas problem by making the airplane asymmetric?"

For the bulk of the 1980s the Reformers disrupted the status quo. "Boyd's whole theory was based on figuring out how to do that more quickly than your adversary . . . and we were doing that in the Pentagon," Spinney explained. But eventually, Spinney said, with the constant opposition, they were "ground down." With more prominence came more vocal critics.

Though there's not one specific moment when the Reformers fell out of favor, in *The Pentagon Wars*, Jim Burton pinpoints an October 11, 1987, op-ed in *The Washington Post* by columnist and reporter Fred Reed, "Let's Reform the Military Reformers."

Reed argued that "much of what prominent adversaries of the military," a.k.a. the Fighter Mafia and Military Reformers, "write is absolute, verifiable nonsense." He labeled them as "evangelical critics of the military" who "by focusing on defects which do not exist, have distracted attention from defects that do exist." Reed recalled how when he was hired as a columnist by the *Washington Times* in 1982, Pierre Sprey gave him a presentation about all the flaws with the Army's new tank, an experience he referred to as being "Spreyed." Reed, who graduated from Camp Pendelton's Marine Corps light-armor school, claimed that "Sprey's notions bore no relation either to the military I had been in or to the engineers I had lived with." Reed traveled to Fort Knox "with [his] own stopwatch and tape measure," to assess the tank himself, going so far as to drive it and fire its cannon. "In every case I could personally verify, from acceleration to effectiveness of turret stabilization, the Army's version proved correct." Reed's damning critiques of the Reformers continued:

One begins to notice a pattern in the writings of the evangelical Reformers: First, a robust disregard for truth. Second, a taste for parody. Observe that the Reformers do not accuse the military merely of bureaucratic ineptitude, poor judgement, and inattention in the expenditure of other people's money—the normal foibles of federal agencies. Instead soldiers are accused of absurdity, of serious unfamiliarity with their profession, of behavior explainable only by clinically substandard intelligence. This is not analysis. It is caricature. . . . The evangelicals are not without agendas of their own.

Reed labeled the work of Sprey, Spinney, Boyd, and others as poorly researched and almost farcical. They had a terrible habit of asking provocative questions, which they followed up with dense answers. "Hubris is an occupational disease of Reformers," Reed wrote. For all the claims the Reformers made about responsible spending and improving equipment for the sake of saving grunts on the ground, Reed felt they compromised their aims. "You don't help our boys by making essentially random charges about a highly complex subject whose fundamentals you have made no attempt to master. In fact it is hard to think of a better way to get troops killed." Reed believed they had insulated themselves into being a group of "zealots" with "hermetically sealed minds."

"Those of us who were hard-core reformers realized that the movement was dead," Burton writes of the moment Reed's op-ed was published. A few years before, in 1985, Sprey had lost his special access to the Pentagon; he was effectively locked out. He had since left defense matters to start his own home recording studio, Mapleshade.[1] Soon Spinney and the rest would follow. Still, the Reformers left an enduring legacy, in particular with the establishment of the Office of Operation Test and Evaluation, which stemmed from Bob Dilger and Lon Ratley's work in the desert, and had been further extended by Jim Burton in his work

---

1. With Mapleshade, Sprey adopted a similar minimalist, human-centered approach to sound recording. He recorded in his home, with no more than four microphones and no noise-reduction equipment. "The wonderful thing about [this method] is the principle that only your ears count," Sprey says on Mapleshade's website. "And that's a way of making brilliant advances in designing anything that has to do with audio, and certainly in designing ways of recording."

investigating another problematic military weapon called the Bradley Fighting Vehicle.

The A-10, meanwhile, remained a black sheep airplane, underfunded, unwanted, and outdated. When Fairchild-Republic shut its doors in 1987, the A-10 was effectively orphaned, too. Without its staunchest supporters to come to its defense, the Warthog seemed destined for a quick death after just a decade of service, an unceremonious—though perhaps fitting—end to an artifact with such a tortuous origin.

Ed Heinemann's A-1 Skyraider
NH 80-G-419474 COURTESY OF THE NAVAL HISTORY AND HERITAGE COMMAND

The B-1B, a.k.a the "Bone"
ETHAN WAGNER

A B-17G in flight over Hill Air Force Base, Utah, August 13, 2015
RONALD BRADSHAW

The F-105 "Thunderchief," a.k.a. "the Thud"
U.S. AIR FORCE MUSEUM WEBSITE VIA WIKIMEDIA COMMONS

Matt Secor the day before the ambush in the Marah Valley
MATT SECOR

The P-47 "Thunderbolt"
DEPARTMENT OF DEFENSE (DOD). DOD VISUAL INFORMATION DOES NOT IMPLY OR CONSTITUTE DOD ENDORSEMENT.

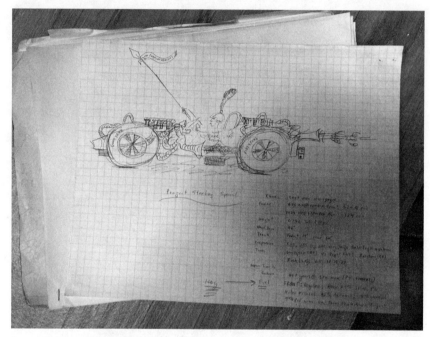

An early Pierre Sprey sketch

PART II

DESTROY

12

"High" Tech

THE QUESTION IRRITATED PIERRE SPREY. IT WAS LATE APRIL 1991, AND Sprey was participating in one of a series of congressional hearings to evaluate the role that new technology served in the U.S. and coalition forces' overwhelming and swift defeat of Saddam Hussein in the Persian Gulf War. Chairing this particular hearing was Wisconsin Democratic Representative Paul Aspin, who asked Sprey, "[D]id anything that happened in this war change your view of high-tech?"

"Well . . . I have a profound disinterest in the abstract concept of high-tech," Sprey replied, "because I don't understand what separates high-tech from low-tech. I have a very deep interest in distinguishing tech that works, and tech that doesn't work." In Sprey's mind, he could not answer the question because no suitable definition for such a distinction existed:

> *It is certainly not the distinction between new and old or the distinction between radically innovative ways of doing things and traditional ways. High versus low is certainly not the difference between simple and complex or between cheap and expensive—after all, I can think of lots of ancient systems that are complicated and expensive, and lots of ultra-modern systems that are simple and cheap.*

The Gulf War had been the ideal stage to showcase the U.S. military's latest "high-tech," especially with respect to airpower. Most every fighter and attack jet saw combat, thoroughly devastating Iraq's forces over the roughly month's-long air campaign spanning mid-January to late February 1991, such that by the time U.S. and coalition ground forces arrived they completed their mission in a matter of days (famously touting one hundred hours).

The war's "star," if there could be such a thing, was the United States' new stealth bomber, the F-117A "Nighthawk" (also referred to colloquially at the time as simply "the Stealth"). The Nighthawk emerged out of the famed "Skunk Works" laboratory of Lockheed Defense Corporation, a secret office in the Mojave Desert. Skunk Works was responsible for some of the most innovative, unusual, and iconic airplanes of the last half century. Their U-2 spy plane gained prominence back in 1960 after U.S. pilot Gary Powers was shot down over Soviet Union territory (on the whole, though, it was a superb spy plane, so effective that it's still in use to this day). SkunkWorks had also built the SR-71 "Blackbird," another spy plane that could fly more than three times the speed of sound. Both the U-2 and the SR-71 looked as though they belonged to science fiction, not the present-day military arsenal.

The F-117 was the strangest-looking SkunkWorks project yet. It appeared wholly un-aerodynamic, angular, and otherworldly, as if a cubist painter had sketched its design blueprint. "Keep in mind that to achieve stealthiness we had to commit a planeload of aerodynamic sins," the F-117's creator, Ben Rich, recounts in his book, *Skunk Works*. "What we came up with suffers just about every kind of unstable flight dynamics." When then Air Force Major Al Whitley saw the F-117 for the first time he remarked, "Boy, it sure is an angular son of a bitch, isn't it?"

All that angularity paired with ultramodern radar-absorbent coating made the F-117 "stealth," or undetectable by radar. It was designed to fly into war zones and drop laser-guided bombs without the enemy ever knowing they were there. One former secretary of the Air Force lauded the F-117 as a miracle of precision: "In World War II it could take 9,000 bombs to hit a target the size of an aircraft shelter. In Vietnam, 300. Today [May 1991] we can do it with one laser-guided munition from an F-117." The F-117's advertised precision inspired a common phrase: "one bomb = one kill." After the war, the Air Force reported that an

F-117 could hit not just a specific structure, but a *vent* or *door* within that structure.

In combat, the F-117 appeared to be as accurate as advertised, with reports that 80 percent of its bombs dropped during Desert Storm landed on their target, an astounding hit rate relative to the guessing game that bombing had been in World War II and Vietnam. Despite making up a tiny fraction of the overall airpower used in Desert Storm (their missions accounted for just 2 percent of all missions flown by U.S. and coalition forces), F-117s were credited with killing 40 percent of all strategic targets. Just as impressive, not a single F-117 was shot down. In the media, the world was treated to footage of laser-guided bombs pulverizing their targets. "The F-117 allowed us to do things that we could have only dreamed about in past conflicts," then Lieutenant General Chuck Horner testified to Congress in April 1991. "Stealth enabled us to gain surprise each and every day of the war."

To no one's surprise, Pierre Sprey doubted the F-117's performance. Ever the contrarian, Sprey argued that none of the tech on display in the Gulf War was actually "new" because its development had begun more than ten years before. Indeed, even the F-117 had taken its first flight at the beginning of the 1980s. Sprey was skeptical, too, of the results that had been presented to the public, imploring to Congress that "the country has been very poorly served by the shamelessly doctored statistics and the hand-selected, tiny number of super success story videos that were shown on the evening news through the war." While the F-117 was not the only weapons system he took issue with, it was the most controversial.

In his presentation to the panel, Sprey noted that accounts from the war indicated "the Stealth is probably not stealthy." He cited allied radars as having been able to track the F-117, and that the F-117 had demonstrated a limited "payload range," meaning it could not fly very far before needing to refuel, which Sprey said "shouldn't be surprising. All you have to do is look at a photograph of the Stealth and know something about aerodynamics to realize that the F-117 has an awfully high drag shape."

Perhaps the most damning of Sprey's testimony came when he said, "[I]t also appears the people most convinced of the fact that the Stealth was being easily tracked were the Stealth pilots." Sprey acknowledged these accounts needed to still be corroborated and confirmed, but if it was true that the F-117 had been easier to track than reported, he wondered why it hadn't been better tested prior to combat. Conversely, if it *had* been tested and discovered that "the Stealth wasn't stealthy: why were those pilot's lives risked in combat in that fashion?" Sprey's speculation had another potential consequence. The United States was now building a much larger stealth bomber, the B-2 Spirit (the Air Force would ultimately purchase twenty-one B-2s at a cost of two billion dollars per airplane when accounting for development expenses and a much smaller than planned production order). "If a little airplane like the Stealth can't be made invisible to radar, there is very, very little hope a huge bomber like the B-2 will be effectively invisible to radar," Sprey said. "I cannot see how one can avoid cancelling the B-2 if that is so."

Sprey's assessment of the F-117 offers a glimpse into what critics most resented (at times perhaps rightfully) about him—his rather consistent opposition. There were a lot of "ifs" in Sprey's statements, and they were vehemently disputed, including by fellow panelist William J. Perry, former secretary of defense, who claimed the need for additional stealth testing "absurd." Perry said they had "conducted hundreds of detection tests on the F-117 in every possible environment you can envision" and reminded those in attendance that the Stealth "is not an invisible airplane," nor did it claim to be, and that to "make it invulnerable to air defense, you have to use it appropriately." Notably, in a hearing the following week, Donald Hicks, former undersecretary of defense for research and engineering, said Sprey's remarks about the lack of stealth testing "may qualify for the most ridiculous comment of the year, at least as one of them."

Sometimes it was not Sprey's credibility in question, but simply the source of his seemingly endless knowledge of all things defense. "Where do you get all your information, Mr. Sprey?" Representative Norman Sisisky of Virginia asked, quick to add that he was not "trying to be facetious," but rather curious as to how Sprey had acquired all this knowledge to which the committee was not privy. Sprey cited his two decades in the defense industry talking with all sorts of folks, both soldiers and journalists who had reported in combat zones. Sprey added, "You get very valuable insights if you start with some basic weapons knowledge, some skepticism, and a lot of interest."

Sprey was not alone in questioning the triumphs of "high tech." In a hearing held the following week (the same one in which Donald Hicks later criticized Sprey), Senator Gary Hart noted, "Some reports of fantastic weapons performance already seem highly inflated, if not grossly exaggerated." Hart reiterated to those in attendance that the current Gulf War data needed much more inspection before it could be seen as a precedent for future spending since "we are dealing almost wholly with claims. History says that claims, even honest ones, are almost always greatly inflated." Hart also used the opportunity to take a dig at the much-maligned B-1 Bomber, which had not deployed to the Persian Gulf. "That was the true Stealth bomber in the Gulf because it literally was invisible," Hart said. "It didn't show up."

Speaking at the same panel as Hart, Sprey's longtime friend and colleague, John Boyd, reminded panelists of the Reformer ethos: people, not technology, were far and above the most important factor in winning a war. In a moment that elicited laughter among attendees, panel chairman Aspin interrupted Boyd mid-answer because Boyd was too far away from the microphone and could not be heard (Aspin had to remind Sprey to speak closer to the mic multiple times the week before, too). Aspin lamented that the mics "don't work a damn." Another panel member, Representative Bill Dickinson added, "Colonel, this is a low-tech committee," to which Boyd quipped, "Are you trying to tell me you've got a technology problem here?"

If the viability of stealth remained up for debate, what had quite literally gone under the radar was the performance of the A-10. At first, the Air Force and General Horner had resisted employing the A-10 in service, opting instead to convert a squadron of F-16s out of Syracuse, New York, into "A-16s." But when A-16s were tasked with taking out early warning radar sites so that allied airplanes could attack Iraqi defenses more easily, the results were miserable. The A-16s flew too fast and too high to bomb accurately.

In looking over the data, apparently someone in the command room suggested to General Horner they give the task to A-10s, even though this kind of mission was not something A-10 drivers trained for. A-10s proved to be so successful in this mission and others that, according to a *Washington Post* report by Jack Anderson and Dale Van Atta, mere days into the war General Horner repented to his staff in a private meeting, "I take back all the bad things I've ever said about the A-10s. I love them. They're saving our asses."[1]

Of course, A-10s did their greatest damage against tanks, devastating Iraq's fearsome tank army, four thousand strong and many of them Russian. Hog drivers utilized a variety of techniques, most notably one called "sandwiching," in which they knocked out the first and last tanks in a long row, trapping the rest in the middle to be easily picked off. One pair of A-10 drivers, Captain Eric Salomonson and Lieutenant John Marks, killed a combined twenty-three tanks over the course of a day. The resulting explosions were "fabulous" Salomonson told William Smallwood in *Warthog: Flying the A-10 in the Gulf War.* "Sometimes star-cluster shells would pop out or real bright magnesium-like stuff would come spewing out on the ground and burn white hot for fifteen or twenty minutes. Turrets were blowing off like tops blowing off pop bottles."

Where Hans Rudel hunted for tanks hidden in houses, A-10s scanned the desert for tanks buried in the sand, like alligators lurking in Florida swampland with just their snouts poking above the surface. A-10 driver Buck Wyndham describes in his book *Hogs in the Sand* how the "landscape below was so barren and lacking in detail that it was all too easy to get slightly 'target-fixated,' a phenomenon where you inadvertently delay dropping a bomb because you can't tell how high you are." Without any trees or mountains for pilots to gauge their altitude, flying over the desert was "like looking at a blank, white wall in a white room, trying to guess how far away it is."

The other A-10s to make an impression were the "Night Hogs," out of the 355th squadron of Myrtle Beach, flying precarious night missions through turbulent and stormy skies. To spot targets, the Night Hogs

---

1. In his testimony at the congressional hearings, Sprey called this about-face a "great tribute to General Horner's objectivity and his courage and his dedication to combat."

adopted an innovative way of seeing in the dark that had first been discovered by A-10 drivers stationed in Korea, using the infrared imaging monitor attached to their Maverick missiles as "a poor man's set of night vision goggles," Wyndham writes. Though A-10 drivers had been specifically directed not to do this in Weapons School because it involved flying with one's head down, the results couldn't be denied.

The Warthog may not have boasted any sophisticated materials, but in a sense it was—to borrow Sprey's phrase—rather "stealthy." With its quiet engines, the A-10 was basically invisible and silent when flying at five thousand feet. And as suspected during the initial design phase, the turbofans didn't give off much heat, making the A-10 difficult to detect via infrared. Waxing philosophically, Wyndham elaborates how even in an airplane most intimately connected with the ground, there can be a perverse sterility about war from the sky:

The radios hum faintly in my helmet, the engines whine steadily, and the warm rays of sunshine stream through the bubble canopy and into my small cockpit. When the missile hits, there is no dramatic chord. No deafening explosion. No screams suddenly stifled. The soundtrack of a pilot's war is mostly silent. . . . It's not horrible or gut-wrenching at all—no more so than when I'm driving down the road and a bug hits my windshield. I feel no disgust or remorse of any kind. As long as there is just that small flash and nothing more, this job is easy.

Ultimately, 144 A-10s would be deployed to Iraq, a figure accounting for just a small fraction of the total number of airplanes used in the war, which made all the more noteworthy the overwhelming damage Hogs inflicted. Curiously, for all the capability the A-10 displayed in the war, they barely flew any close-air support of troops; the ground campaign faced so little opposition and ended so quickly. Instead, A-10s hunted tanks, knocked out radar and missile sites, flew rescue missions, and conducted reconnaissance. A-10 drivers were even credited with shooting down two helicopters, technically making it a "fighter" airplane with air-to-air kills. To reflect all the missions A-10s executed, a cartoon made the rounds suggesting the Warthog be re-designated as a reconnaissance/fighter/observation/attack airplane, or an RFOA-10G.

Just as impressive as the damage A-10s inflicted was the punishment they withstood. One A-10 driver, Captain Paul Johnson, was hit by a surface-to-air missile, which punctured a twenty-foot-diameter hole in his wing, as well as severe damage to his landing gear. Still, he managed to refuel in flight and land (when he got out, he kissed his airplane). What's more, Captain Johnson's airplane was repaired and back in service a couple of weeks later. Colonel Dave Sawyer sustained some five hundred bullet holes that knocked out his airplane's right elevator and damaged its right rudder, left elevator, and tail cone. When asked to assess the damage, Colonel Sawyer told Smallwood his A-10 "was flying almost normally." In all, four A-10s were shot down in combat and two irreparably damaged. Two A-10 drivers died while serving their country: Lieutenant Patrick Olson, age twenty-five, who was posthumously promoted to the rank of captain, and Captain Stephen Phillis, age thirty, who was killed while protecting a downed A-10 driver, who survived.

After the war the reward for a sizable chunk of A-10s was retirement, where they were sent to bake in the "Boneyard" in Tucson, Arizona, sealed with a white vinyl compound called "spraylat" to protect them from the brilliant sunlight and oppressive summer heat that regularly climbs to 105 degrees.[2] A familiar refrain about technology haunted the Hog. In one of the post-war congressional hearings, Representative Norman Sisisky couched his support of the A-10 with a warning. "The world is changing and what's good today may not be good 10 or 15 years from now."

---

2. "The Boneyard" is where airplanes go to die. It spans four square miles, which might not sound like much until you consider it's the equivalent of 596 Walmart Supercenters. Officially known as the 309th Aerospace Maintenance and Regeneration Group out of Davis-Monthan Air Force Base, in Tucson, Arizona, the "Boneyard" houses more than three thousand airplanes and close to six thousand engines. The dry desert air does wonders in preventing the retired airframes from degrading. Some are used for spare parts and, on occasion, others are resurrected and brought back into service. Most every significant military airplane finds its way to the Boneyard, including for a time the B-29 "Enola Gay," which dropped the first atomic bomb, on Hiroshima, Japan. It is now at Udvar-Hazy.

What Sprey, Boyd, and Gary Hart[3] called for in these hearings was an honest assessment of the results of the war, one rooted in data rather than word of mouth. While impressive, the Gulf War's efforts left too many questions unanswered. It would be another Reformer who would take up the burden of sorting through the rubble of testimonials and damage assessments to uncover the war's true insights.

---

3. Hart used these hearings to further debunk misconceptions about the Reformers' stance on technology:

"[C]ontrary to persistent, almost demented mischaracterization of military reform theory, the Persian Gulf war did not prove that high-tech is better than low-tech weaponry. At no time during my more than decade-long involvement with the military reform movement has it ever been argued that technology per se, including high technology, was an evil. The military reform movement has argued that our technological advantage should be used to produce larger numbers of simpler weapons that work in combat conditions, that technological sophistication was not an end in itself, and that the cost of super-technology should not be permitted to drive down the overall numbers of weapons available."

13

To Be Seen

SITTING IN THE AUDIENCE THE DAY JOHN BOYD AND GARY HART TES-
tified before Congress was another ally of the Reformers, a man with a
mustache as extraordinary as his name: Winslow Wheeler. Wheeler's
connection to the Reformers stretched back to the early 1970s, when he
worked as a research assistant on the Foreign Relations Committee for
esteemed (albeit aggressive) New York Republican Senator Jacob Javits.
In 1973, Wheeler helped Javits draft the War Powers Resolution (also
known as the War Powers Act), which requires the president to notify
Congress before embroiling the nation in war. The A-10 first came to
Wheeler's attention just as it entered production because it was being
built nearby, at the Fairchild-Republic factory on Long Island. Throughout his career, Wheeler worked for multiple senators on both sides of the
aisle, but in his mind Javits was the best because "he insisted you disagree
with him when he was wrong." Wheeler recalls one instance when he felt
Javits should challenge then-President Jimmy Carter's veto of the Nimitz
nuclear-powered aircraft carrier. Javits pointed at Wheeler and growled,
"That's not what you said to me six months ago." After John Boyd and
Pierre Sprey, Wheeler felt Javits had the most "raw mental horsepower"
of anyone he'd met.

It was in 1981 when Wheeler first met Pierre Sprey and Chuck
Spinney. They were all sharing a flight from Langley, Virginia, to McConnell Air Force Base in Kansas. Wheeler didn't know either of them yet,
but they quickly got to chatting. "I pressed on Pierre and Chuck my great
idea, which was that the Navy could save itself some money but also have

a much better aviation wing . . . if it just got rid of that stupid F-18 and built more F-14s," the latter of which became well-known in popular culture as the airplane Tom Cruise flies in *Top Gun*. "[Pierre] said something like . . . 'That's a good idea only if you want to ruin naval aviation.'" Nonetheless, they seemed to get on well, and Sprey began bouncing some of his ideas off Wheeler. "The only problem was I couldn't hear almost all of what he was saying because the plane is so noisy," Wheeler remembered. So Wheeler just nodded in agreement with whatever Sprey had to say; Sprey, meanwhile, thought he'd found someone on his same wavelength (indeed he actually had).

Later that day, Wheeler sat in on a meeting with Sprey and Spinney in which they listened to pilots debrief about a recent training mission. Wheeler was struck by how Sprey and Spinney engaged with the pilots. "And they're asking kinds of questions and getting kinds of answers that I had no fucking clue about . . . a whole different level of understanding of airplanes and tactics. . . . And the more I heard, the more I learned, and it was, you know . . . it was an inadvertent tutorial for me about how to learn about airplanes." During that visit, Spinney gave Wheeler a copy of his "Defense Facts of Life" brief, which Wheeler read on the flight back to Virginia alongside Sprey and Spinney in an old cargo plane, sitting two by two in seats facing each other. As Wheeler read—slowly, patiently—he paused on occasion to ask Spinney a clarifying question. "Read the next page," Spinney would reply. On the next page, Wheeler's question would be answered.

By 1992, Wheeler was serving as the assistant director at the U.S. General Accounting Office (GAO). In this role, Wheeler helped lead a small team tasked with assessing the results of the air campaign in Desert Storm. What they found was illuminating, and not a little discouraging for advocates of all that was "stealthy."

From July 1992 to December 1995, the GAO compiled their report. Among the weapons systems they examined was the technological sensation, the F-117 Nighthawk. Wheeler recalled that initially there had been some discussion about not even evaluating the performance of the

A-10, but he pushed for it to be included in the study given the astonishing number of tanks its drivers claimed to have killed.

At first, the GAO's work underwhelmed. After three years of extensive interviews, research, and evaluation, they produced a meager thirteen-page report, a vague overview of the war with few revelations. In truth, the GAO had drafted a 250-page report, but during the declassification process with the Department of Defense it had been neutered, its most pointed findings deemed classified. Among the contentious issues were a series of statements made by the Department of Defense that the GAO proved to be false (the Department of Defense argued the GAO's acknowledgment of these falsehoods was a national security threat). "And we're all crestfallen about what a useless piece of crap that was after years of work," Wheeler remembered. A year later, however, Wheeler's boss, Kwai-Cheung Chan, and Senator David Pryor of Arkansas, pushed for the full report's release (with the exception of a few details that remained classified).

Chiefly, the GAO believed Desert Storm was an unreliable litmus test from which to make judgments. Iraq had demonstrated little air-to-air capability or electronic countermeasures (such as jamming radar), so it was not possible to say exactly how such technology would have affected the U.S. and coalition forces. On the whole, airplanes and the weapons they delivered were flown and fired from higher altitudes than intended and were thus at a safer distance from surface-to-air fire. For these reasons, the GAO claimed, "a number of lessons cannot be drawn directly from Desert Storm because systems were not stressed in ways that could be considered likely and operationally realistic for future conflict."

The GAO used these qualifiers as a means to offer more pointed critiques of the swift defeat of Iraq. "[P]recisely because of the advantages enjoyed by the coalition, the problems that were encountered should be especially noted." Weapons were not as accurate as advertised. Weather had wreaked havoc on targeting sensors. Desert Storm, then, was not solely a triumph of technology. It was also a cautionary tale. Indeed, the war was strange even before it began. U.S. and coalition forces had about a six-month lead time to assemble their forces and plan air assaults, all without being attacked by Iraqi soldiers, an "uncurtailed buildup of forces and military supplies to existing infrastructures on foreign, yet friendly, soil that directly bordered hostilities."

Overall, the GAO's extensive work could be split into two categories: the examination of newer technology and that of older technology. When it came to the F-117, the results were less than flattering.

First, the GAO challenged—and at times outright debunked—a number of the claims about the F-117 that were promoted during and immediately after the war. For one, while the F-117's survivability was championed, with not a single stealth airplane being lost, the GAO noted that F-117s "recorded fewer sorties than any other air-to-ground platform and flew exclusively at night and at medium altitudes—an operating environment in which the fewest casualties occurred among all types of aircraft." The overall loss rate for airplanes in the war had been 1.7 losses per one thousand strikes. Statistically, other airplanes flying the same amount of missions as the F-117 would have been zero losses as well. Indeed, other airplanes like the F-111, the F-16, and, yes, the A-10 were not shot down at night while flying "at least as many night strikes as the F-117." In general, the GAO found that "flying at night was much safer than during the day, regardless of size of radar cross-section or other aircraft-specific characteristics."

A Desert Storm white paper from September 1991 had asserted the "F-117 was the only airplane that planners dared risk over downtown Baghdad," where the air defenses were thought to be formidable. The GAO pushed back on these claims, noting that "the defense systems located in the Baghdad area did not necessarily protect downtown Baghdad at a higher threat level than the rest of the overall metropolitan area." What's more, the "F-117s never faced the defenses that proved to be the most lethal in Desert Storm—daytime AAA and IR SAMs." In fact, the stealth innovations may have not even contributed significantly to the F-117's survivability. "In sum, the factor most strongly associated with survivability in Desert Storm appears to have been the combination of flying high and flying at night—an environment that the F-117s operated in exclusively."

Lockheed had released a statement that "[d]uring the first night, 30 F-117s struck 37 high-value targets, inflicting damage that collapsed

Saddam Hussein's air defense system and all but eliminated Iraq's ability to wage coordinated war. The concept of modern air warfare had been changed forever." When the GAO looked into these claims, they found that the F-117s had actually only hit twenty-one of the thirty-seven targets, and missed 40 percent of the air-defense targets they had been tasked with striking. In other words, the F-117 was not the "silver bullet" that had been advertised.

Part of the evidence for stealth's effectiveness had been that F-117s were undetected until *after* they dropped their bombs on a target, at which point antiaircraft fire would begin. But the GAO found this phenomenon wasn't unique to stealth, and that it wasn't always the case. In fact, this had been a commonality even with the low-tech A-10s dropping bombs "in most cases" and in "the majority of first passes," according to an Air Force after-action report. F-16 and F-15E pilots echoed similar sentiments. What was concerning, the GAO noted, was that "F-117 pilots told us that, on occasion, AAA in a target area would erupt 'spontaneously'—before they had released their bombs or the bombs had exploded," indicating they may have been detected.

An oft-used argument in favor of stealth was that it promoted a more streamlined approach to conflict. Because stealth could not be detected, it didn't need extra fighter planes nearby to defend against air-to-air attacks or radar-jamming airplanes to disable radar below. After the war, Air Force General John M. Loh told Congress that "stealth allows us to use our available force structure more efficiently because it allows us to attack more targets with fewer fighters and support aircraft." In this way, stealth had been framed as a "force multiplier," a weapon that could be used to increase efficiency. However, F-117 pilots told the GAO that they "believed that air-to-air, F-15 aircraft were in a position to challenge any Iraqi interceptors that would have posed a threat to the F-117s." During one meeting with F-117 pilots, Wheeler remembers them saying, "Jamming for us is like American Express: don't leave home without it."

The GAO also documented accounts from pilots lamenting how difficult the F-117 had been to fly given its odd aerodynamics. Namely, the F-117 couldn't "jink," or maneuver suddenly (like Hans Rudel in his

Stuka). Doing such a move was outside the bounds of the F-117 computer's ability to maneuver and could lead to a high-G spin.

The F-117 proved to be much less readily available than other airframes. On that oft-cited first night attack of Baghdad, fifteen F-117s were tasked with hitting Integrated Air Defense Systems targets, but because "of weather aborts and misses, only 9 of these 15 F-117 targets (60 percent) were reported hit by the F-117s on the first night of the campaign." "So, when you look at an airplane's design it's not just the costs, the schedule, and the performance," Wheeler told me. "It's not just effectiveness per sortie. It's also . . . How many times did you show up? . . . You're not effective if you're not there." Wheeler likened this problem of sophistication to what Germany dealt with in World War II. Germany was renowned for its roughly fifteen hundred highly advanced Tiger tanks compared to the United States' more primitive Sherman tanks, of which there were closer to fifty thousand. Unquestionably, the Sherman was the lesser tank. But it was easier to maintain, and at least it was available (this is what Chuck Spinney referred to in "Defense Facts of Life" as "presence").

On average, F-117s flew 0.7 missions per day, which was less than F-15Es (one mission per day) and F-16s (1.2). Both dropped considerably more bombs than the F-117s, though to be clear, dropping more bombs is not necessarily a measure of an airplane's effectiveness. Part of this disparity could be attributed to the F-117's design; it had to keep all weapons in internal bays to maintain its stealth profile, whereas other planes hung bombs and missiles off their wings.

This difference in weapons load wouldn't have been so noticeable if the F-117s didn't have to be housed so far away from the action, at an airbase more than a thousand miles from Baghdad, "which meant a round-trip mission as long as 6 hours with multiple refuelings," the GAO wrote. There were multiple explanations for F-117s being kept at such a distance, including one by the Air Force that it was to protect them from being hit by missiles. "Another explanation," the GAO noted, "was that the air base at Khamis Mushayt was one of only a select few in-theater bases with sufficient hangars to house the F-117 fleet and protect its sensitive radar absorptive coating from the elements."

One success attributed to F-117s had been an attack on the Baghdad Nuclear Research Facility at Osirak, a target which F-16s had previously failed to destroy. What was hailed as a quick, destructive strike by F-117s cleaning up F-16s' mess, however, wasn't true as "48 F-117s were tasked seven more times against the target over the next 32 days, dropping 66 more bombs." F-111s later revisited the same area more than a week later. "Therefore," GAO argued, "the scenario described by the Air Force—an unsuccessful, large conventional package strike using unguided munitions, followed by a successful, small package of stealth aircraft using guided munitions—neither fully presents the results of the two missions, nor fully presents the weight and type of effort expended to achieve success at this target."

After Desert Storm, the Air Force claimed that the "Gulf War illustrated that the precision of modern air attack revolutionized warfare. . . . In particular, the natural partnership of smart weapons and stealth working together gives the attack unprecedented military leverage." Lockheed briefed the GAO in September 1993 that "stealth, combined with precision weapons, demonstrated a change in aerial warfare . . . one bomb = one kill." But the GAO found that "approximately one-third of the bomb drops assessed to be hits either lacked corroborating video documentation or were in conflict with other information in the database." It was just too difficult to accurately assess the extent of the damage and would therefore be too difficult for folks to so boldly support the lofty claims made on stealth's behalf.

If the GAO's faith in all the promises of "high tech" was shaken, their analysis revealed an enthusiasm for "low tech," like the B-52 bomber (in service since 1952) and the A-10, both of which "were cited by Iraqi prisoners of war as the most feared of the coalition aircraft." The GAO concluded that the cost of a weapons system had no meaningful impact on how effective it was in battle and that "neither cost nor stealth technology was found to be a determinant of survivability."

Given the higher number of missions flown by A-10s compared to the F-117, for example, the rate at which A-10s were hit was effectively zero, just like the F-117. Of note, the "Night Hogs," flying against the same kinds of defenses the F-117 faced at night, were not shot down either. For all the clamoring that the A-10 was a flying fossil, it had demonstrated superior capability in modern combat. Maybe just as impressive, the A-10s flew mostly with dark-green paint schemes, which stuck out against the bright sky during the day and "may have been responsible for some of the casualties," according to the GAO.[1]

To be clear, the GAO deliberately stated that they were not trying to grind a particular axe. "Each aircraft of the various types has both strengths and limitations; each aircraft can do things the other cannot . . . we find it inappropriate, given their use, performance, and effectiveness demonstrated in Desert Storm, to rate one more generally 'capable' than the other." In effect, the GAO was arguing for what the Reformers had been imploring for decades, that a "high-low" mix made for the best military arsenal. The F-117 *had* demonstrated effectiveness as part of a team, but it was not the cure-all solution.

The risk of investing so much in relatively few pieces of sophisticated technology—what Chuck Spinney cautioned against in his "Defense Facts of Life" brief—could lead to a kind of analysis paralysis in which commanders did not want to "waste" expensive airplanes or bombs on targets that weren't deemed valuable enough. In comparison, the GAO noted that if you allocated one billion dollars in defense spending, you could buy nine F-117s or 85 A-10s. Given the statistics from Desert Storm, nine F-117s would fly an average daily total of seven missions. Conversely, the same number of A-10s would amount to 119 missions in a day. "While the design missions of the two aircraft differ substantially," the GAO writes, "their use in Desert Storm demonstrated that they are not necessarily mutually exclusive." Ultimately, the GAO wanted the Department of Defense and the weapons manufacturers to be more responsible in the claims they made about these weapons systems because these statements shaped the public's perception of the war.

In an essay years later circulated widely across Capitol Hill, Winslow Wheeler, writing under the pseudonym "Spartacus," discusses how the

---

1. A-10 drivers had actually painted their airplanes a lighter color but were soon ordered to change back.

Department of Defense "asserted to GAO, 'No one has ever seriously attempted to argue that one-shot, one-kill is a realistic expectation for our platforms and weapons.'" However, this phrase had indeed been repeated often, promoting the misguided belief in the "one bomb = one kill" philosophy in later years, whether it be via stealth, unmanned drone, or some other means. Such a belief carries with it a troubling cost, one that blinds from the actual horrors of war. As Wheeler explained recently, "the magic of precision munitions . . . makes [war] just antiseptic enough."

14

The Joint Strike Fighter

IN 1995, THE COMMERCIAL AIRLINE GIANT BOEING BEGAN A FIVE-YEAR competition with Lockheed Martin to build the fighter jet of the future. Designated the Joint Strike Fighter (JSF), this jet would serve numerous missions across all three major military branches while doubling as a lucrative export to U.S. allies around the world. The JSF would come in three varieties: a baseline model for the Air Force, a Navy version modified with a larger wingspan and more rugged landing gear to perform the short takeoffs and withstand hard landings required on aircraft carriers, and an iteration for the Marines that could land vertically like the Harrier jet. The JSF would be stealth, it would be fast, and it would be lethal. Best of all, it would be (relatively) affordable, just a third the cost of the Lockheed F-22 Raptor, then the most advanced fighter jet of the time with a price tag to match.[1] The F-22 had once been projected as the mainstay of the Air Force before its costs became untenable—one hour of flying time in an F-22 cost about seventy thousand dollars. Now, the JSF would rectify this problem, satiating the U.S. military's air-superiority needs for decades to come.

---

1. Publicly, the Air Force reports the cost of the F-22 at 143 million dollars per airplane, but other estimates accounting for all of the initial research and development expenses placed this figure closer to between three and four hundred million dollars. "There's a third way to calculate the F-22's burden on the taxpayer," wrote David Axe for *WIRED* in 2011. "'Lifecycle cost' adds up the price of fuel, spare parts and maintenance during the jet's projected 40-year lifespan. The Government Accountability Office estimates it will cost $59 billion to fix and fly the F-22s until they retire. If you add unit cost and per-plane lifecycle cost, you get the total amount the United States spends to design, produce and operate a single Raptor: a whopping $678 million."

The very notion of the JSF went against most everything for which the Reformers stood. Designing an airplane to do many things across military branches with vastly different needs and unique challenges might seem like a panacea. But to the Reformers it just sounded too good to be true. Setting out to build a jack-of-all-trades tool from the start was bound to cause problems: the systems of conflict, technology, and design were just too complex, with too many variables for everything to align. Pierre Sprey believed any secondary missions an airplane happened to succeed in performing were merely a side effect of designing that airplane to first be good at one specific thing. "When you have an airplane that's a good airplane . . . people always make multi-mission use of it," Sprey told me.

Still, there was precedent for something like the JSF. In the early 1960s, Secretary of Defense Robert McNamara and his Whiz Kids (before Sprey's time) lobbied for an airplane that could solve the needs of both the Air Force and the Navy: the F-111 "Aardvark," equipped with afterburner engines and variable "swing wings" that extended for takeoff and lift and retracted at high speeds or when being stowed on an aircraft carrier. With equal aplomb, the Aardvark promised to perform bombing, air-to-air combat, and close-air support. In actuality, it suffered mightily in meeting these competing demands.[2]

In 2001, Lockheed Martin was awarded the JSF contract. While Boeing had constructed a capable prototype, it sure was ugly, with a large scoop engine intake resembling a pelican with mouth agape. Lockheed's design, on the other hand, fit the ideal profile of a "next generation" fighter. Officially designated the F-35, it was sharp and smooth, a chef's knife slicing through the air. "If you were to go back to the year 2000 and somebody said, 'I can build an airplane that is stealthy and has vertical takeoff and landing capabilities and can go supersonic,' most people in the industry would have said that's impossible," C.T. "Tom" Burbage, Lockheed's general manager for the JSF program from 2000 to 2013, told *The New York Times* years later. "The technology to bring all of that

---

2. Though notably the F-111 eventually found great success in Desert Storm as a tank killer.

together into a single platform was beyond the reach of industry at that time."

But problems arose during production of the F-35 because of the conflicting demands of the various military branches it was supposed to serve. An eighteen-month delay ensued after it was discovered that the design for the Air Force could not easily be applied to the Marine model since it was three thousand pounds overweight and would be too heavy to perform short takeoffs and vertical landings. For his part, Chuck Spinney felt the JSF embodied the worst of what he called the "survivalist needs of the Military Industrial Congressional Complex." Spinney always insisted on adding *Congressional* when discussing the vicious cycle of weapons development, procurement, and spending because he believed the whole process to be inexorably linked to government legislation. In fact, when then-President Dwight Eisenhower coined the term "Military Industrial Complex" in his final presidential address on January 17, 1961, he had originally included "Congressional" in the name, but took it out at the last moment for worry of reprisal. Whatever you called it, the Military Industrial Congressional Complex fueled the "political engineering" of defense contracts, ensuring a project became too big to fail.

"Our weapons typically have jobs in more than 40 states and hundreds of congressional districts," Spinney explained to me. "That's basically to lock it in . . . [to create jobs]. . . . It's a bait and switch operation. The first stage is what we call front-loading. And basically that's putting the camel's nose into the tent. You say, 'It isn't gonna cost very much. And we can get this thing fielded quickly.' So they basically make optimistic predictions about scheduled cost and performance. That's the camel's nose into the tent."

Once the camel's nose is in the tent, a process called "concurrency" begins. With concurrency, a product—in this case, an airplane—begins construction while its design might still be in progress. The thinking behind concurrency is that it expedites production and makes the process more efficient. However, it can create huge problems if serious design flaws are discovered after the airplane has been built. What follows, then, is the convoluted process of "retrofitting," or implementing changes and improvements to an existing design. In step, costs rise.

When a weapons project utilizing the concurrency method reaches a near-untenable state, the government can't simply cut and run. By this point, the weapon under scrutiny has distributed its manufacturing needs across the country such that politicians who want to curb defense spending can't do so without also sending a message that they will be killing jobs. Spinney added, "And that's political engineering. . . . The Joint Strike Fighter is a classic case in point."

A decade later, in 2010, the JSF would go so far over budget—nearly 90 percent more expensive than originally projected—that it forced the Pentagon and Congress to decide if the JSF had violated the Nunn-McCurdy Amendment, requiring defense contractors to notify Congress of cost overruns. At this point, Winslow Wheeler was working as director of the Strauss Military Reform Project in the Center for Defense Information. He quickly became one of the more outspoken critics on the JSF, often seeking editorial advice from Pierre Sprey, who was staying busy with his successful Mapleshade recording company. "You know, he can understand what the hell you're trying to say and put it into simple English," Wheeler told me. "He also had an irritating habit of snarking up stuff and using adjectives and stuff, you know, [that] weren't necessarily wrong, but just pushing the envelope a little bit more than I wanted to." On many occasions, Sprey returned drafts to Wheeler "dripping in comments."

Motivated by the dire state of defense affairs, Wheeler decided to organize and edit a small book called *The Pentagon Labyrinth*, a collection of essays by defense analysts and Reformers. Of course, Wheeler wanted Sprey to contribute. Sprey accepted the invitation, but Wheeler noticed it took Sprey a while to get going on his essay, which was strange given how prolific of a memo writer Sprey had been in the Pentagon. "Maybe it was the idea of writing anything. . . . For some reason he just didn't relish that at all," Wheeler said, "And it took a long time to write that chapter for *The Pentagon Labyrinth*." Wheeler paused a moment, then added softly, "It was a brilliant piece of work."

Published in February 2011, Sprey's essay begins with a stark declaration: "The world is awash in mediocre or even useless weapons. . . . If you are seriously trying to understand whether a given fighter, destroyer, tank, rifle or truck is worth acquiring, you will soon find yourself buried under a mountain of misinformation—the more expensive the weapon, the deeper you'll be buried. Here are a few guideposts for digging your way out." Throughout, Sprey argues for the value of cheap user-friendly technology ("rifles and machine-guns, cheap as they are, are far more important than fighters or bombers in winning wars. That's as true today as it was in World War II"). Eventually, he takes aim at the F-35, imploring how "cheap $15 million close air support planes [like the A-10] will clearly contribute far more to saving American troops in trouble and winning wars than $2.2 billion B2s or $160 million-plus 'multipurpose' fighters like the F-35—no matter whether we're facing Taliban fighters or massed tanks."

Among the new developments Sprey lamented was the concept of "beyond-visual-range" combat, or the idea that air-to-air combat could be fought using radars and missiles such that two opposing fighters never actually laid eyes on one another. He called beyond-visual-range combat a "beguiling dream"; air-to-air combat almost always required getting visual confirmation that a target was an enemy before firing. In this way, beyond-visual-range combat was yet another example of how "combat is separated by a chasm" from the technologist's point of view. The consequence of trying to realize such "beguiling dreams" was building airplanes of "unimaginable complexity."

At its core, Sprey's message remained the same—the design of a tool needs to be simple such that it eases the life of its user. "For any weapon, the list of essential effectiveness characteristics must include the weapon's direct effect on the user's skill, combat adaptability and training (people first!)," Sprey writes. To facilitate these designs, Sprey again implored unbiased and rigorous testing. "[In-house research and development] tests, though perhaps useful to designers and engineers, are inherently useless for judging a weapon's effectiveness because they suffer from an insurmountable conflict of interest: they are controlled by the weapon's development agency," Sprey writes. He likened the practice of contractors conducting their own evaluations to that of someone writing the questions to their own test. Indeed, according to an illuminating investigative feature in *The New York Times Magazine* by Valerie Insinna published years later, when it came to the F-35, Lockheed "was allowed to manage the test program and had the power, for example, to defer more challenging tests until later."

Probably Sprey's most damning critique of the F-35 appeared in a 2013 feature for *Harper's* by Andrew Cockburn. At the time of Cockburn's story, the F-35 cost $191 million per airplane, which while less than the $242 million it'd been listed at in 2006, was still more expensive than originally quoted. Now, the problem was that the F-35 presented a serious fire hazard. The jet's systems for managing fires were troublesome enough that F-35 pilots had to remain at least twenty-five miles away from thunderstorms at all times (your average commercial airliner, meanwhile, might keep a distance of five to twenty miles from a storm). This, coupled with a bevy of other potential hazards such as the F-35 having trouble purging fuel during emergency situations, prompted Sprey to tell Cockburn, "It's as if Detroit suddenly put out a car with lighter fluid in the radiator and gasoline in the hydraulic brake lines."

While the F-35 made for an easy target, it was also a response to a very real problem. The United States' current fleet of airplanes was getting old. At some point, new airplanes had to be built. What the Reformers objected to was the one-size-fits-all mentality. They agreed more airplanes were needed, but they would need to be separate airplanes to fulfill separate missions.

Even though the A-10 proved to be plenty effective in modern combat, the solution wasn't as simple as just building more. The downside of having a low-cost airplane like the A-10 was that it didn't promise lucrative contracts for weapons manufacturers. When Fairchild-Republic shuttered back in 1987, it made getting upgrades for the A-10 all the more difficult. And with the airplane constantly on the chopping block, contractors were understandably less eager to bid on a project as small and precarious as the A-10. Could you blame them? One 2008 study in *The Journal of Business Logistics* used the A-10 as a model of a "nearly worst-case scenario" for a company failing to anticipate supply chain needs when extending a product's service life, arguing that they should have killed the A-10 for good back in the late 1980s and invested in a new airframe then as opposed to squeezing out more use from the A-10. "In this case," the study notes, "the Air Force's efforts to save money through life extension of existing aircraft actually exceeded the seemingly enormous initial investment of acquiring new aircraft."

By this time, development on the JSF was in full swing and the A-10s that had staved off retirement were continuing to fly—a rather miraculous feat considering they were built to last just six thousand flight hours, a limit they eclipsed in 1997. As Tom "Narly" McNurlin, one of the Hog drivers who was involved in extensively upgrading the A-10[3] told me, the A-10 was (and is) always fighting for funding because it has no bureaucratic ally, no manufacturer to lobby for upgrades that would create jobs. In a way, the A-10 could be viewed almost as a parasite, siphoning away money from other programs' budgets. Put another way, it's not that there's some elaborate conspiracy to kill the A-10 so much as "the system doesn't lend itself to providing much in the way of advocacy for the Hog is the better way to look at it," Narly said.

To be fair, the F-35 was not unique in experiencing development problems. "It's hard to even comprehend how complicated it is to create an airplane from scratch," Narly said, speaking in particular of the F-35, whose software, he remarked, contained "millions of lines of code." Traditionally, it takes about seven years from the time an airplane goes from being an idea on a napkin until it rolls off the production line. Just to get a new project through to development it takes about three years for the Air Force to sign off and allocate funding. Then, an official request for proposal is created and sent out to industry manufacturers to bid. Only then, after the proposals go through extensive review, is a contract awarded. Once a prototype is built, it must be tested, tweaked, and manufactured on scale. All that time adds up, such that even something that's proposed as the most technologically sophisticated weapon on paper is outdated by the time it rolls off the production line; the lengthy "acquisition test execution and fielding renders anything they attempt to do obsolete on day one," Narly said. Just think how the technology you use every day has evolved in the last decade: cell phones, laptops, televisions.

---

3. From the original A-10A model to the A-10C, the latter of which was effectively an avionics overhaul of the original Hogs built in the late 1970s.

"So it's not possible under the archaic acquisition test process of the Air Force Operating Center to keep up with what technology has done in the last really 15 to 20 years."

Such was the case with the F-35, and in particular its weapons targeting sensor. "The newest airplane in the Air Force had the worst sensor," Narly said. "It was worse than any other airplane in the United States Air Force" when it first came out. Because the sensor's requirements had all been developed at the start of the project, the F-35 was beholden to the technology available at the time.

All of this is relevant to the A-10 because it explains how the Hog has been able to keep pace (and at times surpass) newer airframes despite being so starved for funding. The benefits that come with a high-profile program like the JSF are clear: a seemingly endless amount of funding and enough momentum to make the project too big to fail. But all that financial support comes with extreme scrutiny. Meanwhile, through its bizarre service life, the A-10 has functioned as a real-life Ship of Theseus, a modern thought experiment in preserving a structure's overall integrity while continually (and quietly) updating its individual components.

The A-10 relies considerably on something called the National Guard and Reserve Equipment Appropriations, which are protected funds for the National Guard to use on their various weapons platforms as they see fit without having to go through the otherwise laborious Department of Defense approval process. While National Guard and Reserve Equipment Appropriations aren't lucrative, they allow for autonomy within the A-10 community to develop gradual upgrades with little oversight. One such improvement was the Scorpion Helmet-Mounted Cueing System, essentially a highly advanced heads-up display in A-10 drivers' helmets. Such piecemeal upgrades have permitted the aged plane to have some of the most advanced tech right when it became available. "We do iterative approaches to try to keep up with technology on what's going on," Narly said, "rather than try to do one great big monster thing."

By 2013, the grumblings to retire the A-10 again mounted. While an effort from the previous year to retire five squadrons had been fended off, now calls renewed to retire the whole fleet by 2015, a move that would presumably save more than four billion dollars. The same arguments resurfaced: the A-10 was a relic of the past, outdated for modern war. "Well the reality of that, because it wasn't true," Narly said. "It had more digital capability and the most advanced avionics suite of any fighter plane in the Department of Defense at the time. So it had gotten to the point of it being incredibly robust when they decided to shit-can it."

By 2013 the A-10 seemed most certainly to be on its way out. No matter how relevant the airframe may have still been, it just didn't have the kind of political backing required to stave off forced retirement. Its pending retirement functioned as a haunting reminder of the defense spending concerns the Reformers had worried about decades prior. "And so one reason why we can't build planes like the A-10 anymore is because they don't generate enough jobs," Chuck Spinney said. "You can't politically engineer something as simple as an A-10."

An A-10 firing the GAU-8 Avenger cannon

The F-117 "Nighthawk" stealth airplane

Pierre Sprey

Winslow Wheeler (middle) between Senators Nancy Landon Kassebaum (R-KS) and David Pryor (D-AR), who jointly hired Wheeler on their personal staffs

The F-35 Lightning II, or Joint Strike Fighter
SENIOR AIRMAN DUNCAN BEVAN

Part III

Survive

15

Muck Brown

"It was almost embarrassing to be part of something that he was part of, because when it was all over . . . everybody would be sitting there beating their chests, and Muck would be sitting there quietly smiling, just reveling in it."

–David "Rainman" Stephenson

The finest Hog driver of them all didn't earn his reputation killing tanks. No Hollywood director would have thought to cast him as a fighter pilot. With his schoolboy haircut and gentle eyes, he looked more like a minister than the man another A-10 driver told me was "God-like in that airplane."

In one breath he'd proffer aphorisms like "integrity is doing the right thing when nobody's looking." In another, out spilled North Carolina backwoods slang: if someone appeared confused, he'd say, "They look like a goat looking at a new gate" or "it's like a pig staring at a wristwatch." Once, after reviewing the results of another squadron's poor bombing mission, he quipped, "Those boys couldn't hit their dinner plate with a spoon." His call sign had similar backwater origins. During flight training in Louisiana, he went fishing in the bayou where he made the mistake of jumping out of the boat and promptly got stuck in waist-high muck.

Where did Robert "Muck" Brown make his bones? For one, as a flight instructor at the Air Force Weapons School, he was so beloved by his students that they jokingly would ask to fail so they could fly with him again. The worst thing Muck could say to you was, "Wow, I'm a little disappointed in your lack of preparation for this sortie."

Of course, you don't become an instructor at the Weapons School unless you can fly the hell out of your airplane. In 1986 he was named the outstanding graduate of the A-10 Fighter Weapons School, and the following year earned the Robbie Risner Award, given to the top graduate across all airframes. "Part of it is Muck was a great pilot," his close friend and mentee David "Rainman" Stephenson said. "But . . . his skill was vision. The patience and the willingness to do whatever it took without caring who got credit for what." At a time when the military zeitgeist deemed the A-10 outdated and largely useless in future wars, Muck would pitch new uses for the Warthog that would endure for decades to come.

In 2013, the final year of his life, as he battled brain cancer so debilitating it robbed him of his ability to speak, Muck mobilized a coalition of A-10 drivers, politicians, and the Military Reformers to save the Hog from forced retirement. "He just wanted that airplane to keep going because he knew what it could do," his wife, Martha Brown, told me. "Some of his last coherent words were about that airplane, you know?"

Muck's path to the A-10 had been a circuitous one. Though he grew up loving airplanes, as a teenager he dreamed of being a rock 'n' roll drummer; in high school he'd even dropped out of Junior Reserve Officers' Training Corps because he wanted to grow his hair long. A gifted percussionist, Muck was accepted to North Texas State's highly competitive music program. When he got to campus he quickly grew discouraged because inside every practice room he walked by was the best drummer he'd ever heard. "It's not whether you can live with this career," an instructor told Muck when he expressed his doubts about music, "It's whether you can live without it." Muck saw a future, one of playing in grimy bars for years, barely making enough money to eat, all in the hopes of finally being discovered. It wasn't for him.

Muck transferred to Wake Forest University, where he studied political science and then was accepted into Georgetown for graduate school.

On Thanksgiving break from Georgetown, Muck made the surprise announcement to his family that he was dropping out. He wanted to fly planes. Years later, Muck told his daughter, Anna, that the deciding factor had been when he got home one night and heard then-President Jimmy Carter on television discussing the failed UN hostage rescue attempt in Iran. He declared then, "I want to be part of actionable solutions."

Muck spent a month hiking and reading in western North Carolina, then visited an Air Force recruiter's office. "He came so close to never having flown an A-10," Anna told me, "to never having been involved in this story." Muck barely passed his eye exam, and he had a back so balky he'd once been unable to stand the morning of a flight test, so he had to crawl out to his airplane without anyone seeing him; all he needed was to get in the cockpit.

In 1990, Muck published an essay in the winter issue of *Air Power Journal* in which he touted a then-revolutionary role for the A-10. While military brass largely thought the A-10 was well on its way to the bone-yard now that the Cold War had ended, Muck believed the Hog had much more to offer than just killing tanks in the Fulda Gap. Indeed, he argued the A-10 was "near-perfect" for future wars. What could the Hog do? Muck's answer: most everything. The A-10's versatility enabled it to carry the same kinds of precision laser-guided weapons as the most modern airplanes. Because of its long loiter time, the A-10 could be used to escort airlifts and provide combat search and rescue, all while flying out of austere airstrips with little logistical support. With just one C-130 cargo plane, Muck said, a small cohort of A-10s could subsist for weeks at a time without any extra support. He knew, because he'd done it. When he was a member of the 74th Tactical Fighter Squadron at England Air Force Base in Louisiana, they'd flown down to Central America "with six A-10s and only those parts we could carry on one C-130," he wrote. In that time, they "flew a total of 509 sorties with those same six jets in 44 flying days."

Muck showcased his real vision, though, with his next idea: the A-10 was ideally suited for supporting special operations and low-intensity conflict situations. In other words, A-10s could work alongside Special Forces units like the Green Berets and Army Rangers, who performed the kind of specialized and extremely dangerous missions that remain classified for decades—then get made into movies.

It's worth taking a moment here to pause. So much of what the A-10 has done in the twenty-first century falls under the umbrella of this category, "special operations and low-intensity conflict" missions. But in the early 1990s, the notion that the A-10 might fly in such a capacity was more of an afterthought; the A-10 was seen as a tool primarily for supporting massive land wars with Army battalions and hunting tanks in the Fulda Gap, not as a stealth-like weapon that could deploy on covert missions.

However, Muck argued, "this concept is not new," citing guerilla-style operations that A-1 Skyraiders had supported in Vietnam. In this way, Muck felt the A-10 was all the more equipped for these missions thanks to an upgrade called LASTE,[1] which improved the accuracy of the Avenger cannon by reducing its vibrations during firing and further enabled pilots to fly more safely at lower altitudes. He proposed, too, an

---

1. For the technology-inclined: LASTE stands for "Low Altitude Safety Target Enhancement." It's a mechanism originally intended to dampen the violent vibrations on the GAU-8 cannon when it gets up to full rotating speed. An A-10 driver named John "40" Watts was largely responsible for getting the LASTE system funded and implemented, which he did by selling the modification not as one that enhanced the A-10's *lethality*, but rather as one that enhanced its *safety*. "Now I know you're thinking, 'How is it a safety modification?'" Watts told me.

What the A-10 lacked from a safety perspective was a sufficient ground proximity warning system, literally the system that detects when an airplane is about to hit the ground and a voice chimes in the cockpit, "Whoop, whoop, pull up!" LASTE was actually based on another system called—bear with me here on the acronyms—Precision Attitude Control Augmentation Integrated Air Gun Sights System (PACAIAGSS), which lessened the gun's vibrations by correcting for wind gusts and the recoil of the gun, all while triangulating the airplane's position relative to its target.

It just so happens the data needed to determine one's firing position relative to a target was the same as the data needed to warn you if your airplane was about to crash. Because the A-10 is almost never flying straight and level as it approaches its target, they affixed the airframe with a radar altimeter and antennas on the sides of the airplane so that when it rolled from side to side the distance to the ground could still be calculated accurately. "Well, if we can do that," Watts explained, "then all we have to do is take an airline system—me being an old airline pilot, right—take an airline system, their ground proximity warning system, and we put in 'whoop whoop pull up pull up' to keep you from hitting the ground. So now it's a safety modification."

Watts took a secondary benefit for the gun control system (the "whoop whoop, pull up" voice) and promoted it as the primary feature. "The way you sold it was, 'Hey, here's this safety feature procedure. Oh, and by the way, it helps us when we're pulling the trigger.'" Watts capped off his sales pitch with the kind of assurance any budget committee relishes: "We get this at no cost. We get the operational improvement at no cost."

arrangement whereby AC-130 gunships (cargo planes modified with cannons firing rounds as large as 105 millimeters) could essentially function as "Forward Air Controllers," spotting targets for A-10s to sweep in low and punish.

Muck's argument illustrated the burgeoning bureaucratic skills that would make him a legend in the Warthog community. The A-10 would work for such missions not only on a technical level, but because it had "a low political profile," which he felt was a "subtle, yet important, attribute that should make the aircraft attractive to special operations." Moreover, the perceived rudimentariness of the A-10 could work in its favor. "It is 'low tech,' can't carry nukes, and is quiet (ever hear two A-10s fly overhead at 10,000 feet?)." What A-10s offered, then, was a "distinctly American show of force."

Here, Muck first proposed among his greatest contributions to the A-10: enhancing the airframe's nighttime capability. As it stood, the A-10 didn't have any special technology to operate at night. Sure, Hog drivers in Desert Storm would use the infrared cameras on their Maverick missiles to spot targets at night, but this would not be a sustainable method. What A-10 drivers needed were night vision goggles (NVGs). "There is no substitute for the situational awareness gained by being able to see what is going on in battle," Muck writes. NVGs had been rejected in the past because they couldn't handle the high G-forces of flying and would get in the way if a driver needed to eject. But now, Muck pointed out, modernized NVGs existed that could fit under helmet visors, and applying them would be "simple, cheap, and quick, taking no more than one day." Muck's arguments were so compelling that after his article was published, U.S. Special Operations Command even drafted a possible plan for how they might team up with A-10s.

A few years later, as he worked toward his master's degree at the Command and General Staff College at Fort Leavenworth, Kansas, Muck devoted his thesis work to further developing a partnership between A-10s and Special Operations. By now, hundreds of A-10s had been forcibly retired after Desert Storm, deemed too old and too primitive. But Muck was making the exact opposite argument; not only was the A-10 still relevant for the present, it was *the* weapon for the future.

When speaking with Muck's close friend and fellow A-10 driver Jack "Coach" Allison, I likened Muck to the irascible John Boyd in that both were military visionaries. But the comparison didn't quite sit right with Coach. He countered with one key difference, "I would not identify [Muck] with John Boyd, because everybody liked him."

While serving at Langley Air Force Base in Virginia, Muck put his Special Operations ideas into practice. Some three hundred miles south, at Pope Field in Cumberland County, North Carolina, A-10s were stationed alongside various Special Operations units, presenting a unique opportunity: A-10 drivers could train closely alongside Special Operations, a necessity given how complex and high-stakes Special Operations missions could be. "You don't have to authenticate people on the radio because you recognize one another's voice," another close friend of Muck, David "Rainman" Stephenson, said of the unmatched closeness required to work with Special Operations.

Before Hogs, Rainman, a gregarious Minnesotan, had flown helicopters, where he'd gotten hundreds of hours of experience using NVGs in flight. Muck connected with Rainman because he could help realize Muck's vision, which required A-10 drivers to be able to fly with NVGs, too. After all, Special Operations executed highly covert operations under the cover of darkness. "All of our customers, everything they do is at night," explained Rainman.

Despite NVGs being widely used on other airframes, the Air Force was reluctant to approve the use of NVGs in single-seaters like the A-10, and understandably so. If a malfunction with the NVGs caused a pilot to crash-land or spin-out or be decapitated trying to eject, it was the folks at Langley who'd take the heat. Here, Muck's bureaucratic savvy flourished. He understood that the Air Force was actually looking for a reason to say "yes" while managing risk, and the way to get them to say "yes" was to cite a precedent for wearing NVGs in single-seat airplanes. So, Muck *manufactured* precedent, coordinating with the 422nd Test and Evaluation Squadron at Nellis Air Force Base to develop the evaluation criteria for the NVGs. With the official testing squadron on board, they could then travel to Pope Air Force Base and teach the rest of the A-10 squadrons how to use the NVGs safely. If this sounds like a logical workaround, in practice it only worked because Muck could transcend bureaucratic paranoia, serving as a kind of bridge between parties who may have been wary of one another. Muck would say, "Do you trust me? Because I trust these guys, so you should, too." Muck could push forward plans and requests in hours or days that might otherwise take weeks or months to approve.

In many ways, Muck shouldered thankless work. With the NVGs, he inhabited a role akin to Ken Mattingly, stuck behind in the control room on the *Apollo 13* mission: though he was the one making the NVGs happen, he wasn't actually getting to test them out himself. Still, Rainman said, "[Muck] was just as every bit as excited as we were, more excited than we were. . . . He didn't even care whether or not he got to do it."[2]

At his next stop, as commander of the Fighter Weapons School, he set about modernizing the A-10 training program. "We're going to rewrite the syllabus," Muck told Rainman, who he brought in as an instructor. Muck wanted to push the instruction to match up with the "third world conflicts" that he'd written about years earlier, which meant A-10 drivers needed to shift their emphasis from killing tanks to devoting much more time to close-air support missions aiding troops in close contact with enemies (like FATTS and Ras performed with Matt Secor in this book's opening chapter) and combat search and rescue, like A-1 drivers did rescuing downed pilots in Vietnam. Muck felt, too, that A-10 drivers needed to have experience using the GAU-8 Avenger not just for air-to-ground missions, but also *air-to-air* combat. Until then, Rainman told me, A-10 drivers never practiced shooting the gun air-to-air, since the Hog wasn't equipped with the radar to find enemy planes. "I don't know," Rainman and Muck figured while searching for a precedent for such a bold idea, "a lot of airplanes got shot down in World War II by airplanes without radar with guns, so it does work."

So Muck arranged for A-10s to practice air-to-air operations. An F-16 would tow a target at the end of a long cable so that A-10 drivers could fire at the target without hitting the friendly jet. Much like with the NVGs, Muck let another driver do the first test run. "He didn't have

---

2. Once the A-10 was NVG-capable, it made the Warthog a truly "modern" airplane, "good as anything in the software, and better than anything in the combat air forces," Jack "Coach" Allison told me.

the kind of ego that said, 'Okay, I'm going to be the *first* person to ever shoot the gun air-to-air,' even though he was the one who was the boss and did whatever coordination was required and supported it so that we could do it," Rainman told me.

The tests began with low expectations, which the A-10 shattered. On the very first exercise, Rainman remembers an A-10 unleashed thirty rounds with a quick trigger-squeeze, landing twelve hits on the target. "He couldn't believe it," Rainman said of the F-16 driver towing the target. The F-16 driver told him, "You could take a flight of four F-16s and they could shoot 2000 rounds between them and not get 12 hits total."

The second day of testing, during their pre-mission briefing, the usually reserved Muck announced eagerly that he would be the first to fly that day and demonstrate the gun. Jack "Coach" Allison advised Muck to wait and let one of the less-experienced students go up first; the day before the gun had proven to be so accurate for air-to-air that it was actually hard to test it because A-10 drivers kept hitting the hardware connecting the targeting sensor to the cable, blowing the target off the cable and sending it floating down to Earth. "I wouldn't do that if I were you," Coach told Muck. In a rare display of fighter-jock brashness, Muck replied, "Well, it's a good thing you're not me." The practice mission began, and on Muck's first pass what happened? He sheered the sensor right off the cable. "And we all watch," Rainman said, "that thing kind of sailing down to the Gulf of Mexico."

By the end of the decade, Muck was a highly decorated officer, on track to becoming a three-star general, if not the head of the entire Air Force. To everyone's surprise, he abruptly retired. "And nobody could believe it," Rainman told me. "Because this is a guy who had been promoted below the zone [i.e., promoted early] won every single award you could win."

Muck took a job flying for UPS, which he found largely boring. His daughter, Anna, said he kept himself entertained on the dull flights by playing out emergency scenarios in his mind and planning out how he'd react. Not long after joining UPS, the 9/11 tragedy occurred. The Air Force heavily courted Muck, offering him a promotion and the opportunity to continue flying. Muck agreed to return, but refused the perks, insisting that he rejoin at the rank he'd last achieved and declining the opportunity to fly in combat so that younger pilots could gain the necessary experience. Instead, he accepted the thankless work behind the scenes at the Pentagon where he could put his vision to good use facilitating the war-planning efforts. "He said, 'I'm more helpful here, I can do more for you here than I can in an airplane,'" Rainman told me. "Which I would never say I can do more for you on the ground than I can in the air. But Muck would. And he did."

Over in Afghanistan, Rainman helped establish the U.S. air base at Bagram. "What it proved was another theory that Muck had pushed earlier, that A-10s can do remote, rugged, unprepared airfield operations," Rainman said. At Bagram, the tarmac was in such horrible condition that an airfield operations officer told Rainman, "If the rocks [on the runway] are bigger than my fist, pick them up, otherwise leave 'em." "Bagram was nasty," Rainman said. "We were burning our own shit with jet fuel . . . but it was the only place you'd want to be as an A-10 pilot. I mean every A-10 guy in the world wanted to be at Bagram during that time because it's what the airplane was made for. It was what Muck's paper said it could do. We were doing it."

Rainman found himself channeling Muck in a fight to get the A-10s flying at night. Despite the NVGs having been approved years earlier, the Air Force was still reluctant to allow A-10 drivers to take off and land wearing the goggles at night. Because Bagram Air Base was surrounded by hostiles, it operated in complete darkness, with no lights on whatsoever. "If you had a little light leak from your tent, you're going to see . . . a sniper round come through there," Rainman said. This meant if A-10 drivers couldn't wear the goggles on takeoff and landing, they couldn't fly at night *at all*. And if they couldn't fly at night, they couldn't support the Special Operations teams who almost exclusively worked at night.

Rainman wondered, "What would Muck do in this situation? What would it take for the Air Force to say yes?" He arranged for an Air Force official to visit Bagram on a dark moonless night. He guided the official up the steps to the control tower, a decrepit, brutalist Soviet structure with only cheap plexiglass separating them from the outside. Without NVGs, they looked out to the inky darkness. Had it not been so loud, with the whine of C-130 engines and the churning of Blackhawk and Apache helicopter rotors, it would have looked like they were staring into an empty desert. Then Rainman gave the official a pair of NVGs. "And he almost fell off over the railing on the catwalk to his death, shocked, because the airfield was busy as fuck," Rainman said. They saw the ground crews and the choppers and the cargo planes and then, off to the side, all of the A-10s, engines off, doing nothing. "Look, all of the people who were supporting those helicopters, they're getting on those right now," Rainman told the official. "They're going out to do their job. And the only place where you don't see any activity on this entire ramp, guess where it is. It's those A-10s, the fucking A-10s are sitting there, quiet."

It's impossible to describe all that Muck did, especially in his second stint with the Air Force. Given his status and access to classified planning, many of his most impactful accomplishments cannot be divulged and may never come to light. What can be said is he was instrumental in getting a new targeting pod affixed to the A-10 which enabled the Hog to perform more missions with Special Operations. During one conversation, Rainman cited to me Clausewitz's concept of "friction," that is, the inherent chaos of war, the same concept that had informed the work of John Boyd and Chuck Spinney. Muck, Rainman felt, had a unique skill for keeping friction to a minimum because of his extraordinary ability to establish trust across different teams. As it went, if you trusted Muck, you could trust whoever he trusted.

In his second retirement—for good, this time—Muck's life blossomed. He returned to his hometown of Waynesville, North Carolina, where he began working at his alma mater, Tuscola High School. He overhauled the school's Junior Reserve Officers' Training Corps program and channeled his teaching skills into helping the school's most struggling kids find their way. He found love with his second wife, Martha Brown. They married in 2007, and though Muck no longer flew, he retained his Hog driver habits. "Everything was planned every day," Martha told me. Muck outlined grocery shopping trips with the same intensity he'd orchestrated A-10 missions, creating lists in map form so he could devise the most efficient route through the store. "He could draw these perfect little squares and check them off," Martha remembered. They had fifty-two photos of airplanes in their home, and whenever they watched movies with airplanes, he'd pick them apart frame by frame, identifying where Hollywood had gotten it wrong (*Top Gun* drove him crazy).

In 2010, Muck was diagnosed with bladder cancer. He endured grueling chemotherapy and his bladder was removed in the spring of 2013. That summer, he received a clean bill of health. But in time, he began feeling a kind of funny tingling in his fingers. His doctors suspected it was a side effect of the chemo, but Muck had never felt this way before. Headaches and fatigue followed. One night, after driving home from Washington, DC, he kept repeating to Martha that his head just felt so weird. He went to the doctor again. This time, they found eleven lesions on his brain; the cancer had spread. After the diagnosis, Muck drove to the grocery store to pick up some broth and medicine for his daughter, Anna, who was run down with a cold. She hadn't yet heard the news about her dad. When he arrived at Anna's home and told her what the doctors said, he didn't express any anger or resentment. Instead, the first thing Muck told Anna was, "I felt so bad for that doctor. I don't think he's ever had to give anyone that bad of news before."

A little over a month before his diagnosis, on October 21, 2013, Muck emailed a coalition of A-10 allies wanting to better understand why a number of Warthog drivers were being quietly transferred over to flying F-16s. He worried over what seemed to be "very well-developed plans . . . to yank the plug out of the wall," which included not only moving pilots to different airframes, but also halting software and hardware upgrades to the A-10. That is, he feared there was an initiative to whittle the A-10 force structure down to nothing bit by it, something that Pierre Sprey often called "salami-slicing."

Indeed, the Air Force was facing a budgetary crisis, and they needed to come up with twenty billion dollars in savings. One idea gaining steam was to divest from an entire weapons system: the A-10. As such, other airframes like the F-35, F-16, and even the B-1 bomber would be used to pick up the close-air support duties.

"I've never been more ashamed and incensed by what MY Air Force is doing," Muck wrote in an email. What he most feared was that such cuts, with no suitable close-air support replacement for the A-10, would spell tragedy for the soldiers on the ground, including the Special Operations soldiers who would "pay for the [Air Force's] arrogance, malfeasance, and deception in blood."

In their fight to save the A-10, Muck and the Reformers had recruited a powerful ally: Senator Kelly Ayotte of New Hampshire, whom Pierre Sprey called "the real hero" in the fight to save the A-10.[3] Working alongside Ayotte was her defense advisor, Bradley Bowman, a West Point graduate who'd flown Blackhawk helicopters in the Army. Bowman and Senator Ayotte drafted a letter to be sent to then-Secretary of Defense Chuck Hagel and Joint Chiefs of Staff Chairman General Martin E. Dempsey, in which they wrote it "would be unconscionable to further cut an asset like the A-10 for budget reasons." They argued the cuts could happen elsewhere, in places that would less directly risk service members' lives (such as "conferences, air shows, and bloated headquarters staffs"). Given the ways the A-10 had been modernized in recent years, it was still very much a relevant weapons platform. Indeed, they argued it would be unwise for the United States to cut the A-10 based on projections of how it would fare in future wars given that "the United States has had a poor track record of predicting conflict. When the U.S. military enters a conflict without sufficient training, resources, and capabilities, the cost is measured in the lives of our brave service members. We have a responsibility to not make those mistakes again."

Muck forwarded the letter to A-10 allies, imploring them to sign: "I pray that sanity, common sense will prevail."

If you recognize a familiar tone in Muck's emails, it's because he was now operating on the same wavelength as Pierre Sprey, with whom he began

---

3. Coincidentally, Senator Ayotte's husband, Joseph Daley, was a Hog driver.

collaborating along with Winslow Wheeler to organize an event in the DC area to educate politicians and the media about close-air support and the A-10. "Pierre had the original idea," Wheeler told me. Wheeler then helped shape the idea so that it would be palatable to as wide an audience as possible. "The way to set it up [was] not just to have a bunch of A-10 yahoos out there screaming about the A-10," Wheeler said, knowing full well the skepticism many on Capitol Hill and in the Pentagon had toward the Reformer ethos. Wheeler thought it best to structure the event as a series of presentations, with two presenters offering opposing sides of an argument. When Sprey learned he would be paired up with the journalist Bill Sweetman,[4] he told Wheeler, "Well I guess I'll have to be careful with what I say." "And that was precisely the effect on Pierre I want[ed] to have," Wheeler told me. "It wasn't just Pierre unrestrained."

On November 23, 2013, the Strauss Military Reform Project and the Project on Government Oversight sponsored the seminar, officially titled: "Close Air Support with and without the A-10: Will U.S. Troops Get the Help They Need?" In his presentation, Sprey briefed audiences on Giulio Douhet's exploits promoting strategic bombing and enlightened the attendees on Pete Quesada's revolutionary close-air support tactics in World War II. He derided attack helicopters and the Harrier jet, which he felt were simply too vulnerable to ground fire to adequately provide close support (Sprey once told me of helicopters, "You can't make them survive"). Mirroring his testimony from the congressional hearings after Desert Storm, he reiterated, "There is indeed a lot of interesting technology, but we need 'good tech,' not 'high tech,' and it should go nowhere before it is tested to standards of performance realism that do not currently exist in [the Department of Defense]."

In a sense, the seminar featured an interdisciplinary panel, showcasing not only the Reformers and combat veterans, but also the scholarship of Dr. Jonathan Shay, a psychiatrist with an extensive history working with veterans and a prolific scholar on the subject of trauma. Dr. Shay had experienced trauma of his own, suffering a stroke that sent him into a coma when he was forty years old. When he awoke, the whole left side

---

4. The co-author alongside Lindsay Peacock of a highly informative book about the A-10, *Combat Aircraft Series: A-10 Thunderbolt II.*

of his body was paralyzed. In his recovery, he immersed himself in the study of Greek epics and later published two books connecting these to the subject of trauma. In working with soldiers who suffer from trauma, Dr. Shay's "approach is woven out of the different strands of his life: part neuroscience, part evolutionary theory, part psychiatric empathy and part Homer," *The New York Times* wrote in 2003, adding that he "may well be the world's only author who has appeared in *Nature, The American Journal of Physiology, Ancient Theater Today* and *Parameters: Journal of the U.S. Army War College*." Shay made for a compelling speaker, one who extended the Reformers' ethos on prioritizing people over technology, particularly when it came to war, and most particularly when it came to something as intimate and necessary as close-air support.

What Dr. Shay and others helped illuminate for the audience was that the real loss in retiring the A-10 so quickly, without a strong replacement, wasn't so much the airframe itself, but the *people* associated with it. It was the people who'd gone through years of intensive close-air support training to understand every movement, worry, and challenge the troops on the ground were experiencing. That kind of intimate knowledge couldn't simply be swapped out and easily replaced, hurriedly and without deserved thought. When it came to something as debilitating as friendly fire, Dr. Shay emphasized that such tragedies are "not a technological problem, but a social problem," one that crushed morale in incalculable ways. "Ideally," Dr. Shay said, for any team to provide true support of another "they should eat together and 'live in each other's armpits.'" When it came to close-air support, what the soldiers on the ground needed was to feel trust in the airplanes flying overhead, and they trusted the A-10.

A few weeks after the seminar, Muck Brown traveled back to DC to speak to a smaller group of legislators about the A-10. By now he'd received his brain cancer diagnosis, and his health was quickly worsening so Martha drove him, which "was really unnerving for him," she said, "because, you know, he was the driver and he liked to be in control. He was definitely a pilot, not a copilot."

The trip did have a highlight: they got to dine with Pierre Sprey. "[Muck] was like a two-year-old because he was gonna get to meet Pierre Sprey," Martha said. "We went to get in [Pierre's] car . . . and it was a small car, but it was filled with records, with albums and vinyl." Sprey and Muck were destined to hit it off: two A-10 advocates with a shared obsession for jazz. A friendship instantly formed. Sprey began researching medical treatments for Muck's cancer, calling Martha, and offering her suggestions and working to get them connected with physicians at other hospitals. "I remember looking at [Muck] and saying, 'You know, this person that you looked up to so much . . . such an important person is doing research [for you] now.' . . . I would say meeting Pierre was one of the highlights and bought him joy in those last couple months."

As Muck's cancer intensified, he lost his ability to communicate verbally. Still, he wrote letters advocating for the A-10. On January 24, 2014, Senator Ayotte penned a letter to Secretary of the Air Force Deborah Lee James citing section 143 of the 2014 National Defense Authorization Act, which "state[d] that you 'may not retire, prepare to retire, or place in storage' any additional A-10 aircraft before December 21, 2014," and that any attempt to retire the Warthog sooner would be "in violation of current law." Some three weeks later, Secretary James wrote back: "In response to your concerns, I have directed that [A-10 development] continue in Fiscal Year (FY) 14." In other words, Muck and the Reformers had bought the Hog some time.

Just a few months later, on March 18, 2014, at age fifty-six, Muck died. It was the day after his and Martha's anniversary, and the day before her birthday. "So in typical fashion, he didn't want to leave on one of those days, so he went in-between," Martha told me. "Like I said, he was so meticulous."

The receiving line at Muck's funeral was so long, mourners waited for up to seven hours in a line that stretched down the Main Street of Waynesville, North Carolina. At the service, the minister asked Muck's daughter, Anna, to give one word to describe her dad. She said, "Well, it takes two: excellence and honor."

In the A-10 community, Muck's legacy endures. At the Hawgsmoke competition held every two years, Hog drivers from across A-10 units in Active Duty, Air Force Reserves, and the Air National Guard vie for the "Lt Col Robert H. 'Muck' Brown Award,"[5] given to the competition's most outstanding pilot.

Hog drivers who flew alongside Muck remember him as much for his drumming as they do his flying. "Any of his friends that were stationed with him can tell the same story," Rainman said, "but we're at the bar, the band takes a break. Muck gets up from the table, goes and gets a couple of beers . . . he's talking to the guys in the band and the next thing you know, the band comes back from the break and Muck is sitting at the drums, playing."

Anna Brown remembers her father always with a grease pencil in hand, jotting down notes on the window of their Honda Accord. On road trips, he insisted on traveling with the most detailed map available. "He would complain if the cartographer had done a poor job." He was "relentlessly thorough," a man so humble that if he pulled an all-nighter at the office he would still come home to shower, shave, and change his clothes so no one knew he hadn't stopped working. Once, Anna asked her dad if all that humility ever bothered him, if he ever craved more credit. He replied, "My thanks is the lives that I've saved."

Martha remembers how her stepchildren would ask before bed, "Can Robert tell us a story?" and he would, expounding on how magical it was to fly in an airplane, breaching the fluffy clouds into an endless blue sky. Each time the story might vary, but Muck's source material remained the same: his favorite poem, "High Flight," by John Gillespie Magee Jr.

> Oh! I have slipped the surly bonds of Earth
> And danced the skies on laughter-silvered wings;
> Sunward I've climbed, and joined the tumbling mirth
> of sun-split clouds,—and done a hundred things
> You have not dreamed of—wheeled and soared and swung

---

5. Muck's own highly decorated career included the following honors: Top Gun, Top Graduate, the Robbie Risner award, the Meritorious Service Medal with four Oak Leaf Clusters, the Aerial Achievement Medal, the Air Force Commendation Medal with one Oak Leaf Cluster, the Air Force Achievement Medal, the Combat Readiness Medal with two Oak Leaf Clusters, the National Defense Service Medal, the Armed Forces Expeditionary Medal, and the Armed Forces Service Medal.

High in the sunlit silence. Hov'ring there,
I've chased the shouting wind along, and flung
My eager craft through footless halls of air . . .
Up, up the long, delirious, burning blue
I've topped the wind-swept heights with easy grace
Where never lark nor ever eagle flew—
And, while with silent lifting mind I've trod
The high untrespassed sanctity of space,
Put out my hand, and touched the face of God.

16

The Hammer and the Nail

"A good A-10 guy is a student of warfare in general, and all the lessons that go with it."

–BRIAN "MASTER" BOEDING

ABOUT A MONTH BEFORE MUCK BROWN'S PASSING IN FEBRUARY 2014, the journalist and longtime friend of Pierre Sprey, Andrew Cockburn, published a story in *Harper's* chronicling the most recent efforts to retire the A-10. But it's what Cockburn's piece had to say about another airplane, the B-1—the airplane the Reformers had been speaking out against for decades now—that was most striking.

Cockburn recounted a tragic incident from May 2012 in which a pair of A-10s declined to attack a target near the border of Pakistan. Video imaging suggested enemies in the area, but when the A-10s flew down close using their own eyes and binoculars they cited "normal signs of life." Amid the A-10 drivers' objections, a B-1 crew chimed in over the radio saying they would bomb the target. Relying on the grainy video from their cockpit thousands of feet in the sky, the B-1 released its ordnance and obliterated the target, which turned out to be a farm, killing a husband and wife and five of their seven children.

This was not the first incident of B-1s firing upon noncombatants; in 2009 B-1s mistakenly killed 140 innocent people in Farah, Afghanistan. But crucially, these kinds of incidents were *not* caused by a malicious crew gone suddenly mad. Rather, what such tragedies illuminated was a deficiency in both training and technology. "If you want to know what the world looks like from a drone feed," a former Air Force colonel involved in the drone program told Cockburn, "walk around for a day with one eye closed and the other looking through a soda straw." For Cockburn, the practice of deferring something so intimate as close-air support to bombers and their rough video feeds, or even unmanned drones, signified "a drive to eliminate direct connection with outside reality—the sort of connection that prevents children from being mistakenly bombed as Taliban fighters."

In late April of that year during a hearing with the Senate Armed Service Committee, Arizona Senator John McCain[1] grilled then-Secretary of the Air Force Deborah Lee James and Air Force Chief of Staff General Mark Welsh (himself a former Hog driver) about the Air Force's close-air support proposals in the event the A-10 was retired.

"Secretary James, so far this committee has not received anything like a complete and comprehensive or detailed plan," McCain said in a smoldering tone. When he asked for James' and Welsh's opinions on what would fill the role of the A-10 should it be retired, Secretary James replied, "what is intended to replace the percentage that the A-10 was doing in terms of close-air support in the immediate future would be the other aircraft such as F-16, 15-E and so forth."

"What's 'so forth'?" interjected McCain. "Tell me again the 'so forth' here." Secretary James repeated the first two jets and then added, "B-1 bombers."

"The B-1 bomber will now be used for close-air support?" replied an incredulous McCain. Secretary James looked to her left toward General Welsh, then confirmed, "So it is my belief that the B-1 bomber has done some close-air support in Afghanistan."

"That's a remarkable statement," McCain again interrupted. "That doesn't comport with any experience I've ever had nor anyone I know has ever had." Now McCain was riled up. "See this is an example: you're throwing in the B-1 bomber as a close-air support weapon to replace the A-10. This is the reason why there is such incredible skepticism here in

---

1. Senator McCain had been flying in Ed Heinemann's A-4 Skyhawk when he was shot down during the Vietnam War; he was a prisoner of war for more than five years.

the Congress. And believe me . . . I can only speak for myself and several others, you will not pursue the elimination of the finest close-air support weapons system in the world with answers like that. So I hope you will come up with something that is credible to those of us who have been engaged in this business for a long, long time."

"Senator," General Welsh chimed in, "May I offer some additional data?" General Welsh explained that B-1s had been doing close-air support in Afghanistan "for some time now, for a number of years—"

McCain cut him off, "And it has been able to perform a limited, a very extremely limited number of missions of close-air support. General, please don't insult my intelligence." If it sounded like McCain had been primed, it's because he was—by a cohort of A-10 drivers who'd been recruited by Pierre Sprey and Muck Brown to travel to Capitol Hill to save the Hog.

Just days before, McCain had been briefed in his office by a small group of A-10 drivers who had "preloaded" the Senator with the questions to ask General Welsh about the B-1 bomber. "And so we got McCain's support," Hog driver Billy "Smitty" Smith told me. Smitty grew up an Air Force brat (his father had been a gunner flying in B-26 Invaders during Korea), and by his own admission, he wasn't a very good student; he estimated his GPA was "one-point something." After high school, from which he says he "barely graduated," he saw a commercial to be an Army helicopter pilot with a catchphrase along the lines of "from high school to flight school." "I am one of those people that can point to the U.S. Army and say that they saved me," Smitty said.

While flying Chinook helicopters in the Army, Smitty went to night school to finish his degree. About a decade later, he joined the Maryland Air National Guard, where he started flight training for the A-10. The once-beleaguered student routinely finished at the top of his class. In 1989, he began flying for the airlines, but he went on military leave whenever he could because he loved flying the Warthog so much (in the 1990s, he'd helped Muck Brown with testing the night vision goggles for the Hog).

Before he died, Muck Brown had recruited Smitty to join their save-the-A-10 campaign, believing Smitty made for an ideal advocate on Capitol Hill. He was a skilled pilot with an Army background, and a great talker who could distill military jargon for a lay audience. Take for example a different B-1 tragedy that resulted in the death of five U.S. Green Berets and six Afghan allies. "We talked about this a lot," Smitty told me of the friendly fire incident. "How do we discuss this on the Hill without us seeming like we're taking advantage of a crisis, which we always criticize politicians for? And so we came up with it as an illustration of the culture and the training differences in those two communities, and particularly the culture part." Even if a given political representative didn't understand the fundamental principles of close-air support, or the difference between depleted uranium rounds and tungsten rounds, or the distinction between laser-guided and free-falling munitions, Smitty and others could talk about the A-10 community in human terms, as a culture of people who do "nothing but live, breathe, eat, sleep, and crap close-support."

Smitty could convey the difference between a bomber that is orbiting five miles in the sky and trying to distinguish between friend and foe while looking through the soda straw that was the targeting pod video display, compared to an A-10 driver who would have a deep institutional knowledge of how U.S. ground forces operated and, upon studying the formation of the unidentified troops below, would have thought to himself, "Wow, the enemy does not deploy his troops in that type of sophisticated manner." Crucially, Smitty exuded genuine empathy for the bomber pilots involved in such tragedies. "Again I can't fault the B-1 crew," Smitty told me, "because they didn't know what they didn't know. They knew what they had been trained to do."

Working closely alongside Muck, Smitty, and Sprey was another A-10 driver, Brian "Master" Boeding (when I asked him how he got his callsign, he said his last name is pronounced "baiting"; no further explanation was needed). Master and Smitty had met while both were deployed overseas, where Master made a strong impression after he elected to serve longer than required so that he could learn from Smitty and the other veteran Hog drivers.

In fact, Master had flown under Muck Brown's close friend, Rainman, in 2003, an arrangement that initially frustrated Rainman because Master was a young green lieutenant at the time. "I'm like there's no goddamn way I'm flying with a fucking lieutenant," Rainman exclaimed when he first heard his wingman would be a "Lieutenant Boeding." "[He] won't live through this kind of shit that I'm going to be doing. . . . And they're like, 'no he's good.' I'm like, 'no, he's a fucking lieutenant.'"

When Master joined Rainman's unit, they flew a particularly dicey night mission through heavy enemy air defenses with low clouds obscuring the target below. "There was a bunch of stuff he fucked up," Rainman remembered. After the sortie, Rainman briefed Master on all his mistakes. "I [wasn't] being rude, but I [was] being harsh and like, 'This is what I was fucking talking about,'" Rainman said. "But . . . what we were doing was . . . it was so impossible. . . . And actually, the one pass he was able to make on the target area, this super critical target area, was the biggest secondary explosion I've ever seen, and I've seen a lot of them. So the coolest fucking pass I've ever seen he did—[he] went into the weather and almost lost control of the airplane when he did it."

During this whole briefing, as Rainman picked apart Master's flying, Master maintained a big smile. "He's smiling at me," Rainman said, "I'm like, 'What the fuck is your problem? What's so fucking funny?' He looks at me and he says, 'Well, Rainman, this was my first combat sortie ever.' I'm thinking 'Holy fuck! *See this is what I was talking about.*'"

But Master had taken his lumps and survived. "And he just kicked ass after that," Rainman said. "And did all these other things, a lot like Muck. I mean, I had him work in the mission planning cell, and he just came up with all these ideas and did all the stuff that no one asked him to do but made everything better. . . . He was the best wingman I ever had. . . . He was by far the best wingman[2] I ever had."

2. "He's one of those guys who was like born in the back of a Cessna 172," Rainman said of Master's love for flying. Meanwhile, Rainman hasn't flown since he left the military. "I don't fly airplanes for food or for fun. I flew for my country. . . . I don't know if I've met more than four or five guys that love flying in airplanes as much as Master."

Back in October 2013, just as Muck Brown and Pierre Sprey began collaborating on the close-air support seminar to be held the following month, Master emailed Sprey on a whim. He was on an airline trip to New Delhi when he went down a rabbit role reading about the Fighter Mafia and the Reformers. At that time, Master was also flying for the Maryland Air National Guard out of Baltimore, and he was surprised to learn that Sprey lived close by. "I am writing to you as . . . a veteran of 4 combat pilot tours in your A-10 Warthog," Master's email to Sprey began. *Would Sprey visit the 104th Fighter Squadron to talk about the origins of the Hog?* Master wondered.

The next day, Sprey replied, saying he'd be "delighted and honored to speak to—and to learn from—Hog drivers who've been there." But Sprey's agreement came with a caveat: would anyone from the 104th be able to attend the close-air support seminar the following month to discuss the "overwhelming importance of close-air support and the disastrous consequences of shutting down the A-10 force"? A deal was made.

Master made for a natural Hog advocate on the Hill. He has a midwestern demeanor that can only be described as laconically congenial (he grew up in Iowa), and the build of a quintessential fighter pilot, tall and broad-shouldered, with striking blue eyes. His father had been a lobbyist, so he understood the political game. And he loved the A-10. "I love anything that's a smart design," he told me. "My newest favorite thing is this thing that hooks into your door latch of your car; it's a foot rest, you could stand on it."

He was also a fitting Sprey disciple, a voracious reader who as a kid devoured books about World War II submarines and the battles between Germany and Russia on the Eastern Front, the same terrain where Hans Rudel had fought. "Which is odd," Master thought of his childhood reading habits. "What 15-year-old grows up reading about that stuff?"

On Capitol Hill, Master had a go-to technique to illustrate the differences between the F-35 and the A-10 to Congressional staffers. In every meeting, he'd bring in a ten-penny nail, which he'd place on the table. "If your job is to hammer in this nail," Master would ask, "would you rather use your iPhone . . . or would you rather have a hammer?" His point was not that the hammer was the only tool that could do the job;

rather, it was that the iPhone *could* be used to hammer in a nail, but it wouldn't make sense: it would be much less effective and get all beat up in the process. Plus, it would be prohibitively expensive. In other words, why use the iPhone when you could use the hammer right next to it?

At the end of his spiel, Master would play audio for the staffers of a Joint Terminal Attack Controller, like Matt Secor from chapter 1, in a particularly hairy situation radioing back to air command headquarters. "This situation is so complex," the voice hollers from the ground, "recommend [that if you send] the Bone [B-1], you do nothing but shows of force," he says (translation: if only B-1s could show up on scene, they were strictly directed to fly above, but not actually bomb the target area). "That's why I recommend an A-10," the voice continues. "I don't even recommend F-15s for this. It's so difficult to figure out what he's saying, and they're so trigger-happy, I don't know how else to say it. This is not a fight to have a fast-moving jet in." Without intending to, the Joint Terminal Attack Controller on the recording was making the perfect sales pitch for the A-10.

To stave off the perception that they were just a group of cranky fighter jocks irrationally devoted to their hunk-of-junk airplane, the save-the-A-10 group got the idea that it shouldn't just be the pilots going to these meetings, but also the ground troops they served.[3] (Smitty thinks it was Muck Brown's idea "because it sounds like something Muck would have said"). Soon enough, they were flanked by service members who could directly attest to being saved by the Warthog. "And I mean," Smitty said, "we have people who were awarded Silver Stars, who called . . . airstrikes . . . 15 meters from their position, and those airstrikes by the A-10 allowed this group of Americans and their Afghan allies the ability to escape."

If they had a midday gap with nothing scheduled, they'd perform "drive-bys," dropping into any representative's offices whose doors were open. In fact, this is how they'd gotten Senator McCain on board. At times, though, Smitty noticed Sprey would stop just before entering

---

3. To make this happen they collaborated with the Tactical Air Control Party and a man named Charlie Keebaugh, whom Smitty said "became instrumental with our attack plan."

certain offices. "I can't go into that office with you," Smitty remembers Sprey saying, "because I'm toxic waste."

"Pierre had such a reputation of being 'anti' a lot of things . . . not in a bad way," Smitty explained. "I mean, he fought for what he thought was right, and as you are aware, a lot of times on the Hill that's not what their interests are." By the mid-2010s, Sprey had spoken out against enough politicians' initiatives that it was common for him to arrive at an office only for him to spring on the driver: "Oh, I'm not going in there."

Ultimately, what Smitty, Master, and the rest of the A-10 advocates tried to get Hill staffers to see was that they weren't simply clamoring to protect an inanimate object. In fact by then, Smitty said, "Pierre did not really like the A-10 . . . and I heard that from him every time we met. You know, 'I don't like this thing.'" "Yeah, I know," Smitty would reply. What they were so desperate to save was the culture of close support around the airplane. "You need to protect that culture because it's what A-10 pilots live and breath and understand of how to support the Army," Smitty said. "It's a finite skill."[4]

Outside of their work on Capitol Hill, the A-10 advocates functioned with a level of slyness akin to the Military Reformers who'd come before them. One of their tactics was to have huge email threads—on the order of a thousand email addresses, enough that no one emailer could be singled out—from folks around the country in different congressional

---

4. The A-10 Weapons School functions as a kind of "charm school" for Hog drivers to refine their abilities to communicate directly with ground forces. To understand the ground force's perspective, they practice missions where they land on dry lakebeds and camp outside under their airplanes alongside Joint Terminal Attack Controllers. Ultimately, the ideal A-10 driver strives to be "humble, credible, and approachable."

"We teach our guys if you make a mistake, be the first person to talk about it in the debrief," Major Ridge "KELSO" Flick told me during a visit to Nellis Air Force Base. "Don't let somebody else highlight your own mistake. Fess up to your mistake right out of the gate, teach people how you could have done this better. . . . [A]s soon as you teach people how to actually do it better, not only does your credibility improve, but also it shows that you have the humility to own your mistakes. . . . And if we're all open about our mistakes and were all learning from each other's mistakes, everybody's kind of rising in performance-level together."

Brigadier General Michael "Johnny Bravo" Drowley described the A-10 community as "translators between both worlds [of ground and air]. . . . So when you look at, again, warfare or some of the conflicts that we get into, there's a very down, dirty, ugly side of that, and we can live in that world, and we are exposed to that world just based off of the missions that we do. But we can also communicate and translate to the other side of the Air Force because that's part of our world as well."

districts asking them to write their representatives and request they meet with the save-the-A-10 cadre. These requests designated the Hog advocates as proxies for the constituents, thereby granting them an audience with congresspeople outside their own districts.

Smitty added that he couldn't tell me everything they did (and still do) in the fight to save the Hog: "Because I don't want to give away our tactics to the Air Force . . . it's still an ongoing fight."

17

Survivable

WHEN ISIS MILITANTS PLUCKED LIEUTENANT MUATH AL-KASASBEH from the Euphrates River, al-Kasasbeh knew his fate. He was a fighter pilot from Jordan, a member of the coalition of nations executing bombing missions against ISIS since September of that year. On this particular day, December 24, 2014, al-Kasasbeh had been flying near Raqqa, a Syrian city under ISIS rule, when his F-16 lost control. ISIS claimed they'd hit al-Kasasbeh's jet with a missile; the United States believed he had experienced mechanical failure. Whatever the cause, al-Kasasbeh had been forced to eject, parachuting into the river, where he'd gotten stuck. After being dragged among the crowds like some horrific trophy, al-Kasasbeh was interviewed by the ISIS propaganda *Dabiq*, who asked him what he thought his captors would do now. Al-Kasasbeh replied, "They will kill me."

As the weeks passed, ISIS tried negotiating a prisoner swap—al-Kasasbeh in exchange for Sajida al-Rishawi, an attempted suicide bomber in line to be executed. Meanwhile, the United Arab Emirates halted their missions against ISIS, arguing that they could no longer count on the United States' search-and-rescue efforts for downed pilots.

Some six weeks after he was captured, on February 3, 2015, ISIS released a video of al-Kasasbeh locked in a cage being burned to death. In Raqqa, the heinous execution was projected on a building wall, where crowds cheered. Only later was it revealed that ISIS has been negotiating in bad faith. The video was old: al-Kasasbeh had been executed a month prior.

Al-Kasasbeh was twenty-six and recently married. A year earlier, he'd traveled with his parents on a pilgrimage to Mecca, Saudi Arabia. He was one of eight siblings, and his brother, Jawat, told the Associated Press, "Since his childhood, he wanted to be a pilot."

A blinding fog of fine sand surged thousands of feet into the air, conjured by a turbulent thunderstorm and its fifty-knot winds. Haboobs, as such sandstorms are known, occur throughout the world, from the Middle East to the American Southwest. Their name comes from the Arabic term for wind, "haab" ("haboob" translates to "strong wind"). These strong winds manifest without warning, and they are brutal.

Ryan "Jinks" Mestelle and his wingman, Clint "Voodoo" Hoover, bobbed above this particular haboob in their respective A-10s, straining to identify viable ISIS targets along the Syrian border. But the haboob was making such detection impossible; they'd been flying for two hours without seeing a mark.

Jinks and Voodoo ascended above the storm to link up with a KC-135 tanker to refuel before moving to another "kill box," or target area, where they hoped the weather would be more cooperative. These missions usually lasted around six hours, so they still had plenty of time to salvage what had thus far been a goose egg of a sortie. Above the storm, it was a different world: the air clear, the sun bright, the visibility restricted only by one's eyesight.

Jinks latched onto the tanker first. A long, rigid boom transferred fuel from the KC-135 into the receiver in the nose of his A-10. After five minutes, Jinks detached from the tanker, fully loaded with gas. Until now, it had been a routine mission, uneventful aside from the weather and the fact that it happened to be Jinks's hundredth combat sortie.

Then—disaster.

"Immediately my jet lunged forward, [the] caution light panel erupted, and the jet began shuddering uncontrollably," Jinks recounts in his mission journal. "The stick began slamming left and right while the rudder pedals were violently swapping [in] both directions." Over the radio, the tanker crew hollered, "Holy shit, dude, you're on fire!" A twenty-foot flame streamed off Jinks' left engine as he wrestled with an airplane weighed down by a full load of ordnance and fuel. His A-10 lurched forward. Below, the haboob churned.

Jinks was now losing altitude at a thousand feet per minute. To slow the fall, he jettisoned his rockets and bombs, briefly admiring the surreal scene as they tumbled into the spiraling sandstorm. His descent eased to 250 feet per minute, still a dire situation, but at least he'd bought himself some time. What he couldn't dump were the eleven thousand pounds of fuel he'd just taken on from the tanker. He had two options: find a nearby airstrip or eject.

It was April 9, 2015, and the tragedy of Lieutenant Muath al-Kasasbeh was at the front of Jinks' mind. Ideally, he wanted to land his plane. Given how much his A-10 was shuddering, Jinks suspected both his engines were destroyed, but a systems check revealed encouraging news: only the left engine had been damaged; the right one was still good to go. "And I look outside, I'm looking at the motor," Jinks told me years later, "Because one thing, I mean, Pierre built the airplane so you can sit in the seat and really look over your shoulder and see the engines. And the whole front of the engine is gone. And there's a little piece of the core of the engine sticking out still, and it's still rotating and it won't stop. And there's chunks of metal and fire and crap coming off of it." Jinks asked Voodoo for his assessment. "So, you know, [Voodoo's] words are, 'It's all fucked up. . . . You have chunks falling off the airplane.'"

If Jinks needed hope that he could make it home, he might have recalled the exploits of Lieutenant Colonel Kim Campbell from April 2003, whose A-10 sustained damage from enemy fire that disabled all of her hydraulic controls. In that instance, Campbell couldn't bail out because she was directly over a target she had just attacked; ejecting would have been suicide. Instead, Campbell rather miraculously flew her A-10 to safety using the airplane's ingenious but grueling manual reversion mechanism.

Jinks had one thing going for him that Campbell didn't: he still had partial hydraulic controls. He hopped on the radio and sent out a wide broadcast for help: "Sandy One," the code for a downed airplane. A pair of F-16s and F-18s picked up his call, hit their afterburners, and headed his way. When the fighter jocks arrived on scene, the first thing they did was refuel with the tanker still flying above the haboob. Voodoo would have liked to refuel, too, but he couldn't leave Jinks' wing by even a few feet or else he would have most certainly lost sight of him in the haboob. When the F-16s and F-18s asked where the downed airplane was, Jinks replied, "Why, I'm the downed airplane. I'm just not there yet."

Jinks hoped he could land at an airstrip in Baghdad but given his rate of descent he knew he couldn't make it. Perhaps a nearby highway? Jostling around in the haboob, it was impossible to spot a viable strip of road. Jinks pinged the Air Operations Center, effectively his and Voodoo's "mission control," who identified a working airbase not far from their position: Al Assad, a former Iraqi airbase that was now a no-man's land with ISIS and coalition encampments scattered around it. Jinks set his course for Al-Assad, fifteen miles away.

Al-Assad had three airstrips, two of which were barricaded: no one knew which was unobstructed. If Jinks and Voodoo chose one of the two blocked runways, they would essentially be crashing their planes directly into concrete. Still, Jinks liked those odds better than his chances of being rescued after ejecting into the haboob.

During this fiasco Jinks discovered that he couldn't power his A-10 any faster than two hundred knots or the airplane would pitch forward and begin to nosedive. If he slowed to below 185 knots, the plane dipped sharply to the left at an almost ninety-degree angle. He steadied his speed at 195 knots, the upper limit his landing gear tires could withstand before they would completely shred their rubber.

At the ten-mile mark Jinks could still only see one mile ahead (compared to, say, the twenty or more miles one might see looking out an airplane window on a clear day). From his cockpit he saw only the illuminated box from his heads-up display projected onto a wall of unending sand. If he removed his hands from the stick or his feet from the rudder pedals, the airplane would lose control. If he looked over his left shoulder, he could see an engine spinning errantly, shedding fragments into the sandstorm. With the damage to his airplane, Jinks had lost control of the left hydraulics that powered his landing gear. He would have to use the emergency gear extension, a byproduct of the Hog's clever and resilient design: because the A-10's wheels retract forward into the airframe, the gear can be manually released so that the gear partially lowers, at which point the incoming headwind "pushes" it down.

With the emergency gear extension, it takes about thirty seconds for the landing gear to fall into place. To be safe, an A-10 driver will usually initiate the gear extension about ten miles away from the intended landing spot. However, Voodoo suggested Jinks hold off until they got closer to Al-Assad. With the landing gear lowered, Jinks' airplane would experience more drag, causing him to fall short of the airstrip. "That's why we fly in two ships," Jinks said of Voodoo's suggestion, "the collective mind—you know what I mean?" So Jinks waited to extend the gear until he was three miles out from Al-Assad. Fifty-knot crosswinds howled. "So I put a hand on the ejection handle and I put a hand on the metal gear extension," Jinks said. "I just pulled the lever because I didn't know what would happen. And it just worked totally as advertised." At one mile, the gear fell into place, and soon after, the runway materialized through the storm. Jinks and Voodoo had guessed right; this runway was open.

Once on the ground, Jinks and Voodoo tried radioing coalition forces. No answer. It seemed they were alone on an abandoned airfield in a sandstorm with one airplane that couldn't take off and another so dangerously low on fuel that even if it got in the air, it wouldn't stay there for long. They may have made it safely on the ground; now they needed to make it out alive.

Two white pickup trucks appeared on the horizon, which Jinks and Voodoo found strange; after all, U.S. and coalition military forces didn't drive shabby white pickups. "And so like any good A-10 pilot you have your binoculars on," Jinks told me. "So I pull my binoculars out. I'm looking out there. I'm like 'Those are clearly not good people.'" It was only now, with the trucks approaching, that Voodoo noticed Jinks was missing the top of his right tail. This explained why his airplane kept tipping over at slower speeds. "The engine cowling had separated, bounced off the top of the right motor and severed the top portion of my right vertical stabilizer," Jinks explained in his after-action journal.

With the mysterious white pickups closing in, fuel remained a problem for Voodoo. He could only taxi on the runway for so long before his airplane simply gave out. Across the airbase, Jinks and Voodoo spotted a few tan hangars that resembled those of allied forces. But when they taxied over they discovered the hangars were abandoned. "And this was, like, two miles away," Jinks told me. "So mind you, it's 50-knot winds and a sandstorm, and I only have one engine and my wingman is almost out of gas still."

At this point, Jinks' fight-or-flight mechanism kicked in, a decision made easier by the fact that neither he nor Voodoo could fly. Jinks decided both drivers would manually arm their Avenger cannons and fire them into the open desert. Both drivers were still strapped into their cockpits, so they were effectively turning their tank-killing airplanes into, well, *tanks*. They figured if they fired and the trucks stopped, it would mean they were friendlies. But if the trucks continued, the fight would be on.

Just as Jinks and Voodoo steered their A-10s into position to fire their warning shots, six armored Marine "Stryker" troop transports mounted with 0.50-caliber machine guns manifested through the sandstorm. Possibly scared off by the Marines, or the two Avenger cannons pointed their way, the trucks swerved off course, disappearing south into the storm.

A Marine colonel sidled up to Jinks' airplane and tapped the cockpit. "This airplane is a beautiful airplane in the air," Jinks recalled the colonel saying, "but it sure is a pain in the ass on the ground." The Marines planned to tow the two A-10s out of Al-Assad, onto the highway, and down to a nearby camp in a valley gorge. To accommodate the A-10's fifty-eight-foot wingspan, the Marines brought in bulldozers to widen the road. When Jinks expressed concern about what would happen if his A-10's wheel-brakes failed during the tow operation, the Marines told him not to worry. "'We'll just get in formation with our Strykers," they said. "If you lose brakes, just hit the car in front of you." "Only the Marine Corps think of this," Jinks marveled years later.

The Marines towed Jinks and Voodoo into an old aircraft hangar carved out of the side of the mountains, a contingency that Saddam Hussein had ordered years earlier in case his primary airstrips were destroyed. A handful of Marine snipers perched on top of the A-10s to keep watch as Jinks and Voodoo went inside. "The Marine hospitality was impeccable," Jinks wrote in his journal. Now safely under Marine protection, Jinks asked to borrow a satellite phone. "It was my one phone call home from prison, you know?" Jinks told me. He dialed Pierre Sprey's number.

Jinks had first met Sprey a few years prior on Capitol Hill in the bottom of the Rayburn Building, where he was lobbying alongside Master and Smitty to save the A-10. They struck up a friendship, and whenever Jinks was in the DC area he would invite Sprey out; regardless of the company, Jinks was sure they'd get a kick out of Sprey. Once, Sprey joined Jinks while he was with folks from the Defense Advanced Researched Projects Agency (DARPA). After dinner, Sprey suggested they all go to a spot nearby. "Really fantastic music, good drinks, you guys are going to love it," Sprey assured them. They walked down the street and climbed the stairs of another building, at which point they realized they were in a full-on nightclub: dark, music-thumping, everyone around them in their twenties. Sprey turrned to everyone and said, "Isn't this great? The acoustics are fantastic."

Sprey answered the phone and, unfazed that Jinks had just told him he was calling from a satellite phone in Iraq, went straight into making small talk. "It's common Pierre," Jinks said. Finally, Jinks cut off Sprey. "Sir, I've just got to thank you. . . . Without your design, I would be dead."

As for Jinks' mangled A-10? Just like Sprey had envisioned, the A-10 could not only take off and land from austere airfields, but also undergo a good deal of repairs under the haggard conditions like the ones Jinks and Voodoo now found themselves in. Thus, he would have been tickled—but not surprised—to learn that a maintenance unit removed the damaged tail and engine from Jinks' airplane and arranged for repair parts to be flown in on a cargo plane. Once the replacement parts were delivered, maintainers stacked mattresses on one another to form a makeshift ladder up to the tail where they affixed the new engine and built an impromptu crane, which they used to set the new tail section in place. Four days later, Jinks' A-10 was back in the air.

18

The Fathers of the A-10

WHEN THE FATHER OF THE A-10, AVERY KAY, DIED ON OCTOBER 29, 2015, Pierre Sprey remembered receiving a call from Kay's family, asking for details about arranging the funeral services at Arlington National Cemetery. Colonel Kay, of course, was deserving of a proper military burial with full honors. And given his rank, Kay was entitled to a military flyover, too. "So I started to look into the flyover business," Sprey said. "Obviously the only thing we wanted was an A-10 flyover."

Around the time Sprey heard of Kay's passing, he was on Capitol Hill lobbying for the A-10 with his friend and fellow advocate, Dan Grazier. "Hey, I've got something for you," Sprey told Grazier as they stood inside the lobby of the Hart Senate Office building. "Whenever Pierre said that, that way," Grazier told me, "it always made me stop because I'm like, 'Alright this is gonna be good.'" Sprey wanted Grazier's help getting the word out to national news media outlets that the "father of the A-10" had died.

In a previous life, Grazier had been a television reporter before joining the Marine Corps where he studied the work of John Boyd and his OODA Loop in Officer Candidate School. Years later, eager for more stability for his family, Grazier started looking for a job outside the Marine Corps. A mentor advised him to get in touch with Winslow Wheeler and the Project on Government Oversight, which had a fellowship opening that perfectly aligned with Grazier's experience, both as a soldier and a reporter. After interviewing with Wheeler, Spinney, and

Sprey—"the most interesting, exciting job interview that I will ever have," Grazier told me—he got the job.

In the role, Grazier did (and still does) the kind of work that makes the Military Reformers proud, dissecting convoluted government documents packed with code phrases and legal jargon to uncover the truth about military defense spending. It was Sprey who taught Grazier how to translate these documents, Grazier told me, adding, "And so like to the Lockheed Martins and the generals in the Pentagon's perspective, you know, me in that position was just a match made in hell . . . Because I hassle the shit out of them."

Despite possessing Sprey's *je ne sais quoi*, Grazier was skeptical the A-10 flyover would get approved. "And Pierre smiled and chuckled a little bit," Grazier told me. "And he said, 'Oh don't worry, I know how to make that happen.'"

Sprey called on his friends in the 104th Fighter Squadron, the A-10 Air National Guard unit stationed out of Baltimore with whom he'd become close in recent years while lobbying to save the A-10. Couldn't they just arrange a scheduled training mission for that day and divert briefly for the flyover, Sprey wondered? "I thought it'd be real simple," Sprey said. "The squadron knew better."

While getting a flyover approved for Kay would be no problem, ensuring that A-10s performed it would require some bureaucratic finagling. To get the flyover, Avery Kay's family had to put in a request with the Air Force, at which point the call would go out to all available squadrons in the area. This meant other airplanes (like F-16s) could do the flyover if they accepted the request first. So a plan set in motion: the 104th Fighter Squadron advised Kay's family to notify them the moment they put in the request; the 104th would have someone monitor the communication channel the whole time, ready to pluck up the request the instant it went out.

Given all the turmoil around the A-10 at the time, Sprey and others were concerned that advertising Kay as the "father of the A-10" might dissuade the flyover. So they kept that part a secret. "In essence," Sprey said, "we had to create a conspiracy," which Sprey thought was an appropriate tribute to an airplane borne out of intrigue. Once the flyover was secured, the public relations push began. Grazier contacted a friend who worked at CNN and told them he could get them all the access they needed, including cameras inside the Warthog cockpits during the flyover.

At the funeral, Grazier stood next to Sprey as the A-10s streaked past; CNN viewers were treated to views from the ground and the cockpit as the A-10 formation buzzed the Pentagon. Grazier deemed the whole event "a great old Pentagon caper." After the service, Grazier and Sprey "started laughing our asses off," Grazier remembered. "I was just so privileged to have played a small role in it and to have been there to experience that with him."

Some five years later, on August 5, 2021, Pierre—"None of this Mr. Sprey business," he was often quick to correct—died at his home in Glenn Dale, Maryland. He had suffered a heart attack while working at his desk. Rightfully, his disciples and the living members of the Fighter Mafia and the Military Reformers felt he deserved an A-10 flyover as well. But arranging this for Pierre would be trickier than it had been for Avery Kay. Unlike Kay, Pierre wasn't technically entitled to a flyover at all. But in a kind of twisted irony, Pierre's cadre learned that they could get the flyover approved for him if he was declared a "dignitary" by the Pentagon. Miraculously, the request was approved the day before Pierre's memorial.

The following day, Pierre's memorial was held on an unimaginably clear afternoon at a vineyard in Upper Marlboro, Maryland. The sun shined bright and hot on Pierre's friends—old and new—from his lives in the defense world and his many years in the music recording business. Pierre's son, John, spoke briefly, along with Smitty, who gave a brief history about the A-10 to those in attendance. In honor of Pierre, Smitty poured shots of Jeremiah Weed, one-hundred-proof gut-rot whiskey,[1] a

---

1. There are various iterations of the story, but the account by C. R. Anderegg in *Sierra Hotel: Flying Air Force Fighters in the Decade After Vietnam* explains how during a training mission on December 1, 1978, a student and instructor had to eject from their F-4E. The resulting crash left a crater in the desert. A year later, one of the pilots who survived the crash and another pilot who had been flying that day revisited the crash site, camping out in the crater for the night while polishing off a bottle of Jeremiah Weed, the only liquor that a nearby bar had stocked that was high enough proof to do

tradition among fighter and attack drivers. They poured an extra glass to honor Pierre; though he never flew, he was certainly one of them.

So many A-10 drivers requested to participate in the flyover that a lottery system was used to select who would fly. Actually, they used *two* lotteries: one to determine who would get to be in the four-ship flyover and another to decide who would perform the ceremonial "fallen man" maneuver, where one airplane symbolizes the person being honored by splitting off from the group straight up into the sky.

The night before he died, Pierre had met with Dan Grazier, who was working on a story for the Project on Government Oversight that would be published the following month detailing the A-10's grim prospects. Nearly half the active A-10 fleet was currently unflyable due to a lack of support for maintaining and upgrading the airplane, resulting in a "kind of de facto retirement" for the Hog without any dedicated close-air-support replacement in development. "A source within the A-10 community says that many of the flight-worthy aircraft can't shoot their iconic GAU-8 cannons because the squadrons can't get needed replacement parts," Grazier wrote.

In the coming months, the fight to save the A-10 would intensify, and its continued relevance in the theater of "modern" war would be proven yet again. In February 2022, Russia would invade Ukraine with tanks, an assault reminiscent of the Fulda Gap scenario that had inspired the A-10's development more than fifty years earlier.

Amid the ongoing fight to save the A-10, one thing advocates have emphasized is that it is unhelpful (and illogical) to pit the Hog against the F-35. One driver I spoke with, Dan "Fife" Nagle, has had the unique opportunity to fly both airframes. He described the transition from A-10 to F-35 "like going from a 1980s Ford F-150 three-on-the-tree pickup truck to a Tesla," and he, like other drivers I talked to who have flown both airplanes, actually had much to recommend about the F-35. But problems arise when the F-35 (or any other airplane for that matter) is positioned as being able to simply pick up the slack of close-air support. "To say that we're going to get rid of the A-10, we're not going to make

---

"afterburner" shots, in which the alcohol in the shot glass is lit on fire and drank while still flaming. When emptied, just a blue flickering flame remains in the shot glass.

anything like it, we're going to make 2,000 F-35s, I think we then have a large void/vacuum/capabilities gap, whatever you want to call it," Fife told me. "When it comes to doing some of the fights that I've personally been involved in, having flown both airplanes, I can unequivocally say the F-35 could not accomplish almost all of those close-air support type of fights that I've had [in the A-10]. And I'm talking about a *fight*, I'm not talking about 'we're going to bomb a cave entrance,' because technically that would be called close-air support. . . . So I've got dozens of stories, my friends have dozens of stories of executing these missions where the only thing that could have saved these guys' lives was that airplane."

But these were battles for another day, for the remaining members of the Military Reformers and their younger allies to fight. For now, on this warm October afternoon, it was a time to reflect on a life fully lived. The A-10s came into view over the treeline, barely making a sound until they were directly overhead. The fallen man split off into the sky. Nearby, in a gesture that would have delighted Pierre, a small cohort of A-10 drivers jokingly critiqued the flyover's formation. Then Pierre was laid to rest.

19

Mud

"I'm only telling you this because you're writing a book, but it's poor etiquette to ask an attack/fighter pilot how they got their call sign."
—KATHERINE "SLAM" CONRAD

PIERRE AND THE REFORMERS ALWAYS INSISTED THAT PEOPLE MATtered more—much more—than equipment. When it came to current A-10 drivers, Pierre spoke glowingly of many, but the one he seemed to most respect was Katherine "Slam" Conrad, whom he first met some years earlier, when Pierre visited the Maryland Air National Guard. In the last year and a half of his life Pierre began attending Slam's monthly dinner parties, where he quickly endeared himself to guests with what Slam called "a delightful combination of ruthless data analytics and velvet patrician charm." He was the perfect dinner party guest: he could talk music, art, wine, medicine. "I remember him insisting that when I buy yogurt," Slam said, "I have to leave it out on the counter for a couple of days to let the bacteria grow because that's the whole point of yogurt is that it's supposed to keep without refrigeration [compared to] the silly American concept of refrigerating your butter and your cheese and your yogurt . . . it was just always entertaining conversation."

At one dinner, Pierre turned to Slam and, unprompted, asked her, "What wins wars?" Before she could answer Pierre interjected, "Trucks." Slam saw this as an example of how Pierre could take something as innumerably complex as war and boil it down to its essence, to its "baseline unit," as she put it: trucks, that most necessary vehicle to transport troops and weaponry from point A to point B.

These dinners began early in the COVID-19 pandemic when lockdowns were still in effect. Ever the contrarian, Pierre found the strict lockdown rules to be illogical, so he welcomed the invitation. "Why would I care how big the group is—the bigger the group, the more satisfying the revolt against stay-at-home," Pierre wrote to Slam in an email. "No problem with dietary restrictions. I'm omnivorous though I have a strong preference for unsubtle, in-your-face garlic and spicing, kind of like my taste for in-your-face big wines." He would later remark, "I look forward to an evening well-spent outside the bounds of the law."

Slam had given Pierre and me a tour of the Maryland Air National Guard A-10 squadron less than a week before he died. That day I was struck when Slam asked me about my favorite book. *The Orchid Thief*, by Susan Orlean, I told her. Only later did I learn that Slam was testing my literary taste to see if she could trust my sensibilities as a writer. At the end of the day, she gave me a copy of her favorite book, *Tribe*, by Sebastian Junger. She kept a whole stack of *Tribe* copies on a tall bookshelf in her home so that she could give them to anyone with whom she felt the book might resonate.

Tribe is a difficult book to describe. In a mere 130 pages Junger explores what it means for humans to form bonds and connection, post-traumatic stress disorder, humanity's relationship to violence and war, and the manner in which our divisive political system furthers the alienation soldiers feel upon returning from combat. Slam's favorite line appears at the end of the introduction: "Humans don't mind hardship, in fact they thrive on it; what they mind is not feeling necessary."

A little less than a year after Pierre died, in late May 2022, I reached out to Slam. I was visiting my mother in Delaware at the time, a short drive from Slam's home in Baltimore. The timing was serendipitous. Slam had recently accepted a job at Virgin Galactic, with the hopes of fulfilling her dream of becoming an astronaut, and she would soon be moving to New Mexico. For a few more weeks, though, she was still out east, and in a week she would be flying in an air show in Ocean City, Maryland. If I could make it down that weekend, she said, we could find time to chat.

Slam seemed to embody what an A-10 driver was at their best: poised, selfless, confident, and secure in the way one must feel when their purpose is clearly defined. She exuded feeling *necessary*. Perhaps she could help me. I was struggling with something that maybe you've been too if you've made it this far: how do you reckon spending so much time focused on something meant to kill and destroy?

Slam's origins as an attack pilot began when she was in junior high school in Cincinnati, Ohio. While sitting in her seventh-grade classroom, what she suspects was an F-18 jet having engine trouble roared overhead on the approach to the Cincinnati airport. "And I just heard this noise and I was, like, plastered against the glass of the classroom trying to glimpse it as it went by." Her heartrate spiked. For a second she couldn't remember her name. All she could think about was "swirling noise." "And then I remember turning around and my classmates were all looking at me, like, what the hell? And I was looking at them, like, 'What the hell? Why am I the only person that's up here looking at this plane?' So that was kind of the first moment where I thought I might have a passion that was unusual or not something that everybody else felt." Her father had flown C-130s, and she went to air shows a lot as a kid. But the A-10 quickly caught her interest because, as she and so many A-10 drivers often say, "the mission really spoke to me."

After attending the airshow in Ocean City, I met up with Slam on a small deck of the home that she and her family had rented for the weekend. Nearby, partygoers drank beer and pop music echoed down the street.

"Fighter pilots don't relish violence, actually," she began. "It's certainly an element of our job and an important element of our job. But the precision and the appropriateness of the application of violence is very much what we're all about, specifically in the A-10 community. It's never been about who I'm killing, it's about who I'm protecting," she explained, noting that the missions she was usually tasked with flying were in support of U.S. troops under attack. "In general, I sleep very well at night because I feel strongly that people are alive because of the violence that I enacted responsibly on their behalf."

I struggled to find the right phrase. What did it mean to praise something that—Slam interrupted. "That's designed to kill people." Exactly. "I think you and I probably have a similar reaction to most Americans," she continued, "which is an instinctual baseline understanding that conflict is a certainty amongst human beings and that conflict will occasionally rise to violence and that you have to be ready for that violence."

And what about Pierre? Did she ever wonder if he struggled with the morality of it all, that he'd spent so much of his life and intellect on national defense? "I don't think he was a man plagued by self-doubt. But as I told you earlier, I think Pierre was a realist, that war is, frankly inevitable. . . . You must be responsible in your preparation for that inevitability. And so I think he held a similar viewpoint of war to me, which is to, you know, hit it hard, hit it heavy and get it over with soon because these prolonged wars, low grade wars are more detrimental than the alternative. And I think that's why he felt it was important to have repeatable technologies to keep America safe."

Before we left off, I told Slam about an A-10 driver I'd met a few months earlier who said his most memorable mission involved protecting a small Army unit pinned down inside a Humvee. When the A-10s radioed down to ask what they needed most, their answer was simple: sleep. So the Hog drivers told the soldiers to crawl under their Humvee and close their eyes while they flew in circles for hours above, keeping the enemy at bay: the Flying Gun was now the Flying White Noise Machine.

"That's the sort of stuff that just it's so humbling," Slam said, bringing her hand to her heart. "It makes me so proud to be part of this community. Like that level of—I'm sure dudes would be offended to hear me say this—but almost feminine care, almost a mothering instinct to say like, 'I'm here to care for you. And if you are tired, then let me take your worries. Let me take your stress. Like, let me protect you. And rest.'"

At the Ocean City air show, it occurred to me how odd it is to showcase A-10s at flying demonstrations. For obvious reasons they can't "demonstrate" their defining feature. What you're left with as a viewer is a funny-looking plane, flying slow. I understand how a child can look at an F-18 Super Hornet or the Air Force's Thunderbird demonstration team, which currently flies F-16s, and be wowed by the awesome power of aviation, the thunderous roar of their afterburners. Meanwhile, an A-10 is so quiet it doesn't even require you to wear earplugs during its flight routine. Strange, I thought, how a young person could watch these kludgy planes crawl quietly across the sky and decide *that* was what they wanted to fly.

There is a moment in *Tribe* where Junger works to capture the "crippling alienation many soldiers feel at home." He finds the most apt description in the poem "Sick Leave" by World War I soldier and poet Siegfried Sassoon: "In bitter safety I awake, unfriended; / And while the dawn begins with slashing rain/ I think of the Battalion in the mud."

On his last visit to the Maryland Air National Guard, just a few days before his death, Pierre stood next to Slam on the flight line. An A-10 glided past. Pierre craned his neck and followed the arc of its flight. What was he thinking about as he watched his airplane in flight, I asked. He told me he appreciated how tight the A-10 could turn, just as it had been designed, which allows the pilot to stay over the battlefield and keep their eyes on the ground. In other words, his answer was the same as it had always been: he was thinking of the battalion in the mud.

Pictured left to right: Jeremy "Frogger" Stone, Pierre, Ryan "Jinks" Mestelle

Brian "Master" Boeding and
David "Rainman" Stephenson
during Operation Iraqi Freedom
in 2003
BRIAN "MASTER" BOEDING

Night austere field
operations on Mud Lake,
Nevada
BRIAN "MASTER" BOEDING

A-10 drivers at Bagram
Airfield wearing t-shirts of
Jeremiah Weed, a favorite
drink among fighter and
attack pilots
BRIAN "MASTER" BOEDING

A-10s from the Michigan Air
National Guard in 2019
BRIAN "MASTER" BOEDING

Brian "Master" Boeding and Pierre
BRIAN "MASTER" BOEDING

Texas lake austere field
landing
BRIAN "MASTER" BOEDING

An A-10 landing on a highway in Estonia
BRIAN "MASTER" BOEDING

Another angle of a highway landing
BRIAN "MASTER" BOEDING

The Warthog's "nose"
BRIAN "MASTER" BOEDING

What an A-10 driver called "true power projection" on Mud Lake, Nevada
BRIAN "MASTER" BOEDING

Robert "Muck" Brown and Pierre advocating for the A-10
MARTHA BROWN

A memorial to Muck Brown at his alma mater, Tuscola High School, in Waynesville, North Carolina, where he also taught Air Force Junior Reserve Officers' Training Corps. Air Force and Army colleagues came from across the country to honor Muck (a display honoring Muck can also be found at the Pima Air & Space Museum in Tucson, Arizona)
MARTHA BROWN

Pierre enjoying his visit to the Maryland ANG
104th Fighter Squadron
KATHERINE "SLAM" CONRAD

Signing the inside of an A-10
KATHERINE "SLAM" CONRAD

Katherine "Slam" Conrad and Pierre
KATHERINE "SLAM" CONRAD

Acknowledgments

I emailed Pierre Sprey on a whim in April 2020. At the time, I was surprised to learn that the person largely responsible for the A-10 was even still alive. He emailed back right away, and over the next year we had many lengthy phone calls (COVID-19 prevented us from meeting in person at the time), during which I'd put Pierre on speakerphone, sprawl out on the floor, and take notes as he recalled with stunning clarity the details of his life in the Pentagon and his work on the A-10. He'd rattle off books I should read and people I needed to contact. He was relentless in his generosity and patience with me, and I felt a tremendous gratitude that he trusted me with his story. The extraordinary life that he lived gave me the opportunity to do something I never thought would be possible: write a book.

Pierre died unexpectedly just three days after I'd spent a long weekend with him in Maryland. That Friday, we visited the 104th Fighter Squadron, and the next day we met at my hotel where, as always, I turned on the recorder and let Pierre drive the conversation. Usually he spoke from memory, but for these interviews he came prepared with a list of topics he wanted to be sure to address. I was on the floor again, this time with my feet elevated on a desk chair, reeling from a back injury I'd suffered earlier in the summer. Pierre was unfazed by the odd arrangement; he even offered me a pillow from behind his back so I could prop my legs up higher. It turned out he, too, once had serious back problems and professed the secret to fixing them was drinking exorbitant amounts of water, which he said helped regenerate cartilage (I never fact-checked him on this, but I did up my water intake regardless).

After what would be our last interview the next day, I walked Pierre to his car, a beat-up silver coupe, where we sat against the hood in the hotel parking lot and split a chicken salad sandwich from Wegmans, a grocery store highly recommended by Pierre. I felt embarrassed that this was all I had to offer him, a grocery store sandwich out of a plastic bag with no napkins or silverware. But he didn't seem to mind; he was, as always, wholly unpretentious. When he finished eating, he gave me a smile, got in his car, and sped off.

Susan Orlean says you know it's getting close to the time to write when you feel the curve at which you're learning new information begin to flatten. With Pierre, that curve never flattened, but that last weekend in Maryland I did feel its slope become slightly less steep, which added to the strangeness I felt when he left this world just as I was beginning to write his story. I still haven't figured out what to do with those feelings except feel them and hope that Pierre would have liked what this book became.

With Pierre vouching for me, I was welcomed by his family, friends, fellow Military Reformers, and the A-10 community, all of whom were so generous with their time and willing to help me understand their perspectives of the Warthog's story: John Sprey, Megan Downes, Winslow Wheeler, Chuck Spinney, Tom Christie, Ray Leopold, Lon Ratley, Bob Speir, Slam, Master, Jinks, Smitty, Martha Brown, Anna Brown, Rainman, Coach, Mike Wyly, Tito, 40 Watts, TC, Bones, Zucco, Narly, Matt Secor, FATTS, Ras, and the 104th Fighter Squadron. This book was also made possible with the help of the U.S. Air Force, who coordinated visits for me at Hill Air Force Base and Nellis Air Force Base, where I had the opportunity to speak with the active-duty service members, engineers, and maintainers affiliated with the A-10.

My agent, Jack Gernert, instilled in me the belief that I was actually capable of writing a book and supported me tirelessly throughout its development. I'm grateful to the folks at Lyons Press, in particular my editors Rick Rinehart, Felicity Tucker, and Katy Whipple, as well as the marketing and publicity team, for turning my dream of writing a book into a reality. I want to also thank all the editors at the publications for which I've written over the years who took chances on me to write something that would go out in the world, and edited me patiently, kindly, and thoroughly: Brian Hurley, Holly Wendt, Willy Staley, Bruce Falconer, Josina Guess, Boris Dralyuk, Rob Latham, Amanda Dobbins, Andrew Gruttadaro, and Vera Titunik (who graciously reminded me of the importance of tension in story!). Along the way, so many exceptional writers have been generous with their time, responding to queries or letting me interview them at length, including Blake J. Harris, Adam Hochschild, and Susan Orlean.

Columbia University's School of the Arts gave me the incredible opportunity to learn from wonderful writers and professors, including Patty O'Toole, Margo Jefferson, Lis Harris, Alana Newhouse, and David Samuels. At Columbia—in the School of the Arts, the Undergraduate Writing Program, and on the basketball court—I found mentors and lifelong friends: Glenn Michael Gordon, Allen Durgin, Jason Ueda, Sue Mendelsohn, Nicole Wallack, Aaron Ritzenberg, Elizabeth Metzger, Bob Blaisdell, Heather Radke, and Noah Gallagher Shannon. Noah, you showed me what it meant to be a professional writer, and I'm so grateful to have you in my corner (or open along the baseline for a fifteen-foot jumper!).

This book was also made possible by a generous grant-in-aid from Oberlin College, an institution filled with so many folks who have supported me in my writing and teaching over the years: Josh Sperling, Jan Cooper, Nancy Boutilier, Ferd Protzman, Gillian Johns, Patty deWinstanely, Anne Trubek, Laura Baudot, and David Kamitsuka.

It was in my first ever college writing course at Oberlin, taught by the incomparable Laurie McMillin, where I was introduced to this thing called "nonfiction writing" (we read a story by Michael Pollan about the beef industry). Laurie's first assignment for that class was nonfiction, too: the prompt was "Where and What I Played as a Child . . ." I remember visiting Laurie's office and expressing my worries about my writing before she'd even had time to read any of our assignments. She invited me into her office, and she asked me to just sit as she read my story aloud, patiently, eagerly, and warmly. I remember thinking, "Oh, that wasn't *terrible*." Then she gave me techniques for revision that I use to this day, both with myself and with students. She told me to open up a new document, put my font on size four—so small that I couldn't even read what I was typing—and write the personal essay again. Laurie taught me that writing is a learned skill, one that you can refine through repeated practice. But more than that, she taught me the value of patience, kindness, and warmth while still holding yourself and others to the highest standards. She taught me that sometimes the greatest difference you can make in someone's life is asking them to have a seat and listen as you read their words aloud.

So many loyal friends and family supported me in this book and my writing aspirations over the years. James Swanson and Dahsan Gary enthusiastically read early chapters of this book. Bryan Kriss and Dave Dahl joined me on a particularly harrowing reporting trip. Dave, without your steadfast enthusiasm, keen editorial eye, and constant encouragement (such as the periodic texts out of the blue like, "Never doubt your book!"), this book would have never happened.

Finally, I want to thank my parents. My dad gave me the blueprint for what it means to work diligently at one's craft, and it's one that I aspire to every day (always sewing those oranges!). He has supported me in my dream of becoming a writer in incalculable ways, and perhaps most germane to this book, he introduced me to military aviation, a subject we have bonded over my entire life, sometimes going entire conversations where we only communicate through lines from *Top Gun*. Papa, I love you.

My mom has read with equal intensity everything I've ever written, from short personal essays in college to every chapter and draft of this book. She introduced me at a young age to her eclectic literary taste, from Pat Conroy to Amy Hempel to Gay Talese to Flannery O'Connor, and so many other writers who she'd just happen to be reading and send my way. Pierre Sprey's close friends would talk about enduring the "Pierre Sprey buzz saw" when asking him to review a piece of writing or set of calculations. Pierre left this world before I could experience this buzz saw, but my mom's editorial blade is razor sharp, too. For as long as I can remember, the final test for my writing has been to sit with her in her living room with a printed-out copy of my draft—always single-sided, always double-spaced—as she reads each sentence aloud while leaning back in her red recliner and twirling her feet. When she comes across a sentence that doesn't quite feel right, she pauses. Her feet stop twirling. Then, the real work begins.

Notes on Sources

Along with personal interviews, a wealth of sources (print, electronic, video, archival) were essential to this book's composition. I often directly reference these sources in the body of the text, but for the instances where I do not, I have included the following notes.

Part I

Author's Note

"named for rhetorician Kenneth Burke": Nordquist

1. West of the Smoke

The details of the Marah Valley attack were pieced together with extensive interviews with the parties involved, along with A-10 drivers' video feed of the attack available on YouTube: "Real A-10C CAS Mission HUD/Litening Unclassified FOUO." YouTube. Lexat News, 2013. https://www.youtube.com/watch?v=29UnZdX42lE.
"In fact, the Bone could fly 1.2 times the speed of sound": "B-1B" Lancer
"and the plane itself can remain in flight with half of one wing blown off, one engine, and a sizable chunk of its tail missing": Sweetman and Peacock 1992, 27

2. The Redeemer

"Now he was toiling in the office of Air Force Doctrine, Concepts, and Objectives Directorate, a smoke screen moniker for the bureau's true role of preserving—and expanding—the Air Force's lucrative budget": Sprey interview
"But when the Institute for Defense Analysis assessed the strategy, they found the campaign was largely unproductive": Newman and Shepperd 2006
"In fact, the primary North Vietnamese supply lines had not buckled under incessant American bombing; they had strengthened": Newman and Shepperd 2006

"Douhet believed you defeated an enemy not by attacking its military forces head-on, but rather by 'totally [cutting] off the arteries of a functioning army': that is, its supply lines": Hippler 2013

"In Command of the Air, *the seminal text of strategic bombing, Douhet argues, '[I]t is not enough to shoot down all birds in flight if you want to wipe out the species; there remain the eggs and the nests. The most effective method would be to destroy the eggs and the nests systematically'"*: Douhet 1998, 34; Donald Miller 2006, 34

"Douhet endorsed the use of poison gas on civilians": Astor 1997, 8

"A projectile that falls on a trench may be limited to making a hole in the ground; one that falls on a city will produce an immeasurably greater material and moral destruction. For that reason, the preferred targets of aerial war will necessarily be cities—the largest, most populous, most industrialized, most intellectual cities": Hippler 2013, 119

"'We could cross the lines of these contending armies in a few minutes in our airplane,' Mitchell notes in his memoir": Donald Miller 2006, 32

"Mitchell received the Distinguished Service Cross . . . he was court-martialed . . . ": Minnie L. Jones

"passing of the Air Corps Act of 1926 functioned as a lucrative consolation. The act infused almost 35 percent of the Army's budget into developing airpower over the next five years, resulting in thousands of jobs and expensive new airplanes. During that time, not one new rifle was bought for ground troops": Hughes 1995, 48

"devoting almost no time or scholarship to the study of supporting ground troops": Hughes 1995, 53

"After all, Douhet, who died in 1930, believed air warfare could be executed "completely independently from the progress of land and sea operations": Hippler 2013, 122

"In 1927, a few years before his death, Douhet noted that 'the true combat plane, able to impose its will upon the enemy, has not yet been invented; nor does it seem likely it will be soon'": Donald Miller 2006, 40

"Along with the B-17, the United States invested $1.5 billion (approximately $27.5 billion in 2020) in the Norden Mark 15 bombsight": Gladwell 2011

"Years later, the Norden company would lean into the fanciful image": LIFE 1943

"General Douglas MacArthur worried over the imbalance of airpower": Hughes 1995, 48

"For their part, Wilbur and Orville Wright had resisted the temptation": Hughes 1995, 55

"A 1941 study found that only one-sixth of explosives dropped from British bombers landed within a five-mile radius of their targets. Further, the Battle of Britain demonstrated the resilience a dedicated population could muster in the face of tremendous airpower. Though Germany mercilessly bombed England, the British did not cower as Douhet had theorized decades earlier. They dug in": Hughes 1995, 75

"In a panic, turret gunners would fire recklessly, striking friendly bombers. Even when smaller aircraft were recognized as viable tools of war, they were frequently unavailable for supporting soldiers because they had been called away to escort bombers": Donald Miller 2006, 68

"Meanwhile, troops desperate for air assistance sometimes waited as long as three hours for close-air support; by then, the fight could be long over, the battle lost": Hughes 1995, 132

"It makes you feel very helpless": Hughes 1995, 178

"The 1st Bomb Wing alone lost thirty-six American bombers and had 352 airmen killed, along with more than a hundred bombers significantly damaged": Astor 1997, 178

"(total losses amounted to 60 bombers and 564 men)": Tillman 2018

"'Had they continued the attacks with the same energy,' Speer said at the time, 'we would quickly have been at our last gasp'": Tillman 2018

"Perhaps the most glaring repercussions of America's bomber fixation played out on June 6, 1944. Prior to the D-Day invasion, bombers dropped six million pounds of explosives on Normandy's beaches in hopes of destroying Germany's defenses and clearing the way for the allied assault. The soldiers who stormed Utah Beach benefited from the awesome potential of airpower, taking control of the beach. But the men assigned to Omaha Beach walked into a slaughter. When the Higgins boats carrying allied platoons crossed the choppy surf, neared the beaches, and lowered their ramps, a largely intact German defense network of heavy machine guns nestled in dense concrete bunkers awaited. The bombs had missed Omaha Beach by miles": Hughes 1995, 5

"air and ground speak a different language . . . ": Hughes 1995, 184

"Quesada did his best to rebuild trust between the ground in the air, first by making sure that there was a representative from the air on the ground who could clearly communicate the ground's position to pilots overhead and direct them accordingly. He also arranged for Army soldiers to fly in planes, such that both sides could appreciate the others' perspectives of war. All these efforts enabled Quesada's 'armored column cover,' in which air units loitered above the battlefield and could be called on in an instant (much like what Matt Secor had done with FATTS and Ras in the Marah Valley of Afghanistan). This ready-made close-air support was not only useful in helping troops get out of a jam, but also enhanced their aggressiveness on ground assaults. If troops were covering ground quickly and their supporting artillery couldn't keep up to shell the enemy ahead, then they could call on the air to serve as de facto artillery to clear the way ahead": Douglas Campbell 2003, 22

"Where the bombers had come up short, his P-47s slowed the encroaching German Panzer tank divisions enough for U.S. soldiers to reach the cliffsides after landing at the beaches. When the air and ground forces set up headquarters in the French countryside, Quesada performed his most controversial move yet; he pitched his tent directly next to Army General Omar Bradley's, signifying his belief that air and ground were intertwined and need to be in close coordination and cooperation": Sprey interview

"But as subsequent changes in defense policy further reduced the importance of non-nuclear air power, Pete Quesada resigned": Hughes 1995, 19

"Avery Kay accepted an assignment teaching aviators how to fly bombers from treetop level at night": Sprey interview

"But his crisis of faith in long-range strategic bombing complicated his path to promotion": Sprey interview

"Pilots flying over North Vietnam received mixed messages for how to drop their ordnance, leading to underwhelming results. Inflict damage on the enemy, pilots were told, but at all costs avoid damage to themselves or America's pricey jets": Newman and Shepperd 2006, 55

"To help with the bombers' accuracy, the Air Force employed pilots to fly aging F-100 Super-Sabre jets in the role of 'Forward Air Control,' or FAC. In this role, FAC pilots flew low to the ground, spotted possible threats, and fired smoke rockets at the targets. The FAC missions

were grueling—often lasting more than four hours—and given the extended exposure to ground fire, extremely dangerous. The fighter-bombers that followed would then drop their ordnance on literal clouds of smoke enveloping the jungle below, like shooting at the suggestion of a ghost in the night. One didn't measure the effectiveness of these sorties so much as guess. All the while, the Vietcong moved through the jungle relatively unscathed": Newman and Shepperd 2006, 31–32

"At the end of yet another meeting filled with bad news, Air Force Chief of Staff John P. McConnell reportedly bowed his head in distress and sighed, 'I'm so sick of it . . . I have never been so goddamned frustrated by it all'": Newman and Shepperd 2006, 79

"Amid this desperation, Avery Kay and his superior, Major General Richard Yudkin, conceived of a shrewd proposition": Douglas Campbell 2003, 63

"When Kay pinged various offices for available engineers to join his team, he was rebuffed": Sprey interview

3. The Whiz Kid

"The Fulda Gap had been where the frostbitten, battered armies of Napoleon Bonaparte retreated after their defeat at the Battle of Leipzig in 1813": Hammerich 2018, 3

"A little over a century later, U.S. General George S. Patton traversed the Gap in the Second World War en route to victory": Wilson 2015

"U.S. service members nicknamed the Fulda Gap the 'wasp waist of West Germany.' More reserved military strategists dispassionately deemed it a 'key-terrain feature'": Hammerich 2018, 3

"In short, Kahn forwarded the idea that in the horrific event of a nuclear war, the first strike would not necessarily be the last. Rather, what really mattered was how a nation could respond to such an attack. Life could indeed go on after such a horror, Khan argued. Most unusual, though, was Kahn's belief that a nuclear attack could inspire morale among survivors: 'It would not surprise me if the overwhelming majority of the survivors devoted themselves with a somewhat fanatic intensity to the task of rebuilding what was destroyed. It is probably worth mentioning that Kahn's work relied on intelligence that overestimated the Soviet weapons arsenal. In the late 1950s, the United States believed the Soviet Union possessed roughly three hundred intercontinental ballistic missiles; in fact, they only had four": Menand 2005

"where fighter pilots were not allowed to engage a foe with missiles until they had confirmed an aircraft belonged to the enemy": Coram 2002, 218–9

"Frustration among pilots mounted, spawning the phrase 'IT TAKES A FIGHTER WITH A GUN TO KILL A MIG-21'": Coram 2002, 219

"Boyd called these evaluative sessions the 'Pierre Sprey buzz saw'": Coram 2002, 200

"Epatko's recent defection had caused quite a stir": The New York Times 1967

"During one bombing mission just south of Hanoi, American airmen were stunned when MiG-17s from North Vietnam's almost comically small fleet of thirty-six jets downed two U.S. F-105 Thunderchiefs, which were weighed down by their six-thousand-pound bomb loads": TIME 1965

4. The System

"like the XB-70 Valkyrie . . . it could actually 'ride' its own supersonic shockwave thanks to variable wingtips that angled downward": Mustard n.d.

"as well as René Descartes' Rules for Direction of the Mind, a lengthy treatise espousing the systems approach first written in 1628 (but only later published in 1701)": Watson 2023

"Such mathematical approaches to analyzing problems guided the field of operations research . . . 'Someone had to devise new techniques for these weapons, new methods of assessing their effectiveness and the most efficient way to use them,' writes Fred Kaplan in The Wizards of Armageddon. *'It was a task that fell to the scientists'"*: Fred Kaplan 1983, 52

"One such precocious mind was Robert Strange McNamara . . . McNamara's insights contributed to reducing the 'abort rate' of bombers, which (understandably) were often finding excuses to avoid flying over their targets for fear of being killed": Kaplan 250

"McNamara was instrumental in the production and promotion of the compact Ford Falcon, and through intensive analyses of car accidents, McNamara and the 'Whiz Kids,' as they'd come to be known, developed safer cars with such innovations as padded instrument panels, steering wheels that wouldn't impale drivers (a leading cause of death in accidents), and, most controversially, seatbelts": Morris 2004

"A stout negotiator, McNamara only accepted the post after being granted the power to appoint every single senior official": Morris 2004

"Among his exacting accounting methods was to directly compare and evaluate military spending across all branches together, which was unprecedented at the time": Kaplan 254

"who cultivated such unsavory nicknames as con-man, dictator, and 'Mr. I have all the answers McNamara'": Harry Reasoner via Morris 2004

"On October 21, 1967, as Sprey was preparing to defend his controversial memo, twenty thousand Americans marched on the Pentagon to protest the war effort. Soon thereafter, McMamara submitted his own memo directly to President Lyndon Johnson urging that the United States absolutely must change course in Vietnam. On February 29, 1968, McNamara resigned from his position as secretary of defense": Morris 2004

5. Simplicate, and Add More Lightness

"The Skyraider belonged to a different era, first conceived in the waning years of World War II as a 'bomber-torpedo' to protect naval aircraft carriers from submarine attacks": Johnson 2008

"On one harrowing occasion, Gray's A-1 sustained more than fifty bullet holes. Other pilots reported taking up to two hundred hits, some leaving holes large enough to fit a basketball or even an entire person through": Rausa 2001, 44–45

"A-1 designers found that a pilot's head was typically two feet away from the instrument panels, so they adjusted the gauges to be easily read at that distance": Rausa 2001, 10–11

"A-1s facilitated the rescue of approximately a thousand downed pilots in Vietnam": Rausa 2001, 178

"He 'never completed a formal degree as an engineer,' notes writer and engineer John Golan": Golan 2015

"Heinemann adhered to the motto of Gordon Hooton, a designer for the Ford Motor Company in the 1920s: 'Simplicate and add more lightness'": Sprey interview; Sprey remembered seeing a plaque with this motto on Heinemann's desk

"Instead, he utilized a simple delta-wing design. There were no unnecessary moving parts, no added complexity, no extra opportunities for something to break. The delta-wing design shaved off about two hundred pounds on the A-4's overall weight, and Heinemann cut an additional fifty-eight pounds by ordering an entirely new ejection seat": Golan 2015

"Like the A-1, the A-4 had an extremely user-friendly cockpit. It was so simple, in fact, that pilots found it disarming.": Golan 2017

All quotations from Rudel are from his book, *Stuka Pilot*.

6. The Thud

"On June 6, 1950, the graduating cadets of the U.S. Military Academy at West Point considered a monumental question: what would the next war look like?": Kenneth Campbell 1950 (first came to my attention through Ogorkiewicz's book).

"Like the airplane that would ultimately be designed to destroy it, the tank has had the peculiar quality of endurance": Richard Ogorkiewicz's (2015) phenomenal *Tanks: 100 Years of Evolution* was immeasurably helpful for my understanding of tanks.

"They had a range of less than twenty-five miles and a top speed of under four miles per hour": Ogorkiewicz 2015, 43

"But as the war progressed, tanks showed promise, especially as mobile artillery that could move behind troops and shell the enemy at a distance, clearing the way for foot soldiers": Ogorkiewicz 2015, 50

"It occurred to me that if I could invent a machine—a gun—that would by its rapidity of fire enable one man to do as much battle duty as a hundred, that it would to a great extent, supersede the necessity of large armies, and consequently exposure to battle and disease would be greatly diminished": Chivers 2010, 25–26

"What Gatling strived to create was a mobile, reliable gun that could be manned by just a few soldiers and fire bullets at an astounding rate": Chivers 2010, 26

"the U.S. Army Air Corps' 'Project Vulcan.' The Vulcan contract was awarded to General Electric, who presented a Gatling-style design that had numerous benefits over the current crop of airplane-mounted guns": Sweetman and Peacock 1992, 37

"A Gatling-style gun could also fire much faster than other guns, which made it more accurate as there was less time between each bullet's discharge and therefore less variation in its placement on the target": Sweetman and Peacock 1992, 36–37

"the trip would be so long and the Thud guzzled so much fuel that a pilot would not be able to fly home after dropping his bomb": Vizcarra 2018

"When these tanks emptied, they contained flammable vapors that the Thud had no way of purging": Chuck Spinney interview

"Fuel itself posed huge problems for Thud. It did not have 'self-sealing fuel tanks,' or fuel tanks coated with a rubber mixture that expanded if the tank was punctured and acted like a sponge to soak up the now-leaking fuel. Self-sealing fuel tanks had been around since before World War

II, but they were bulkier than integral tanks built into the airframe and had thus become less popular in the supersonic jet age, where everything needed to be streamlined for aerodynamic effect": Neubeck 2019, 24; Sweetman and Peacock 1992, 25

"*There was such widespread belief in missiles as the primary weapon of war, too, that the thinking was if missile completely obliterated a jet, it really didn't matter if there was a fuel leak anyway*": Sweetman and Peacock 1992, 25

"*It got worse. Just like its fuel tanks, the Thud's already fragile hydraulic systems were housed around its engine. If they leaked, a fire could easily start. And while the Thud had multiple sets of hydraulic lines, they ran a mere half-inch apart from each other. A well-placed 0.50-caliber round could punch through the Thud's belly and disable all the lines*": Spinney interview

"*In March 1968, Sprey and his team drafted a Concept Formulation Packet for the A-X: a list of parameters, must-haves, and non-negotiables*": Douglas Campbell 2003, 68

7. Fly Before Buy

"*Unsurprisingly, this led to some production debacles, including the C-5A Galaxy, a cargo plane the size of a football field that had gone two billion dollars over its projected cost*": Burton 1993, 18

"*Defense contractors balked at the competitive fly-off idea; a prototype that didn't perform well meant the end of a fat government contract*": Coram 2002, 258

"*What's more, the Marine Corps was working on acquiring the AV-8B Harrier airplane, renowned for its ability to take off from short airstrips and land vertically like a helicopter*": Douglas Campbell 2003, 75–76

"*In the coming years, the A-X project would face scrutiny as the entire fleet of attack aircraft—both existing and in development—came under review*": Douglas Campbell 2003, 83

"*Just before noon on March 12, 1969, a Cheyenne prototype exploded mid-flight along the coast of southern California, killing its test pilot, thirty-two-year-old David A. Beil. In another incident a year prior, a Cheyenne's rotors went off kilter, colliding into the canopy*": Douglas Campbell 2003, 74–75

"*What Sprey cared for the least was the Cheyenne's high-end top speed, reported at more than 240 miles per hour, faster even than the AH-64 Apache attack helicopter in use today*": Hutchinson 2022

"*In May 1970, a request for A-X design proposals went out to twelve contractors. These proposals needed to be 'design to cost,' meaning that contractors were given a fixed cost for their design: they needed to present a working prototype that could be produced at $1.5 million per airplane. The design-to-cost philosophy sought to protect the government from overspending by preventing defense contractors from adding features that might improve an airplane's capability, like flying at night or in bad weather, but also exponentially increase their cost*": Sweetman and Peacock 1992, 23

"*By December 1970, the list of candidates winnowed down to two companies: Northrop and Fairchild-Republic. They would have just over two years to design and build their prototypes*": Douglas Campbell 2003, 81; Neubeck 2019, 4

"*Though Seversky was arrested, he was later permitted to fly, becoming the top 'ace' in Russia's Navy by shooting down thirteen enemy airplanes over the course of the war*": this and all Seversky information in this paragraph from Rumerman n.d.

"*Sprey's superiors clearly thought more highly of him. In response to his resignation, they wrote to Sprey, praising his 'keen conceptual skills and perceived analytical abilities,' which had earned Sprey 'a well-deserved reputation as one of the very best systems analysts'*": Tucker 1970

"*Northrop's design team was headed by Walt Fellers, who had studied under Edgar Schmued, the designer of the P-51 Mustang*": Sprey interview

"*Fairchild-Republic, meanwhile, was headed by Robert Sanator, top executive and then-president, and project engineer Vincent Tizio*": Smallwood 2005, 14

"*Turbofan engines didn't offer great acceleration, but they were more propulsive than a comparable propeller-driven engine, and they didn't burn near as much fuel as jets*": Douglas Campbell 2003, 80

"*In October 1972, Northrop and Fairchild Republic unveiled their competing designs at Edwards Air Force Base in the desert of southern California, where the competitive fly-off testing would take place. Both designs had much to recommend: ultra-survivable fuel tanks, cockpits swaddled in a titanium bathtub to protect the pilot, bubble canopies for enhanced visibility while flying, and a manual-reversion backup flight control mechanism*": Douglas Campbell 2003, 95

"*Like much of the rest of the A-10's parts, its engines were to be the first 'unhanded' engines in Air Force history (either engine could be placed on the left or right side of the aircraft)*": Sweetman and Peacock 1992, 23

"*With the turbofans—which already ran cooler than traditional jet engines—situated up by the tails, it further reduced the amount of exhaust that could be detected from the ground*": Sweetman and Peacock 1992, 20

"*Test pilots also favored the A-10 to the A-9 as it proved more survivable in the outdoor wind tunnel gun testing*": Douglas Campbell 2003, 95

"*The cannon's ammo drum was shielded with 'trigger plates' that would activate if an enemy round penetrated the airframe, essentially exploding the round before it could get to the ammo drum itself (a similar technology existed in tanks of the time). Fairchild-Republic overengineered the A-10 to such a degree that internal structural components that were essential in other airplanes could be disconnected or disabled in an A-10 and it could still remain in flight. The result was a practically unkillable airplane, one that could remain in flight with half the tail and wing blown off, just one functioning engine, and no hydraulic controls*": Sweetman and Peacock 1992, 24–26

"*Sure, the wing pods contributed to the A-10's funny look, but they actually allowed the airplane to be smaller since there didn't need to be extra internal space in the fuselage to stow the landing gear*": Douglas Campbell 2003, 94

"*so if the A-10's landing gear ever failed to lower it could still effectively 'crash-land' without crashing or damaging too much of the airplane; indeed, in later years A-10s and their pilots would survive doing just that*": Douglas Campbell 2003, 95

"*if the gear ever malfunctioned mid-extension, the incoming airstream would literally push the wheels down into place*": Sweetman and Peacock 1992, 22

8. The Military Reformers Assemble

"Both companies were now tasked with constructing a weapon of immense destruction, capable of obliterating tanks, artillery, bunkers, and armored troop transports": all information from this paragraph from National Museum of the Air Force

"Leopold uncovered a much different estimate: sixty-eight million dollars per airplane, the most expensive Air Force project at the time": Coram 2002, 287

"As the B-1's price kept rising (by 1974 it climbed to one hundred million dollars per airplane)": Coram 2002, 304

"Congress wanted yet another fly-off, this time between the A-10 and the A-7 Corsair II . . . Why couldn't the United States just keeping using them? Skeptics of the A-7 wondered if the fly-off was politically motivated to keep manufacturing jobs in Texas": Douglas Campbell 2003, 98

"In April 1974, the fly-off occurred between the A-7 and A-10 at Fort Riley in Kansas. The A-10 won handily, with pilots testifying in June to the House Armed Services committee their unanimous support for the plane": Douglas Campbell 2003, 106

9. Owning an Elephant

"A fearless and crafty airman, Dilger once found himself in a dogfight with an enemy": Flintoff's Funeral Home and Crematory

"Prior testing had already uncovered hidden problems": Douglas Campbell 2003, 113

"At the time, the estimated cost of thirty-millimeter ammunition was quoted at about eighty-three dollars per round": Burton 1993, 107

10. Attack, Revise, Re-Attack

"In May 1978, the Reformers and their allies, Bob Dilger and Lon Ratley among them, convened in a hotel conference room in Springfield, Virginia": "Proceedings of Seminar on Air Antitank Warfare (May 25–26, 1978)" 1979

"Boyd's philosophical approach had been showcased in two famous papers, 'Destruction and Creation' and 'Patterns of Conflict'": in addition to Boyd's papers, my understanding of the context for his work is greatly informed by Robert Coram's biography of John Boyd

"In education, we refer to this as the hermeneutic circle": Le Cunff 2023

11. Friction

"This argument had been reinforced by Riccioni a few years prior, when he examined the flying experience of fighter jets in Vietnam in a 1978 paper": Fallows 1981, 45

"Suspicious that their phone lines might be tapped, they adopted codenames when placing calls. Sprey's identity was 'Mr. Grau'": Burton 1993, 71–72

PART II

12. "High" Tech

"It was late April 1991, and Sprey was participating in one of a series of congressional hearings": "Performance of High-Technology Equipment in Operation Desert Storm" 1991

"In a hearing held the following week (the same one in which Donald Hicks later criticized Sprey), Senator Gary Hart noted": "U.S. Military Reform After Oper. Desert Storm" 1991

"a cartoon made the rounds suggesting the Warthog be re-designated as a reconnaissance/fighter/observation/attack airplane, or an RFOA-10G": Smallwood 2005, 110

"One former secretary of the Air Force lauded the F-117 as a miracle of precision": Chan et al 1997. Of note, the GAO's full report, "Operation Desert Storm: Evaluation of the Air Campaign," was an invaluable resource for me, and I'm indebted to the remarkably thorough and assiduous work of its authors.

"the Air Force would ultimately purchase 21 B-2s at a cost $2 billion per airplane when accounting for development expenses and a much smaller than planned production order)": Prisco 2020

"One A-10 driver, Captain Paul Johnson, was hit by a surface-to-air missile, which resulted in a twenty-foot-diameter hole in his wing": Neubeck 2019, 68

"'The Boneyard' is where airplanes go to die": "Davis-Monthan Air Force Boneyard in Tucson: Layout, Operations, Tours, and Maps" n.d.

13. To Be Seen

"From July 1992 to December 1995, the GAO compiled their report": The GAO's full illuminating report is listed in the bibliography as Chan et al. 1997.

"Doing such a move was outside the bounds of the F-117 computer's ability to maneuver and could lead to a high-G spin": Wheeler interview

"A-10 drivers had actually painted their airplanes a lighter color but were soon ordered to change back": Wyndham 2020

14. The Joint Strike Fighter

"Publicly, the Air Force reports the cost of the F-22 at 143 million dollars per airplane": Official United States Air Force Website 2022

"but other estimates accounting for all of the initial research and development expenses placed this figure closer to between three and four hundred million dollars": Axe 2011

"one hour of flying time in an F-22 cost about seventy thousand dollars.": Ritsick

"In fact, when then-President Dwight Eisenhower coined the term 'Military Industrial Complex' in his final presidential address on January 17, 1961, he had originally included 'Congressional' in the name": Cockburn 2013

"that it forced the Pentagon and Congress to decide if the JSF had violated the Nunn–McCurdy Amendment, requiring defense contractors to notify Congress of cost overruns": Insinna 2019

"(your average commercial airliner, meanwhile, might keep a distance of five to twenty miles from a storm)": Federal Aviation Administration n.d.

"One 2008 study in The Journal of Business Logistics *used"*: Jones, Shawn R., and George Zsidisin

"considering they were built to last just six thousand flight hours, a limit they eclipsed in 1997.": Jones and Zsidisin 2008

"a move that would presumably save more than four billion dollars": Pendelton 2011

Part III

15. Muck Brown

"Dr. Shay had experienced trauma of his own": Berreby 2003

"Muck's own highly decorated career included the following honors": Auffhammer 2022

16. The Hammer and the Nail

"during a hearing with the Senate Armed Service Committee": "Sen. McCain on the A-10: '. . . Don't Insult My Intelligence!'" n.d.

17. Survivable

"They will kill me": BBC News 2015

"they could no longer count on the United States' search-and-rescue efforts for downed pilots": "ISIS Burns Jordanian Pilot Alive | NBC Nightly News" n.d.

"locked in a cage being burned to death": CBS News 2015

"al-Kasasbeh was twenty-six and recently married": Wagner 2015 (along with all information that follows in this paragraph about al-Kasasbeh)

"Their name comes from the Arabic term for wind, 'haab'": "Haboob: Wind Storm" n.d.

"('haboob' translates to 'strong wind')": Miller et al. 2008

"recalled the exploits of Lieutenant Colonel Kim Campbell": Roza 2022

18. The Fathers of the A-10

"CNN viewers were treated to views": "Remembering the Father of the A-10" 2016

"working on a story for the Project on Government Oversight that would be published the following month": Grazier 2021

In addition to our interview, Grazier offers his moving account of his relationship with Sprey on the POGO website, which can be found at this link: https://www.pogo.org/analysis/2021/08/pogo-remembers-pierre-sprey-pentagon-provocateur-and-mentor.

BIBLIOGRAPHY

"3/26: Face the Nation: Gonzales, Warner, Kirby." *Face the Nation*, March 26, 2023. https://www.cbs.com/shows/video/RKsKTSmmfGyrbMsIY4ZbPfzwO40NCb1d/.

"Abraham Wald and the Missing Bullet Holes: An Excerpt from How Not to Be Wrong by Jordan Ellenberg." *Medium*, July 14, 2016. https://medium.com/@penguinpress/an-excerpt-from-how-not-to-be-wrong-by-jordan-ellenberg-664e708cfc3d.

Air War in Vietnam. Video/DVD. MVD Entertainment Group, 2008. https://video-alexanderstreet-com.ezproxy.oberlin.edu/watch/air-war-in-vietnam.

Anderegg, C. R. "The True Story of Jeremiah Weed." In *Sierra Hotel: Flying Air Force Fighters in the Decade After Vietnam*, 210. Washington, DC: Air Force History and Museums Program, U.S. Air Force, 2001. https://nation.time.com/wp-content/uploads/sites/8/2012/05/the-story-of-jeremiah-weed.pdf.

Anderson, Jack, and Dale Van Atta. "The Hero That Almost Missed the War." *The Washington Post*, March 5, 1991. https://www.washingtonpost.com/archive/local/1991/03/05/the-hero-that-almost-missed-the-war/c5859915-52f7-426e-a664-d0acd1febc0f/.

"Antitank Warfare Seminar: Hans Rudel Transcript," 110. Washington, DC, 1976.

Apple, Carolyn. "World War II: America's Heavy Hitter—The B-17 Flying Fortress." Delaware.gov: HCA Delaware Historical & Cultural Affairs, n.d. https://history.delaware.gov/word-war-ii-americas-heavy-hitter-the-b-17-flying-fortress/.

Arizona Republic. "Where Were We When MIG Came?" May 27, 1967. https://www.newspapers.com/clip/6578392/soviet-defector/.

Astor, Gerald. *The Mighty Eighth: The Air War in Europe as Told by the Men Who Fought It*. New York: Dell Publishing, 1997.

Auffhammer, Tyler. "Tuscola JROTC to Memorialize Fighter Pilot Robert 'Muck' Brown." *The Mountaineer*, November 5, 2022. https://www.themountaineer.com/specialreports/veterans_day/tuscola-jrotc-to-memorialize-fighter-pilot-robert-muck-brown/article_ffa82186-5b79-11ed-bdf7-c74ebb48b85e.html.

Axe, David. "Buyer's Remorse: How Much Has the F-22 Really Cost?" *WIRED*, December 14, 2011. https://www.wired.com/2011/12/f-22-real-cost/.

Ayotte, Kelly A. "Letter from Senator Kelly A. Ayotte (NH) to Secretary of United States Secretary of the Air Force Deborah Lee James," January 24, 2014.

"B-1B Lancer." Accessed March 27, 2023. https://www.af.mil/About-Us/Fact-Sheets/Display/Article/104500/b-1b-lancer/.

Battle of the X-Planes. YouTube. NOVA, 2003. https://www.youtube.com/watch?v=J -9ZfpjSyeM; https://www.pbs.org/wgbh/nova/xplanes/credits.html.

BBC News. "Profile: IS-Held Jordanian Pilot Moaz al-Kasasbeh," February 3, 2015. https://www.bbc.com/news/world-middle-east-31021927.

Berreby, David. "Scientist at Work—Jonathan Shay; Exploring Combat and the Psyche, Beginning with Homer." *The New York Times*, March 11, 2003. https://www.nytimes.com/2003/03/11/science/scientist-work-jonathan-shay-exploring -combat-psyche-beginning-with-homer.html.

Boyd, John. "Destruction and Creation." In *Boyd: The Fighter Pilot Who Changed the Art of War*, by Robert Coram, 451–62. New York: Back Bay Books/Little, Brown and Company, 1976.

Broughton, Jack. *Thud Ridge: Air Battle Action against the Heart of North Vietnam*. New York: Bantam Books, 1985.

Brown, Capt. Robert H. "A Real Hog War: The A-10 in Low-Intensity Conflict." *Airpower Journal* IV, no. 4 (Winter 1990): 54–66.

Brown, Major Robert H. "Expanded A-10 Support of Special Operations: An Analysis of Concept Viability." Command and General Staff College, 1993.

Burgess, Rick, and Zip Rause. *US Navy A-1 Skyraider Units of the Vietnam War*. First edition. Combat Aircraft. Oxford: Osprey Publishing, 2009.

Burkey, Kenneth, *The Philosophy of Literary Form: Studies in Symbolic Action* 3rd ed. 1941. Univ. of California Press, 1973. https://www.thoughtco.com/what-is-burkean -parlor-1689042.

Burton, James G. *The Pentagon Wars: Reformers Challenge the Old Guard*. Annapolis, MD: Naval Institute Press, 1993.

Campbell, Douglas N. *The Warthog and the Close Air Support Debate*. Annapolis, MD: Naval Institute Press, 2003.

Campbell, Kenneth. "Pace Urges Army Built on Science." *The New York Times*, June 7, 1950.

CBS News. "WORLD ISIS Video Purports to Show Jordanian Pilot Burned Alive," February 3, 2015. https://www.cbsnews.com/news/isis-hostage-jordanian-pilot -muath-al-kaseasbeh-purportedly-burned-alive-in-video/.

Chan, Kwai-Cheung, Winslow T. Wheeler, Jonathan R. Tumin, Jeffrey K. Harris, and Carolyn M. Copper. "Operation Desert Storm: Evaluation of the Air Campaign." GAO/NSIAD-97–134 Operation Desert Storm Air Campaign. Washington, DC: U.S. General Accounting Office, June 1997.

Chivers, C. J. *The Gun*. New York: Simon & Schuster, 2010.

Cockburn, Andrew. "Flight of the Discords." *Harper's Magazine*, June 6, 2013. https:// harpers.org/2013/06/flight-of-the-discords/.

———. "Tunnel Vision: Will the Air Force Kill Its Most Effective Weapon?" *Harper's Magazine*, February 2014.

Flintoff's Funeral Home and Crematory. "Col. Robert Dilger," n.d. https://www.flintofts .com/obituaries/Col-Robert-G-Dilger?obId=25785187.

Coram, Robert. *Boyd: The Fighter Pilot Who Changed the Art of War*. New York: Back Bay Books/Little, Brown and Company, 2002.

Corum, James S. "On Airpower, Land Power, and Counterinsurgency Getting Doctrine Right." *JFQ: Joint Force Quarterly*, no. 49 (Spring 2008): 93–97.

"Davis-Monthan Air Force Boneyard in Tucson: Layout, Operations, Tours, and Maps." n.d. https://www.airplaneboneyards.com/davis-monthan-afb-amarg-airplane -boneyard.htm.

Descartes, René. "Rules for the Direction of the Mind." In *The Philosophical Writings of Descartes*, translated by John Cottingham, Robert Stoothoff, and Dugald Murdoch, 1:7–78. Cambridge: Cambridge University Press, 1985.

Douhet, Giulio. *The Command of the Air*. Washington, DC: Air Force History and Museums Program, 1998.

"Executive Summary Proceedings." In *Close Air Support with and without the A-10: Will US Troops Get the Help They Need?* Straus Military Reform Project and the Project on Government Oversight, 2013.

F 105 Thunderchief: Wings & Discovery Documentary. YouTube. Discovery Channel, Wings & Discovery, n.d. https://www.youtube.com/watch?v=8vZE9t65WKQ&t=2092s.

Fallows, James. "Muscle-Bound Superpower: The State of America's Defense." *The Atlantic*, October 1979. https://www.theatlantic.com/magazine/archive/1979/10/muscle -bound-superpower-the-state-of-americas-defense/666965/.

———. *National Defense*. New York: Vintage Books, 1981.

Federal Aviation Administration. "Thunderstorms—Don't Flirt . . . Skirt 'Em." n.d. https: //www.faasafety.gov/files/gslac/library/documents/2011/Aug/56397/FAA%20P -8740-12%20Thunderstorms[hi-res]%20branded.pdf.

"Fulda Gap." In *Britannica Academic*, n.d. https://academic-eb-com.ezproxy.oberlin.edu/ levels/collegiate/article/Fulda-Gap/606278.

Fulda Gap: Battlefield of Cold War Alliances. Lanham, Maryland: Lexington Books, 2018. https://books.google.com/books?hl=en&lr=&id =OwRBDwAAQBAJ&oi=fnd&pg=PP1&dq=fulda+gap&ots=jeBPc1aN0w&sig =JxgZ4QbNVcB0IqL9QV2MeSDT7K8#v=onepage&q&f=false.

Gladwell, Malcolm. "Malcolm Gladwell: The Strange Tale of the Norden Bombsight." TED, October 26, 2011. https://www.youtube.com/watch?v=HpiZTvlWx2g.

———. *The Bomber Mafia: A Dream, a Temptation, and the Longest Night of the Second World War*. New York: Little, Brown and Company, 2021.

Golan, John. "Heinemann's Hot Rod." *Aviation History, Property of Weider History Group*, January 2015.

———. "What Made Heinemann's Hot Rod So Sensational?" HistoryNet, March 3, 3017. https://www.historynet.com/heinemanns-hot-rod/?f.

Grazier, Dan. "New Document Shows How the Air Force Is Starving the A-10 Fleet." *Center for Defense Information at POGO*, September 13, 2021. https://www.pogo .org/analysis/2021/09/new-document-shows-how-the-air-force-is-starving-the-a -10-fleet.

Hammerich, Helmut R. "The Fulda Gap: A Flashpoint of the Cold War between Myth and Reality." In *Fulda Gap: Battlefield of the Cold War Alliances*. London: Lexington Books, 2018.

"Haboob: Wind Storm." In *Haboob*, n.d. https://www.britannica.com/science/haboob.

Hippler, Thomas. "Part 1—Douhet's Strategic Thought." In *Bombing the People: Giulio Douhet and the Foundations of Air Power Strategy, 1884–1939*, 25–148. Cambridge: Cambridge University Press, 2013. https://www-cambridge-org.ezproxy.oberlin .edu/core/books/bombing-the-people/douhets-strategic-thought/2BECABE88A 64EB18F8CE3BC6F5128251.

Hoffman, David E. *The Dead Hand: The Untold Story of the Cold War Arms Race and Its Dangerous Legacy*. New York: Anchor Books, 2009.

Hollway, Don. "How the Low, Slow A-1 Skyraider Earned Its Place in the Hearts of US Troops in Vietnam." *Military Times*, December 15, 2017. https://www .militarytimes.com/off-duty/2017/12/15/how-the-low-slow-a-1-skyraider-earned -its-place-in-the-hearts-of-us-troops-in-vietnam/.

Hughes, Thomas. *Over Lord: General Pete Quesada and the Triumph of Tactical Air Power in World War II*. New York: The Free Press, 1995.

Hutchinson, Harold C. "The Impressive Cheyenne Attack Helicopter Was Way Ahead of Its Time." *We Are the Mighty* (blog), August 1, 2022. https://www.wearethemighty .com/popular/ah-56-cheyenne-helicopter/.

Insinna, Valerie. "Inside America's Dysfunctional Trillion-Dollar Fighter-Jet Program." *The New York Times Magazine*, August 21, 2019. https://www.nytimes.com/2019 /08/21/magazine/f35-joint-strike-fighter-program.html.

International Atomic Energy Agency. "Depleted Uranium." n.d. https://www.iaea.org/ topics/spent-fuel-management/depleted-uranium.

Isaacson, Walter. "U.S. Defense Spending: Are Billions Being Wasted?" *Time*, March 7, 1983. https://content.time.com/time/covers/0,16641,19830307,00.html.

"ISIS Burns Jordanian Pilot Alive | NBC Nightly News." YouTube. NBC News, n.d. https://www.youtube.com/watch?v=cfdasSFz1v0.

James, Deborah Lee. "Letter from United States Secretary of the Air Force Deborah Lee James to Senator Kelly A. Ayotte," February 12, 2014.

Jayne, Randy. "The Last Prop Fighter: Sandys, Hobos, Rifeflies, Zorros, and Spads." *Air & Space Power Journal*, June 1, 2017. https://web-s-ebscohost-com.ezproxy .oberlin.edu/ehost/pdfviewer/pdfviewer?vid=0&sid=76ee791d-1093-4b99-884f -d489c7a5679e%40redis.

Johnson, E. R. "Able Dog." *Aviation History, Property of Weider History Group*, September 2008.

Jones, Minnie L. "William 'Billy' Mitchell — 'The Father of the United States Air Force.'" U.S. Army, October 17, 2019. https://www.army.mil/article/33680 /william_billy_mitchell_the_father_of_the_united_states_air_force#:~:text=In %20November%201925%2C%20Mitchell%20was,discredit%20upon%20the %20military%20service.%22.

Jones, Shawn R., and George Zsidisin. "Performance Implications of Product Life Cycle Extension: The Case of the A-10 Aircraft." *Journal of Business Logistics* 29, no. 2 (September 2008): 189–214.

Junger, Sebastian. *Tribe: On Homecoming and Belonging*. New York: Twelve, 2016.

Kaplan, Fred M. *The Wizards of Armageddon*. New York: Simon & Schuster, 1983.

Kaplan, Robert D. *Hog Pilots, Blue Water Grunts: The American Military in the Air, at Sea, and on the Ground.* New York: Vintage Books, 2008.

Le Cunff, Anne-Laure. "The Hermeneutic Circle: A Key to Critical Reading." *Ness Labs* (blog). Accessed March 27, 2023. https://nesslabs.com/hermeneutic-circle.

LIFE. "New York Bomb: Norden Company Takes over Circus to See Bomb Hit Pickle in Barrel," April 26, 1943.

Magee, John Gillespie. "Letter to Parents." September 3, 1941. John Magee Papers, Library of Congress, Washington, DC. Manuscript. In *Respectfully Quoted: A Dictionary of Quotations Requested from the Congressional Research Service*, edited by Suzy Platt, 117–18. Washington, DC: Library of Congress, 1989.

Mapleshade. "About Us," n.d. http://www.mapleshadestore.com/aboutus.php.

Menand, Louis. "Fat Man: Herman Kahn and the Nuclear Age." *The New Yorker,* June 19, 2005. https://www.newyorker.com/magazine/2005/06/27/fat-man.

Mestelle, Ryan. "Jinks Mission Journal, Mission: 100," April 9, 2015.

Miller, Donald. L. *Masters of the Air: America's Bomber Boys Who Fought the Air War against Nazi Germany.* New York: Simon & Schuster, 2006.

Miller, Kent. "Skyraider 2? The Air Force May Bring Back Vietnam-Style Combat Plane." *Air Force Times,* October 17, 2017. https://www.airforcetimes.com/news/your-air-force/2017/10/17/skyraider-2-the-air-force-may-bring-back-vietnam-style-combat-plane/.

Miller, Steven D., Arunas P. Kuciauskas, Ming Liu, Qiang Ji, Jeffrey S. Reid, Daniel W. Breed, Annette L. Walker, and Abdulla Al Mandoos. "Haboob Dust Storms of the Southern Arabian Peninsula." *Journal of Geophysical Research: Atmospheres* 113, no. D1 (January 12, 2008). https://agupubs.onlinelibrary.wiley.com/doi/full/10.1029/2007JD008550.

Morris, Errol, director. *The Fog of War.* Prime Video (streaming online video), Historical Documentary, Military and War. Sony Pictures Classics, 2004.

Mustard. *The World's Fastest Bomber: The XB-70 Valkyrie.* YouTube, n.d. https://www.youtube.com/watch?v=Yl32c352thE.

Mutza, Wayne. *The A-1 Skyraider in Vietnam: The Spad's Last War.* Atglen, PA: Schiffer Military, 2003.

National Museum of the US Air Force. "GAU-8/A Avenger," April 16, 2010. https://web.archive.org/web/20100416063452/http://www.nationalmuseum.af.mil/factsheets/factsheet.asp?id=1019.

Neubeck, Ken. *A-10 Thunderbolt II: Fairchild Republic's Warthog at War.* Legends of Warfare: Aviationzsx. Atglen, PA: Schiffer Military, 2019.

Newman, Rick, and Don Shepperd. *Bury Us Upside Down: The Misty Pilots and the Secret Battle for the Ho Chi Minh Trail.* New York: Ballantine Books, 2006.

Nordquist, Richard. "What Is the Burkean Parlor?" *ThoughtCo.* (blog), August 10, 2018. https://www.thoughtco.com/what-is-burkean-parlor-1689042.

Norman, Don. *The Design of Everyday Things.* Expanded and revised edition. New York: Basic Books, 2013.

Official United States Air Force Website. "F-22 Raptor." August 2022. https://www.af.mil/About-Us/Fact-Sheets/Display/Article/104506/f-22-raptor/.

Ogorkiewicz, Richard. *Tanks: 100 Years of Evolution*. Oxford: Osprey Publishing, 2015.

Ormes, Harold. *Go Ugly Early: A-10 Warthog Close Air Support Fighter*. Monee, IL: CreateSpace, 2021.

Pendelton, John H. "Force Structure: Preliminary Observations on Air Force A-10 Divestment." GAO-15–698R. Washington, DC: U.S. Government Accountability Office, June 25, 2011.

"Performance of High-Technology Equipment in Operation Desert Storm." Washington, DC, April 22, 1991. https://ift.onlinelibrary.wiley.com/doi/10.1111/1541–4337.12024.

Prisco, Jacopo. "B-2 Spirit: The $2 Billion Flying Wing." *CNN.com*, January 29, 2020.

"Proceedings of Seminar on Air Antitank Warfare (May 25–26, 1978)," 169. Springfield, VA: Battelle, Columbus Laboratories, Tactical Technology Center, 1979.

Ratley III, Lonnie Otis. "A Comparison of the USAF Projected A-10 Employment in Europe and the Luftwaffe Schlachtgeschwader Experience on the Eastern Front in World War Two." Naval Postgraduate School, 1977. Lon Ratley's personal archives.

Rausa, R. M. "Portrait of a Warplane." *Naval Aviation News*, August 2001. https://web-s-ebscohost-com.ezproxy.oberlin.edu/ehost/detail/detail?vid=0&sid=188229eb-0625-4bf4-b062-93691136c39e%40redis&bdata=JnNpdGU9ZWhvc3QtbGl2Z SZzY29wZT1zaXRl#AN=5124192&db=f5h.

Rausa, Rosario. *Skyraider: The Douglas A-1 "Flying Dump Truck."* Charleston, SC: The Nautical & Aviation Publishing Company, 2001.

Real A-10C CAS Mission HUD/Litening Unclassified FOUO. YouTube. Lexat News, 2013. https://www.youtube.com/watch?v=29UnZdX42lE.

Reed, Fred. "Let's Reform the Military Reformers." *The Washington Post*, October 11, 1987, sec. Op-Ed. https://www.washingtonpost.com/archive/opinions/1987/10/11/lets-reform-the-military-reformers/64b9fed4-dc2a-4ef0-ae61-5d459254d866/.

"Remembering the Father of the A-10." YouTube. CNN, March 21, 2016. https://www.youtube.com/watch?v=ZGRhkA9OfA4.

Riccioni, E. E., "Information Circular on GE-430 Gun, and Maverick," October 31, 1978. Pierre Sprey's personal archives.

Riccioni, Everest E. "The Blitzfighter Concept for a New Air-to-Ground Aircraft." Slides, May 1981.

Rich, Ben R., and Leo Janos. *Skunk Works: A Personal Memoir of My Years at Lockheed*. New York: Back Bay Books/Little, Brown and Company, 1994.

Richards, Chet. "Boyd's Ooda Loop." *Necesse* 5, no. 1 (2020): 142–65.

Ritsick, Colin. "How Much Does an F-22 Raptor Cost." Military Machine, February 1, 2021. https://militarymachine.com/f-22-cost/

Roza, David. "How an Air Force A-10 Pilot Pulled off a Miracle Landing with Much of Her Tail Shot Off." *Task & Purpose*, March 11, 2022. https://taskandpurpose.com/news/air-force-a-10-pilot-kim-campbell/.

Rudel, Hans Ulrich. *Stuka Pilot*. London: Black House Publishing Ltd, 2016.

Rumerman, Judy. "Alexander de Seversky and Seversky Aircraft." U.S. Centennial of Flight Commission, n.d. https://centennialofflight.net/essay/Aerospace/Seversky/Aero42.htm.

Schudel, Matt. "Pierre Sprey, Pentagon Analyst Who Battled Brass to Produce A-10 Warplane, Dies at 83." *The Washington Post*, August 20, 2021. https://www .washingtonpost.com/local/obituaries/pierre-sprey-dead/2021/08/20/fe995430 -ff6e-11eb-ba7e-2cf966e88e93_story.html.

"Sen. McCain on the A-10: " . . . Don't Insult My Intelligence!" YouTube, n.d. https:// www.youtube.com/watch?v=_up7IHd3LDs.

Sherman, Charles D. "Uranium Bullets: NATO Loves and Fears the New Ammunition." *International Herald Tribune*, 1979. Original copy accessed via Pierre Sprey's personal archives.

Simonds, Merilyn. *Gutenberg's Fingerprint: Paper, Pixels and the Lasting Impression of Books*. Toronto, Ontario, Canada: ECW Press, 2017. https://ebookcentral.proquest .com/lib/oberlin/reader.action?docID=5180512.

Smallwood, William L. *Warthog: Flying the A-10 in the Gulf War*. Sterling, VA: Potomac Books, 2005.

Spartacus. "How Washington Deals with Defense Facts and Other Inconvenient Intrusions: The Revealing Story of GAO's Desert Storm Air Campaign Report," n.d.

Spinney, Franklin C. "Defense Facts of Life." Washington, DC: Defense Technical Information Center, December 5, 1980.

Sprey, Pierre. "Re: Birth of the Video That Helped Us Save the A-10," May 14, 2020.

———. "Re: Does Lockdown Work? Expect a Tsunami of Fraudulent Statistics," April 23, 2020.

———. "Evaluating Weapons: Sorting the Good from the Bad." In *The Pentagon Labyrinth: 10 Short Essays to Help You through It. Edited by Winslow T. Wheeler*, 141. Washington, D.C.: Center for Defense Information, 2011.

———. "Memorandum for Dr. Selin, F15 Meeting at Wright Patterson," October 22, 1969. Pierre Sprey's personal archives.

———. "Memorandum for Dr. Tucker, DRPC RDT&E Paper," September 9, 1969. Pierre Sprey's personal archives.

———. "Memorandum for Dr. Tucker, Subject: Resignation," October 23, 1970. Pierre Sprey's personal archives.

———. "Notes on Close Air Support," April 18, 1968. Pierre Sprey's personal archives.

Staff Writer. "T-62." www.MilitaryFactory.com, May 24, 2022. https://www .militaryfactory.com/armor/detail.php?armor_id=21.

Sweetman, Bill, and Lindsay Peacock. *Combat Aircraft: A-10*. New York: Crescent Books, 1992.

The Insane Engineering of the A-10 Warthog. YouTube. Real Engineering, n.d. https://www .youtube.com/watch?v=wk6Qr6OO5Xo.

The New York Times. "Soviet Flier Asks for Asylum," June 3, 1967. https://www.nytimes .com/1967/06/03/archives/soviet-flier-asks-for-asylum-in-us.html.

The Smithsonian's National Air and Space Museum. "Stalin's 'Essential Aircraft': Ilyushin Il-2 in WWII." September 26, 2016. https://airandspace.si.edu/stories/editorial/ stalins-ilyushin-il-2-shturmovik.

Tillman, Barrett. "Back to Schweinfurt." *Air&Space Forces Magazine*, August 31, 2018. https://www.airandspaceforces.com/article/back-to-schweinfurt/.

TIME. "Armed Forces: How It Happened," April 16, 1965. https://content.time.com/time/subscriber/article/0,33009,841817,00.html.

Treichler, Don. *Night Hecklers: VC-35's Korean Air Campaign during the Hours of Darkness*. Fifth edition. Monee, IL: Don Treichler, 2017.

Tucker, Gardiner L. "Mr. Pierre Sprey," November 3, 1970. Pierre Sprey's personal archives.

"U.S. Military Reform After Oper. Desert Storm." Rayburn House Office Building, Washington, DC, April 30, 1991. https://www.c-span.org/video/?17753-1/us-military-reform-oper-desert-storm.

Vizcarra, Mark, director. *Thud Pilots*. Speed & Angels Productions, 2018.

Wagner, Meg. "Muath Al-Kaseasbeh, Jordanian Pilot Burned Alive by ISIS, Always Dreamed of Flying Planes His Close-Knit Family Says." *New York Daily News*, February 3, 2015. https://www.nydailynews.com/news/world/jordanian-pilot-killed-isis-dreamt-flying-article-1.2101801.

Watson, R. A. "René Descartes." *Encyclopedia Britannica*, March 27, 2023. https://www.britannica.com/biography/Rene-Descartes.

Welch, Ivan B. "Fulda Gap." In *Encyclopedia of World Geography*. New York: Facts on File, Inc. Golson Books, Ltd., 2005. https://archive.org/stream/encyclopediaofworldgeography_201909/Encyclopedia%20of%20World%20Geography_djvu.txt.

Wheeler, Winslow. *Mr. Smith Is Dead: No One Stands in the Way as Congress Laces Post-Sept. 11 Defense Bills with Pork*. Washington, DC: Center for Defense Information, 2022.

———. *The Wastrels of Defense: How Congress Sabotages U.S. Security*. Annapolis, MD: Naval Institute Press, 2004.

White, Harry J., and Selmo Tauber. *Systems Analysis*. Philadelphia: W. B. Saunders Company, 1969.

Wilson, W. B. *The Fulda Gap*, n.d. https://www.blackhorse.org/wp-content/uploads/2018/10/fuldagap.pdf.

Wyndham, Buck. *Hogs in the Sand: A Gulf War A-10 Pilot's Combat Journal*. Virginia Beach, VA: Köehler Books, 2020.

Zabecki, David T. *Journal of Cold War Studies* 18, no. 3 (Summer 2016). https://muse-jhu-edu.ezproxy.oberlin.edu/article/632300.

INDEX

Page locators in italics indicate figures.

9/11 tragedy, 170

A-1 Skyraider (Douglas), 49–52, 77, *123*, 168
A-4 Skyhawk, 51–52, 62n1, 70
A-6 Intruder, 70
A-7 Corsair II, 90, 97
A-7 Crusader, 70
A-9 prototype, 78–79
A-10 Thunderbolt II, 134, *212–16*; at air shows, 210–11, *215*; ammo drum "trigger plates," 79; attempts to retire, 156–57, 166, 175–79, 183–86; as black sheep airplane, 120–21; "bottoming out" at seventy-five feet, 9; bubble canopy, 52, 66–67, 96, 135; cult status of, 12; damage inflicted by, 52, 61, 94–95, 134–36; damage sustained by, 5, 11, 52, 78–79, 136, 195; and "destructive deduction," 108; engines, 5, 77–79, 96, 135; as exhibit of duality, 12; fixed wing, 5; flight controls, manual reversion, 5, 66, 67, 78, 80, 195; as "Forrest Gump" of airplanes, 12; Hawgsmoke competition, 179–80; hydraulic controls, 195; landing gear, 79–80, 196–97; loiter time, 167; low political profile, 169; maintenance of, 72, 79, 105, 136, 199; maneuverability, 104–5; nicknames ("The Warthog," "The Hog," "The Flying Gun"), 5; "Night Hogs," 134–35, 146; night vision goggles (NVGs) on, 169–74, 185; paint schemes, 146; piecemeal upgrades, 156–57; retirement of, 136, 169, 204; rudders, elevators, and ailerons, 5; in service, 11; special operations, 167–70, 174, 176; as "stealthy," 135; successor proposal, 107, 117–18; supply chain for, 154–55; survivability, 5, 11, 79–80, 136, 194–99; targeting pod, 174; turning radius, 66, 105, 211; unprepared airfield operations, 173–74; versatility of, 156,

167; as weapon for the future, 169; wingspan, 52, 198. *See also* A-X research; GAU-8 Avenger cannon

"Aerial Attack Study" (Boyd), 33

Afghanistan: Bagram Air Base, 173, *214*; Marah Valley, 3–13, 23

AH-56 "Cheyenne," 24–25, 70–71

AH-64 Apache, 71

Air Corps Act of 1926, 18

Air Corps Tactical School (Maxwell Field, Montgomery, Alabama), 18

aircraft performance, 33–34

Air Defense Command, 50

Air Force Doctrine, Concepts, and Objectives Directorate, 15

Air Force Operating Center, 156

Air Force Scientific Advisory Board in, 67

Air Force Weapons School, 165–66, 190n4

Air Operations Center, 196

Air Power Journal, 167

air-to-air combat, 35, 37, 135, 141, 143, 150, 153, 171–72

air-to-air refueling, 74, 194

air-to-ground weapons, 82–83, 101

AK-47 assault rifle, 60

Al Assad air base (Iraq), 196–98

Allison, Jack "Coach," 169–70

American exceptionalism, 35, 36

ammunition: twenty-millimeter round, 61; thirty-millimeter round, 9, 10, 35, 61, 94–95; 105-millimeter, 168; ammo loader, 101–2; armor-piercing rounds, 59; cost of, 102; DU (depleted uranium), 94–95, 95–96n1, 99–101, 105; testing, 98–102, 105

Analytic Services, Inc., 49

Anderegg, C. R., 203–4n1

Anderson, Jack, 134

Apollo 13 mission, 171

Arlington National Cemetery, 201

Armament Laboratory (Eglin Air Force Base), 82

armor, 40–41

"armored-column-cover," 23

Army Air Corps, 40, 97; Statistical Control Office, 41

Army-Navy "E" award for excellence, 19

Aspin, Paul, 129, 133

Avenger cannon. *See* GAU-8 Avenger cannon

Aviation History Magazine, 51–52

awards and medals, 10, 19, 102, 180n5

Axe, David, 149n1

A-X research, 49, 50, 55, 59, 61–67; Concept Formulation Packet, 65–66; engine design, 77; request for proposals, 74. *See also* A-10 Thunderbolt II

Ayotte, Kelly, 176, 179

B-1 bomber, 87–89, 133, 175, 183–86, 189
B-1B Lancer ("the Bone"), 4–5, *123*
B-17 "Flying Fortress," 15, 16, 19, 21, 24, 27, 39, 83, *124*
B-26 Invader, 185
B-29 bomber, 42; "Enola Gay," 136n2
B-52 bomber, 145
Baghdad Nuclear Research Facility (Osirak, Iraq), 145
Bagram Air Base (Afghanistan), 173, *214*
The Baltimore Sun, 13
Beil, David A., 70
"beyond-visual-range" combat, 153
"The Blitzfighter Concept of a New Air-to-Ground Aircraft" (Riccioni), 116–17
Boeding, Brian "Master," 183, 186–90, 199, *214, 215*
Boeing, 149
"Bomber Mafia," 87–88, 94
bombing: inaccuracy of, World War II, 19–22; long-range strategic bombing (interdiction bombing), 16–18, 22, 27–28; polarity of theory, 22; target selection, 16–19, 21; World War I, 16–18
bombs, 39, 53, 62, 145–48; hit rate, 16, 22, 130–31; laser-guided, 130, 131; nuclear, 57

"The Boneyard" (309th Aerospace Maintenance and Regeneration Group), 136, 136n2
Bonner, Jeff "Bones," 80n2
bootstraps innovation, 12
Bowman, Bradley, 176
Boyd, John, 33–36, 82, 84–91, 106–10, 119, 169–70; at congressional hearings, 133; "Destruction and Creation," 106–9; "Patterns of Conflict," 106, 109
Bradley, Omar, 24
Bradley Fighting Vehicle, 120
Broughton, Jack, 57, 62–63, 65
Brown, Anna, 167, 175, 179, 180
Brown, Martha, 166, 174–75, 178–79
Brown, Robert "Muck," 165–81, 185–86, *217*
bubble canopy, 49, 52, 66–67, 96, 135
Bulge, Battle of, 114
Burbage, C. T. "Tom," 150–51
Burton, Jim, 117, 119, 120
"button hook turn," 105

C-5 Galaxy, 31, 69
C-130, 167–68, 174, 209
Campbell, Douglas, 90
Campbell, Kim, 195
Camp Pendleton, 119
car accidents, analyses of, 42
Carter, Jimmy, 139, 167

Center for Defense
Information, 152
Central Intelligence Agency
(CIA), 37
Chan, Kwai-Cheung, 141
Cheyenne helicopter, 24–25,
70–71
Chivers, C. J., 60
Christie, Tom, 33n3, 81–87, 89,
96, 100, 106, 110
Civil War, 60
Clausewitz, Carl von, 114, 174
close-air support, 5–7, 87, 93;
Air Force deal with Army, 15;
B-1 as, 183–85; as community,
186, 190, 209; as contradiction
of Air Force ideology, 15–16;
ineffectiveness of in Vietnam,
16, 25; long wait times for, 16,
20; slow speed as factor, 66; in
World War II, 20, 23
"Close Air Support with and
without the A-10: Will U.S.
Troops Get the Help They
Need?" (seminar), 177–78, 188
CNN, 201
Cockburn, Andrew, 45, 154,
183–84
Cold War: Fulda Gap concerns,
27, 32, 98, 204; intelligence, 30;
and West Point training, 57
Command of the Air (Douhet),
16–18
complex systems, 39–40, 73,
114–15

computer modeling programs,
72–73
concurrency, 151–52
Congress, 199; "Close Air Support
with and without the A-10:
Will U.S. Troops Get the
Help They Need?" seminar,
177–78, 188; congressional
hearings, 129, 131–33, 136–
37; House Armed Services
Committee, 90; Senate Armed
Services Committee, 70, 184;
Senate Foreign Relations
Committee, 139
Conrad, Katherine "Slam,"
207–10, 218
Coram, Robert, 33–34, 69, 109
COVID-19 pandemic, 206
Cruise, Tom, 140

Davis-Monthan Air Force Base
(Tucson, Arizona), 136n2
Defense Advanced Researched
Projects Agency (DARPA), 199
defense contractors: A-X request
for proposals, 74; competitive
ammunition testing, 102;
"fly before buy" procurement,
69–70; fly-off between
airplane manufacturers, 69–70,
77–78, 90; Nunn-McCurdy
Amendment, 152; testing by,
153–54
"Defense Facts of Life" (Spinney),
113, 115, 140, 144, 146

defense spending, 70, 74, 82, 85–89, 113, 116, 148, 152, 157, 202; McNamara as auditor, 42–43; Sprey's memo, 27–28, 32

delta-wing design, 52

Dempsey, Martin E., 176

Department of Defense, 30–31, 47, 107, 141, 146–47, 156. *See also* Pentagon

Descartes, René, 40

Desert Storm, 131, 140–47, 169, 177

The Design of Everyday Things (Norman), 113

design-to-cost philosophy, 74

"Destruction and Creation" (Boyd), 106–9

deterrence theory, 30

"dialectic cycle/engine," 108–9

Dickinson, Bill, 133

Dilger, Bob, 93–94, 96–102, 103, 105, 110, 117, 120

dogfighting, 33–36

Douglas, Donald, 51, 177

Douhet, Giulio, 16–19, 21, 28

drivers (A-10 pilots), 5–13, 44–45n1, 80n2; Hawgsmoke, 179–80; Iraq incident, 194–99; night vision goggles (NVGs), 169–74, 185; "sandwiching," 134; Scorpion Helmet-Mounted Cueing System, 156; transferred to F-16s, 175. *See also specific drivers*

Drowley, Michael "Johnny Bravo," 80n2, 190n4

DU (depleted uranium), 94–95, 95–96n1, 99–101, 105

Edwards Air Force Base (California), 77–78

Eglin Air Force Base (Florida), 82, 83, 100

Eisenhower, Dwight, 151

Ellenberg, Jordan, 40

energy-maneuverability (E-M) theory, 33–35, 82, 84, 85

engines: afterburner, 150; liquid-cooled, 23; radial, 23; turbofan, 5, 77–78, 96, 135

England Air Force Base (Louisiana), 167

Enthoven, Alain, 33, 43

Epatko, Vasily Ilyich, 36–37

"escapable" aircraft, 12

Estienne, J. E., 58

F-1 Mirages, 4, 6

F4F-Wildcat, 29

F-4 Phantom, 93, 97

F-5 Freedom Fighter, 74

F6F-Hellcat, 29

F-14 Tomcat, 47–48, 140

F-15E Strike Eagle, 6, 47–48, 117, 143, 144, 189

F-16 Fighting Falcon, 6, 28, 89–90, 133, 143, 145, 171–72, 195–96, 175

F-18, 140, 195–96, 209

F-22 Raptor, 149
F-35 Lightning II (JSF), 149–56,
  175, 188, 204–5, *213*
F-100 Super-Sabre, 25
F-105 Thunderchief ("The Thud"),
  36–37, 62–66, 74, 82–83, 90,
  97, *124. See also* Vietnam War
F-111 "Aardvark," 145, 150
F-117A "Nighthawk" ("the
  Stealth"), 130–32, 140–46, *159*
Fairchild Hiller Corporation, 74
Fairchild-Republic, 74, 77, 90,
  120–21; Long Island factory,
  139; and supply chain for A-10,
  154–55
"fallen man" maneuver, 204
Fallows, James, 50
FATTS. *See* Stone, Andy
  ("FATTS")
Fellers, Walt, 77
fighter-bombers, 25
"Fighter Mafia," 87, 100–101, 116,
  119, 188, 203. *See also* Military
  Reformers
Fighter Weapons School (Nellis
  Air Force Base, Nevada), 6,
  33, 171
fixed-force structure, 89–90
Flick, Ridge "KELSO," 190n4
flight controls, manual reversion,
  5, 66, 67, 78, 80, 195
fly-off between airplane
  manufacturers, 69–70,
  77–78, 90
The Fog of War (documentary), 42

Ford, Gerald, 90
Ford Motor Company, 42, 51, 81
Forward Air Control (FAC), 25
"friction," 114
friendly fire: and B-1, 183–84,
  186; and communication
  between air and ground, 23;
  fears of, 7, 9–10n1, 10, 178; in
  World War II, 20
fuel tanks, self-sealing, 63, 66, 79
Fulda Gap, 27, 32, 98, 204
future: A-10 as weapon for,
  169; focus on to exclusion of
  present, 63–64, 87–88, 113–14
F-X fighter development, 35, 36

Gatling, Richard, 60–61
GAU-8 Avenger cannon, 9, 10,
  93, 94, 96, 101, 105, 116, *159,*
  168n1, 171, *216*
General Accounting Office
  (GAO), 140–47
General Electric (GE), 60–61, 81
Germany: Blitzkrieg and anti-
  tank strategies, 98; Panzer
  tank divisions, 23–24; Tiger
  tanks, 144. *See also* Rudel, Hans
  Ulrich
Gnat (British plane), 116, 118
Golan, John, 51
"gold-plating," 48, 51, 70, 73–74
Gray, Paul, 50
Grazier, Dan, 201–204
Greeks and Romans, 40

Grumman Aircraft Engineering Corporation, 29–30
"Gs" (forces of gravity), 34, 66, 97, 105
Gulf War veterans, 95n1
guns: 30-millimeter cannon, 79, 80, 91, 101; 75 millimeter, 58; 115-millimeter "smoothbore" barrel, 59; AK-47 assault rifle, 60; in fighter jets, Boyd's advocacy of, 34; four-barrel Gatling gun, 117; Gatling gun, 5, 60–61; GAU-8 Avenger cannon, 9, 10, 93, 94, 96, 101, 105, 116, *159*, 168n1, 171, *216*; M-16 assault rifle, 75; Vulcan cannon, 60–61, 81
The Gun (Chivers), 60
gyroscopes, 20, 74

haboobs (sandstorms), 194–96
Hagel, Chuck, 176
Hallock, Richard, 76–77, 89, 109
Harper's, 154, 183
Harriers, 4, 6, 70, 149
Hart, Gary, 133, 137n3
Harvard Business School, 41
Hawgsmoke competition, 179–80
Heinemann, Ed, 51–52, 62n1, 70, 74, 77, *123*
Heisenberg, Werner, 108
helicopters, 15, 175; AH-56 Cheyenne, 24–25, 70–71; AH-64 Apache, 71; Apache, 174; Blackhawk, 173; Chinook, 185
hermeneutic circle, 107
Hewlett-Packard, 71
Hicks, Donald, 132, 133
Higgins boats, 22
high-tech, 129–33, 177; General Accounting Office (GAO) audit, 140–47. *See also* F-117A "Nighthawk" ("the Stealth")
Hillaker, Harry, 87n2
historical approach, 77
Hitch, Charlie, 43
Hitler, Adolf, 55
Hogs in the Sand (Wyndham), 134–35
Hooton, Gordon, 51
Hoover, Clint "Voodoo," 194–95
Horner, Chuck, 131, 133–34
How Not to Be Wrong: The Power of Mathematical Thinking (*Ellenberg*), 40
Hudson Institute, 30
Hughes, Howard, 51
Hughes, Thomas Alexander, 20, 23
human-centered design, 44, 44–45n1
Hussein, Saddam, 129, 143, 198

Ilyushin-2 Sturmovik, 66n2
infantry, 58; on Capitol Hill, 189–90; in Marah Valley, Afghanistan, 3–13, 23
Insinna, Valerie, 154
Institute for Defense Analysis, 16

interchangeable parts, 78–79
interdiction bombing, 16
International Atomic Energy Agency (IAEA), 95n1
Iran hostages, 167
Iraq, 129–30, 134, 140–47
ISIS, 193–94

James, Deborah Lee, 179, 184
Javits, Jacob, 139
Johnson, Lyndon, 28, 43–44
Johnson, Paul, 136
Johnson-McConnell Agreement of 1966, 15–16, 15n1
Joint Munitions Effectiveness Manual, 32, 82
Joint Strike Fighter (JSF) (F-35), 149–52, *213. See also* F-35 Lightning II (JSF)
Joint Terminal Attack Controller (JTAC), 3, 6, 189, 190n4
Journal of Business Logistics, 154–55
Junger, Sebastian, 208, 211
Junkers Ju-87G dive-bomber ("Stuka"), 52–53, 59

Kahn, Herman, 30
Kaplan, Fred, 41, 42
al-Kasasbeh, Muath, 193–95
Kassebaum, Nancy Landon, *161*
Kay, Avery, 15–16, 21, 24–26, 49; flyover at funeral of, 201–3; offers job to Sprey, 37–38
KC-135 tanker, 194

Kellet, Wallace, 74
Kennedy, John F., 41, 42
Khamis Mushayt air base (Saudi Arabia), 144
Kiba, Charlie, 189n3
Kirby, John, 95–96n1
Kishlein, Sam, 81
Korean War, 35, 50; tank invasion by North Korea, 59

landing gear, 79–80, 196–97
Langley Air Force Base (Virginia), 170
LASTE (Low Altitude Safety Target Enhancement), 168, 168n1
Leipzig, Battle of (1813), 27
LeMay, Curtis, 42
Leopold, Ray, 81, 86–89
lethality, 79, 96, 114–16, 168n1
"Let's Reform the Military Reformers" (Reed), 119–20
linear programs, 31, 39
lines of production, targeting, 21–22
Ling-Temco-Vought, 90
live-fire survivability testing, 72–73
Lockheed, 130, 142–43, 145
Lockheed Martin, 149
Loh, John M., 143
Lot Acceptance Verification Program, 96
"Lt Col Robert H. 'Muck' Brown Award," 179–80

M-16 assault rifle, 75

M46 tanks, 99

MacArthur, Douglas, 19–20

Magee, John Gillespie, Jr., 180–81

maneuverability, 104–5; energy-maneuverability (E-M) theory, 33–35, 82, 84, 85; of F-117, 143–44

Mapleshade recording studio, 120, 152

Marine "Stryker" troop transports, 198

Marks, John, 134

Maryland Air National Guard, 185, 188, 207, 211

Masters of the Air (Miller), 18n3, 19

mathematics: differential equations, 40; operations research, 30, 40–42; vector analysis, 40

Mattingly, Ken, 171

Maverick missile, 83–84, 100–101, 135, 169

"Maverick" missile, 83–84, 100–101, 135

Maxwell Field, Montgomery, Alabama, 18

McCain, John, 184–85, 189

McConnell, John P., 25, 37

McConnell Air Force Base (Kansas), 139

McLucas, John, 71–72

McNamara, Robert, 12, 30, 41–45, 150; at Ford Motor Company,

42; as lead auditor for U.S. military, 42–43; memo to Johnson, 43–44; "total package procurement," 69. *See also* Whiz Kids (Pentagon)

McNurlin, Tom "Narly," 155–56

Mestelle, Ryan "Jinks," 194–95, *213*

MiGs, 33; and F-105 "Thud" losses, 36–37, 62–66; MiG-17, 36–37, 93; MiG-21, 35; North Korean, 35

"Military Industrial Complex," 151

"Military Industrial Congressional Complex," 151

Military Reformers: defined, 87n3; as "dialectic engine," 109; lectures delivered by, 111; media criticism of, 119–20; meeting of and early work, 81–91; members of, 86–87; and OODA Loop, 109; "Reform Movement," 102, 117, 137n3; and Rudel, 103; sense of being spied on, 117–18; "Wheel of Satan," 117–18; willingness to be challenged, 111–12. *See also* Christie, Tom; Dilger, Bob; "Fighter Mafia"; Hallock, Richard; Ratley, Lon; Spinney, Franklin "Chuck"; Sprey, Pierre

Miller, Donald, 18n3, 19

missiles, 63; limitations of, 35; Maverick, 83–84, 100–101, 135, 169
Mitchell, Billy, 17–18
Morris, Errol, 42
Muck. *See* Brown, Robert "Muck"
"Musclebound Superpower" (Fallows), 115
Myers, Chuck, 89

Nagle, Dan "Fife," 204
Napoleon Bonaparte, 37
National Defense (Fallows), 50, 115
National Defense Authorization Act (2014), 179
National Guard and Reserve Equipment Appropriations, 156
Naval Postgraduate School (Monterey, California), 97
Nellis Air Force Base (Las Vegas), 6; 422nd Test and Evaluation Squadron, 170
Nellis Range (Nevada desert), 98–100
Nelson, William, 20
New York Times, 57, 178
New York Times Magazine, 154
night vision goggles (NVGs), 169–74, 185
Nimitz nuclear-powered aircraft carrier, 139
Nixon, Richard, 71
Norden, Carl, 19

Norden Mark 15 bombsight, 19, 20
Norman, Don, 113
Norris, Tom "TC," 44–45n1
Northrop, 74, 77
Northrop, Jack, 51
nuclear warfare, 22–23, 32, 62
Nunn-McCurdy Amendment, 152

Office of Operation Test and Evaluation, 120
Ogorkiewicz, Richard, 58
Olson, Patrick, 136
On Thermonuclear War (Kahn), 30
OODA Loop (Observe, Orient, Decide, Act), 109, 115, 201
operations research, 30, 40–42
Over Lord (Hughes), 20, 23

P-47 Thunderbolt, 23, 49, 74, 76, *125*
P-51 Mustang, 23, 77, 118
Pace, Frank C., Jr., 57–58, 59
Packard, Dave, 71
"Patterns of Conflict" (Boyd), 106
Patton, George S., 27
Peacock, Lindsay, 175n4
Pentagon, 13, 43; Sprey declared "dignitary" by, 201; Sprey locked out of special access to, 120; Sprey's resignation from, 75–76. *See also* Department of Defense; Whiz Kids (Pentagon)

The Pentagon Labyrinth (ed. Wheeler), 152–54
The Pentagon Wars (Burton), 117, 119
Persian Gulf War, 129–33
Philco electronics, 81
Philco-Ford, 81
Phillis, Stephen, 136
"Pierre Sprey buzz saw," 36
pilots: difficulty seeing the ground, 6–10, 23–25, 49–51, 66, 75, 76; tactical vs. test, 72. *See also* drivers (A-10 pilots); specific pilots
Pope Field (Cumberland County, North Carolina), 170
Powers, Gary, 130
presence, more valuable than lethality, 114
Project on Government Oversight, 175, 201–2, 204
Project Vulcan, 60–61
prototyping, 69–75, 80
Pryor, David, 141, *161*

Quesada, Pete, 23–24, 49, 50, 74, 177

radar, 24, 27, 50, 62, 117, 130–33, 135, 141–43
radio, importance of, 50–52
Rainman. *See* Stephenson, David "Rainman"
RAND Corporation, 42

Rasmussen, Reid ("Ras"), 5, 7, 8, 10, 171
Ratley, Lon, 97–101, 103, 105, 111, 120
Rausa, Rosario, 50
"readiness" problems, 89, 113
reattack time, 105, 116
Reed, Fred, 119–20
Reformers. *See* Military Reformers
Republic Aviation Corporation, 74
retrofitting, 151
Riccioni, Everest E., 87n2, 100–101, 116–17
Rich, Ben, 130
al-Rishawi, Sajida, 193
risk assessment and mitigation, 9, 170
Rolling Thunder (Vietnam War), 16
Royal Air Force, 18
Rudel, Hans Ulrich, 47, 52–55, 59, 71, 74, 98, 102, 134, 188; insights on A-10, 103–4
Rules for Direction of the Mind (Descartes), 40
Russia: invasion of Ukraine, 204. *See also* Soviet Union
Rutan, Burt, 118–19

safety, 168n1
Salomonson, Eric, 134
Sanator, Robert, 77
Sassoon, Siegfried, 211
Sawyer, Dave, 136

Schlesinger, James, 89, 90
Schmued, Edgar, 77
Schweinfurt Raid, 21
Scorpion Helmet-Mounted
    Cueing System, 156
Secor, Matt, 3–13, 6–8, *125*,
    171, 189
Senate Foreign Relations
    Committee, 139
Seversky, Alexander de, 74
Seversky Aircraft Corporation, 74
sewing machine phenomenon,
    20–21
Shay, Jonathan, 177–78
Sherman, Charles D., 95
shot-line analysis, 72–73
"Sick Leave" (Sassoon), 211
*Sierra Hotel: Flying Air Force
    Fighters in the Decade After
    Vietnam* (Anderegg), 203–4n1
Sisisky, Norman, 132, 136
Skunk Works (Rich), 130
"Skunk Works" laboratory
    (Lockheed), 130
*Skyraider: The Douglas A-1 "Flying
    Dump Truck"* (Rausa), 50
Smallwood, William, 134, 136
Smith, Billy "Smitty," 185–91, 199
Smith, Roland, 118
Smithsonian Air and Space
    Museum, 118
smoke grenades, 7–9
Soviet Union, 24, 27–28,
    66n2, 95–96n1, 98, 104,
    188; defectors from, 36; and

Seversky, 75; tanks, 52, 59,
    98–99; weapons of used in
    testing, 72, 73. *See also* Russia
special operations, 167–70, 174,
    176. *See also* U.S. Special Forces
    in Afghanistan (Bearded Ones)
speed of aircraft, 89; air response
    time, 105; and "Gs" (forces
    of gravity), 34, 66, 97, 105;
    Mach 1.6, 117; Mach-2,
    33–34; Mach-3, 39; slowness,
    12–13, 116–17; SR-71's, 130;
    Stuka, 52, 103; and wingspan
    design, 50
Speer, Albert, 21
Speir, Bob, 47, 84
spies, 24
Spinney, Franklin "Chuck,"
    62–63, 74, 84–87, 90–91,
    109–10; and Boyd, 106; on
    constant opposition, 119;
    "Defense Facts of Life," 113,
    115, 140, 144, 146; and Dilger,
    93–94; "Military Industrial
    Congressional Complex"
    phrase, 151; on political
    engineering, 157; on *Time*
    cover, 116; and Wheeler,
    139–40
"spooky missions," 24
Sprey, John, 203
Sprey, Pierre, *161, 213, 215, 217*;
    A-10 successor proposal, 107,
    117–18; analytic mind, 12;
    attacks on by reputation and

intellect by military bureaucrats, 11–12; A-X research, 49, 50, 55; and Boyd, 109–10; bureaucracies, disregard for, 28–29, 47, 77; and Christie, 82–85; at congressional hearings, 129, 131–33, 137; "Countering a Warsaw Pact Blitz" talk, 104–6; criticisms of A-10, 104–5, 190; death of, 13, 203–4; declared "dignitary" by the Pentagon, 203; and Dilger, 93–94, 96, 103–4; educational background, 12, 29–30; as empiricist, 28, 56, 109–10; essay in *The Pentagon Labyrinth*, 152–54; on F-117, 131–32; and Fallows, 115; in "Fighter Mafia," 87; first impression of A-10, 80; "gold-plating," view of, 48, 51, 70, 73–74; and Hallock, 76–77, 89; *Harper's* feature, 154; on Horner, 134n1; isolation of, 44–45; locked out of special access to Pentagon, 120; Mapleshade recording studio, 120, 152; memo sent to Kay, 26, 27–28; memo to Department of Defense, 47–48; and Muck, 176–77, 178–79, 188; on multi-mission use, 150; obituary, 13; reputation of in Congress, 190–91; resignation from Pentagon, 75–76; and Riccioni, 116; on Rutan,

118–19; sketches by, *126*; and Spinney, 106; on Stolfi, 97; trucks considered most important tool by, 31–32, 207–8; on vertical wind tunnel, 74; war, stance toward, 44; Warfield Air Base event in honor of, 13; and Wheeler, 139–40, 152–53; on Whiz Kids team, 30–32, 37

Sprey memo: attempts to discredit, 33, 35–36; sent to Kay, 26, 27–28; "treaty," 33

Squadron Officer School, 86

SR-71 "Blackbird," 130

Stalin, Joseph, 66n2

Statistical Research Group, 40

stealth, 129–33, 131

Stephenson, David "Rainman," 9–10n1, 165, 170–73, 187, *214*

Stolfi, Rusell, 97–98, 100

Stone, Andy ("FATTS"), 5–22, 6–7, 23, 171–73

Stone, Jeremy "Frogger," *213*

Strauss Military Reform Project, 152, 177

"Stuka." *See* Junkers Ju-87G dive-bomber ("Stuka")

Stuka Pilot (Rudel), 52, 55, 103

surface-to-air missiles, 97

survivability, 41, 72–73, 82–83, 142, 145–46; of A-10, 5, 11, 79–80, 136, 194–99; of helicopters, 70, 177

survivor morale, 30

Sweetman, Bill, 177

"swing-wing" technology, 51, 88, 150

systems analysis, 39–40, 43

Systems Analysis (White and Tauber), 40

T-62 (Russian), 99

Tactical Air Control Party, 189n3

Taliban, 3–13

tanks: M46, 99; mathematics of hunting, 71; Sherman (U. S.), 144; T-62, 59; T-62 (Russian tank), 99; Tiger (Germany), 144

Tanks: 100 years of Evolution (Ogorkiewicz), 58

tank warfare, 57–59, 97–98; Persian Gulf War, 134; "sandwiching," 134

target selection, 16–19; lines of production, 21–22

Tauber, Selmo, 40

testing: ammunition, 98–102; by defense contractors, 153–54; live-fire survivability, 72–73

thermodynamics, 34

"Thud." *See* F-105 Thunderchief

Thud Ridge (Broughton, 62–63, 65

Tizio, Vincent, 77

Tokyo, bombing of (March 10, 1945), 42

Top Gun (film), 140, 175

"total package procurement," 69

trauma, 177–78

"tree-falls-in-the-forest" paradox, 22

trench warfare, 58

Tribe (Junger), 208, 211

"trigger plates," 79

truck convoys, 76

trucks, as most important tool for winning war, 31–32

turbofan engines, 5, 77–78, 96, 135

turning radius, 66, 105, 211

U-2 spy plane, 130

U-235 uranium, 95

Ukraine, Russian invasion of, 204

U.S. Air Force: 1st Bomb Wing, 21; 74th Tactical Fighter Squadron, 167; 104th Fighter Squadron, 188; 355th Fighter Squadron, 134–35; Air Corps Tactical School (Maxwell Field), 18; attempts to botch Sprey's data, 33; attempts to separate from Army, 18; Eighth Air Force, 15, 19, 22; Fighter Weapon's School (U.S. Air Force), 6; founding of (1947), 22; McNamara's audit of, 43; and nuclear warfare, 22–23; Tactical Air Command, 24

U.S. Army: budget deal with Air Force, 15–16, 24–25

U.S. Army Air Corps: Project Vulcan, 60–61

"U.S. Defense Spending: Are Billions Being Wasted?" (*Time*), 116
U.S. Marine Corps, 22, 70, 119, 198–99
U.S. Navy, 29, 90
U. S. Navy, 99–100
U.S. Navy, 139–40
U.S. Special Forces in Afghanistan (Bearded Ones), 3–13. *See also* special operations
U.S. Special Operations Command, 169

Valkyrie. *See* XB-70 Valkyrie
Van Atta, Dale, 134
Vietcong, 25
Vietnam War, 25, 90; air fleet, limits of, 49–50; as disaster, 43; machine guns used in airplanes, 35; McNamara's memo to Johnson, 43–44; MiG-17s in, 36–37; Operation Rolling Thunder, 16. *See also* F-105 Thunderchief ("The Thud")
Vulcan cannon, 60–61, 81

Wald, Abraham, 40–41, 78n1
war: as complex system, 39; viewed through lens of aircraft design, 12–13
Warfield Air National Guard Base (Maryland), 11, 13
War Powers Resolution (War Powers Act), 139

Warthog (Campbell), 90
Warthog: Flying the A-10 in the Gulf War (Smallwood), 134
Washington Post, 119, 134
Washington Times, 119
Watts, John "40," 166n1
Welsh, Mark, 184–85
West Point (U.S. Military Academy at West Point), 57
Wheeler, Winslow, 12, 139–44, 146–47, *161*, 176–77; *The Pentagon Labyrinth*, 152–54
White, Harry J., 40
Whitley, Al, 130
Whiz Kids (Pentagon), 12, 30–33, 37, 42–43, 48, 83; North Atlantic Treaty Organization group, 32; Strategic Transportation Group, 31. *See also* Pentagon
"Wild Weasel" missions, 97
wind tunnels, 64, 73–74
wingmen, 7, 8, 10
The Wizards of Armageddon (Kaplan), 41, 42
World War I, 74; Saint-Mihiel, Battle of, 18; tank warfare, 58
World War II, 16; bomber missions, 21–22; Britain, Battle of, 20; close-air support in, 20, 23; D-Day invasion, 22; and Fulda Gap, 27; Normandy offensive, 22, 23–24, 57; operations research, 40; Schweinfurt Raid, 21; tank

warfare, 59; Tokyo, bombing
of, 42
Wright, Orville, 20
Wright, Wilbur, 20
Wright Flyer, 5
Wright-Patterson Air Force
Base (Dayton, Ohio), 48, 62,
73–74, 83

Wyndham, Buck, 134–35

XB-70 Valkyrie, 39

Yudkin, Richard, 25